MODERN LEGAL STUDIES

Drug Injuries
and the
Pursuit of Compensation

.

MODERN LEGAL STUDIES

Drug Injuries
and the
Pursuit of Compensation

Pamela R. Ferguson

LL.B., Ph.D., Senior Lecturer in Law,
University of Dundee

SWEET & MAXWELL

THOMSON REUTERS

Published in 1996 by Thomson Reuters (Legal) Limited
(Registered in England & Wales, Company No 1679046.
Registered Office and address for service:
100 Avenue Road, London, NW3 3PF)
trading as Sweet & Maxwell

Transferred to print on demand in 2010
Printed and bound by Hobbs the Printers Ltd, Totton, Hampshire

For further information on our products and services, visit
www.sweetandmaxwell.co.uk

ISBN: 978 0 421 57070 2
No natural forests were destroyed to make this product;
only farmed timber was used and replanted.

A CIP catalogue record for this book is available
from the British Library.

Preface

My great aunt Naomi worked in a pharmacy and kept me amused when I was a child with her tales of life in a chemist's shop. One of her favourite stories involved a customer who bought "alka-seltzers", and returned later that same day, complaining that he had tried and tried, but just could not swallow them. In later years, when I myself had a Summer job in a local chemist, I wondered who was to blame for this. Surely not the pharmacist? What about the manufacturer of the alka-seltzers? Presumably the customer himself was most at fault for not reading the instructions to dissolve these rather large tablets in water.

My aunt's story was an entertaining one; no real harm was caused to the customer, but some pharmaceutical drugs have caused serious harm to their consumers. Despite this, it is a surprising fact that no one in this country has succeeded in suing a pharmaceutical company for injuries caused by its products. While there have been instances of *ex gratia* payments and other out of court settlements, no court has decided the crucial issue of liability. This book attempts to explore why this might be the case, and examines the hurdles which confront potential plaintiffs.

The gestation of the book has been long and arduous (one set-back included the destruction of the original manuscript in an explosion at the publishers) and I would like to record my thanks to a number of people for their assistance. The book developed out of a Ph.D. which I first began working on as a part-time student at Edinburgh University, under the supervision of Sandy McCall Smith. Combining "part-time" study with full time employment in the Procurator Fiscal Service proved to be less feasible than I had anticipated, and I reluctantly withdrew from these studies. I am, however, indebted to Professor McCall Smith for his help and encouragement during that crucial first stage.

On appointment as a lecturer at Dundee University I re-commenced my studies, under the supervision of Bill McBryde, and am grateful to him also for providing guidance, despite the many other demands on his time. Alastair Bissett-Johnson, Margaret Brazier and Joe Thomson were the examiners of the thesis, and each of them provided helpful comments and suggestions. At the stage at which the thesis was being transformed into a book, Hugh Beale gave vital assistance and encouragement: he read every draft chapter and, when I was least able to see the woods for the trees, provided a clear path out of the forest.

I should like to thank my former and current Heads of Department, Alan Page and Fiona Raitt. Much needed moral support also came from other colleagues, particularly Fraser Davidson and Lynn Ramsey. On a personal level, I would like to thank my friend (now husband) Euan Macdonald who, although not a lawyer, was often able to grasp some of the issues in my work with considerable insight. My family too have offered their support at all times.

As I write this Preface, I am struck by the fact that many eminent people have played a role in the final shape of this book. While I am deeply grateful for all of their help, any errors or "defects" in the final product clearly remain my own.

Pamela R. Ferguson.

Table of Cases

British Cases

American Cases

Other Jurisdictions

Table of Statutes

Table of Statutory Instruments

Contents

CHAPTER 1—DRUG INJURIES

CHAPTER 2—GOVERNMENT REGULATION

"*Drugs represent the class of product in respect of which there has been the greatest public pressure for surer compensation in cases of injury.*" (*Royal Commission on Civil Liability and Compensation for Personal Injury*, Cmnd. 7054, 1978, para. 1273.)

Introduction

In the past decade there have been several mass disasters in the United Kingdom. Among the most prominent are the Lockerbie aeroplane explosion which killed 270 people; the sinking of the *Herald of Free Enterprise* and of the *Marchioness* which claimed 189 and 51 lives respectively; the 95 deaths at the Hillsborough stadium; the 31 people who died in the King's Cross Underground fire and the 167 deaths resulting from the Piper Alpha tragedy. Apart from the fatalities many other people were injured or traumatised.

Some of these cases such as the King's Cross fire, the *Herald of Free Enterprise* and the *Marchioness*, have involved methods of transportation and the carrier is the obvious person to whom the victims look for compensation. Others such as Piper Alpha have involved fixed structures, owned and operated by a company. If one person succeeds in establishing liability this will greatly facilitate the claims of the other victims. Even where liability has not been accepted, the sudden and dramatic nature of these occurrences and the prominent publicity which they have thereafter been afforded have led to public appeals, which have generated large sums of money in the majority of cases.[1]

All of these disasters were "incidents", in the sense that the injuries were sustained at the same time and in the same place. There is, however, a second type of mass disaster in which the *cause* of injury is the same for each person but the victims are injured at different times and in different places. These are commonly referred to as "creeping" disasters.[2] This book considers one particular type of creeping disaster, namely where injuries have been caused by the consumption or use of a pharmaceutical product.

The victims of mass disasters generally encounter problems in achieving

---

[1] See Wells, *Negotiating Tragedy: Law and Disasters* (London, Sweet & Maxwell, 1995). The author points out that *The Marchioness* tragedy was an exception to this, since the victims were portrayed by the media as "rich yuppies".
[2] For a detailed account of the problems faced by victims of "creeping disasters", generally, see Stapleton, *Disease and the Compensation Debate* (Oxford, Clarendon Press, 1986).

compensation[3] but it can be argued that many of these hurdles are exacerbated in cases involving pharmaceutical drugs and devices. This is partly due to the very nature of these products; drugs are inherently dangerous; they are intended to have a biological effect on those who consume them, and therefore offer potential risks as well as possible benefits. It is beyond doubt that great benefits are bestowed by many pharmaceutical drugs and devices. They are a particularly valuable class of products since they can alleviate pain, improve health and even save lives. Many of them do, however, have the potential to cause serious harm. Certain pharmaceutical products may be said to have resulted in "mass disasters" since they have injured large numbers of people. The book aims to explore the potential legal liabilities which arise as a result of these injuries.

When many people are seriously injured by a drug in a "mass disaster" situation this tends to be as a result of some unforeseen, and often unforeseeable, side effect. By contrast, many of the injuries caused by drugs are due to well-known adverse reactions which affect only a small proportion of consumers. One example of this is the brain damage which has been associated with the administration of certain childhood vaccines.[4] This book aims to explore the legal position of persons who suffer recognised drug reactions, also.

It is over thirty years since thousands of people were injured as a result of their mothers' ingestion of the thalidomide drug. This led to the establishment of licensing bodies, such as the British Committee on Safety of Medicine (CSM), to control the manufacture and marketing of drugs. The very existence of official licensing authorities, which provide detailed regulations governing manufacture and supply, is another peculiarity of pharmaceutical products.[5] Despite the existence of these government agencies there have been several major disasters involving pharmaceutical drugs and devices since the thalidomide tragedy. These more recent catastrophes are described, and an attempt is made to determine the extent to which the law has changed since the thalidomide tragedy, and to highlight some of the problems which remain for injured persons in their quest for compensation through the civil courts.

---

[3] For a description of these tragedies and their aftermaths, see Wells, *op. cit.*
[4] See p. 8, below.
[5] See Chap. 2 for a description of the government regulation of pharmaceutical drugs and devices.

The range of persons who may be injured by pharmaceutical products includes patients who receive prescription drugs or other medical devices in hospital, directly from their general practitioners, or from having a prescription filled by a pharmacist. It also includes persons who sustain injury from non-prescription or over-the-counter drugs.[6] The potential legal liability of members of the medical and pharmaceutical professions is explored, as is that of the government regulatory bodies themselves. This book is, however, concerned mainly with the liability of the pharmaceutical industry. To date, no case involving a pharmaceutical drug or device has resulted in compensation being awarded against a manufacturer by a British court. The pattern in this country is for persons to accept relatively small *ex gratia* payments from pharmaceutical companies, or receive no compensation at all.[7] This is in stark contrast to the situation in the United States of America, where plaintiffs in pharmaceutical cases frequently succeed in obtaining generous damages. This book attempts to determine why it has been so difficult for plaintiffs in Britain to recover compensation.

The tort of negligence is assessed,[8] as is the strict liability regime introduced by the Consumer Protection Act 1987. Particular areas of difficulty are explored, including the problem of proving that the product was in some way "defective", of establishing that the injury was *caused by* the pharmaceutical product, of identifying the appropriate defendant, and of conforming to the requirements of statutes of limitation. The book attempts to demonstrate that many of the problems which confront plaintiffs in personal injury actions are particularly acute in respect of suits involving pharmaceutical products, and to suggest that fundamental reform of the law may be needed.

---

[6] See p. 3, below.

[7] *Ex gratia* payments were made in cases involving thalidomide, prednisolone, Opren, Myodil and silicone breast implants. See Chap. 1 below.

[8] The Scots equivalent of "tort" is "delict". The book describes both English and Scots law, and the term "British" is used to refer to these systems. The law in the rest of the United Kingdom is outwith the scope of the present work.

Chapter 1

Drug Injuries

"The large majority of drugs may fairly be described as poisons that heal. They almost always have side-effects in some people, which may appear at once or only after a considerable length of time."[1]

1. Adverse Reactions

There is no such thing as a completely safe drug—almost any drug may produce unwanted or unexpected adverse reactions. Adverse Drug Reactions (ADRs) are commonly divided into two basic categories, types A and B.[2] Type A or "augmented" reactions are pharmacologically predictable and are based on the known activity of the drug or group of drugs to which it belongs. These common adverse reactions tend to be dose related and are rarely serious. Such effects can often be identified before the drug is marketed, hence can usually be warned against. In contrast to this are type B reactions ("bizarre") which are unpredictable, not dose related, and which can be very serious or even fatal in some cases. Thus the risks associated with a pharmaceutical product may be known to its manufac-

---

[1] Burstall, *1992 and the Regulation of the Pharmaceutical Industry* (London, The IEA Health and Welfare Unit, 1990) p. 37.

[2] This distinction is made by Rawlins and Thompson, "Pathogenesis of adverse drug reactions", in Davies, ed., *Textbook of Adverse Drug Reactions* (Oxford University Press, 1977) p. 10.

1

turer prior to being put on the market, or may at least be foreseeable, in the sense that a reasonably prudent manufacturer ought to have been aware of these risks. Alternatively, the risks may be unknown and unforeseeable at the time of marketing.

The injuries caused by certain pharmaceutical drugs can be immediately apparent, such as where persons consume or are exposed to a substance to which they are allergic. However, even where a drug *does* cause immediate harm, the results of this might not be apparent at the time of consumption. It is more common for adverse reactions to pharmaceutical products to be of insidious onset. Indeed, the harmful effects of many medications may not become manifest until persons have been exposed to them for a considerable period. The injuries caused by the anti-arthritis drug Opren[3] and cases of tranquilliser addiction[4] are examples of this.[5] Drugs also interact with the human body in ways that cannot be entirely predicted in advance because of the variety in human metabolism; they are excreted and absorbed differently by different individuals. Since drugs are most commonly taken by people who are unwell,[6] this makes it very difficult to determine whether a patient's symptoms are caused by the side effects of a drug or are part of the underlying illness.

A person may have been taking several different drugs over varying time periods and for a number of ailments, hence may be unlikely to associate the development of new symptoms with an adverse drug reaction. Even where patients do suspect that they may be suffering from the side effects of a drug, this polypharmacy makes it very difficult to determine which of the drugs was responsible for the new illness. It may in fact be the interaction between two or more drugs which has caused the injury.

It is not just the adverse reactions of a drug or device which may harm a patient. A pharmaceutical product which does not work properly also causes harm to its consumer in the sense that it allows the patient's disease or

---

[3] See p. [14], below.

[4] See p. [10], below.

[5] A further example is the development of Creutzfeldt-Jacobs disease (CJD) in adults who were given hormone injections to stimulate growth when they were children. See *The Times* September 5, 1995, p. 6.

[6] Some drugs, such as vaccines and Tamoxifen (prescribed for women who come from families which are prone to breast cancer) are given to healthy people, for the prevention of future illness. Tamoxifen has been associated with blood clotting and liver disorders—see Hutchinson, "Trials and the truth" *The Guardian*, October 17, 1995.

illness to continue unchecked. This is particularly harmful if an alternative and more effective treatment is available.

Pharmaceutical products are divided by law into three categories: "over-the-counter" (OTC) or "general sale" medicines, which can be sold without restriction, "pharmacy medicines" (P) which may only be purchased under the supervision of a pharmacist, and "prescription only medicines" (POM), which require to be procured by prescription, or directly dispensed by a doctor.[7]

It is obvious that medicines which can only be acquired by means of a doctor's prescription tend to be more powerful, hence their potential for causing injury is generally greater than that of non-prescription medications. About 12 per cent of the European Community drug market is for non-prescription drugs.[8] As Hancher has pointed out:

"Cost conscious governments are actively promoting policies of self medication, encouraging the public not to seek medical advice unless necessary. A number of products which had only been available on prescription for a number of years have recently been granted a change of legal status."[9]

At present, however, it remains the case that non-prescription drugs tend to be taken in lower doses by comparatively healthy people. Furthermore, these people are generally suffering from short-term ailments. All of this means that the risk of an adverse reaction from a non-prescription drug is likely to be lower than from one which can only be obtained on prescription.[10] Nevertheless, it is not unknown for non-prescription products to cause injury; thalidomide was originally available without a prescription. Other examples of popular non-prescription drugs which are

---

[7] See the Medicines Act 1968, ss.51 (General Sales list) and 58 (Prescription-only products). See also The Medicines (Prescription Only, Pharmacy and General Sale) Amendment Order (S.I. 1989 No. 1852). This amends the Medicines (Products Other than Veterinary Drugs) (Presciption Only) Order (S.I. 1983 No. 1212) and the Medicines (Products Other than Veterinary Drugs) (General Sale List) Order (S.I. 1984 No. 769). See also the new s.58A of the 1968 Act, which implements Directive 92/26/EEC (L113/5).

[8] Burstall, *ibid*. p. 8.

[9] Hancher, *Regulating for Competition: Government, Law, and the Pharmaceutical Industry in the United Kingdom and France* (Oxford, Clarendon Press, 1990) p. 59.

[10] See "Monitoring the safety of over the counter drugs" Editorial, (1987) *B.M.J.*, 295, p. 797.

capable of causing serious injury are paracetamol,[11] ibuprofen[12] and Tagamet[13] (cimetidine hydrochloride).[14]

The term "pharmaceutical product" may include medical devices, as well as drugs. Some of these, such as intrauterine contraceptive devices, pacemakers, silicone breast implants and heart valves, have been implicated as being responsible for personal injuries.[15]

2. Infamous Products

Some pharmaceutical products which have been marketed in Britain and/or in the United States of America have become notorious. These include thalidomide, Diethylstilbestrol (DES), intrauterine devices such as the Dalkon Shield, and certain vaccines.

(A) THALIDOMIDE

Thalidomide, which led to "the greatest drug tragedy of our time",[16] was discovered in 1953 by Ciba, a West German pharmaceutical company. Preliminary animal tests indicated that the drug had little pharmacological effect, so the company did not continue with its development. Thereafter, Chemie Gruenenthal, also a German company, marketed the drug as a sedative and allowed other companies to produce and sell thalidomide using their own brand names. It has been estimated that over one million people in West Germany took this sedative per day. The first report of suspected damage to the foetus was published in that country in 1961. The

---

[11] It has been argued in an editorial in *The Lancet* that poisoning by paracetamol is one of the most common causes of liver failure in this country. Indeed, its editor has suggested that if paracetamol were to be discovered today it would not be approved by the CSM. See "Paracetamol Hepatotoxicity" (1975) *The Lancet*, p. 1189. See also Moore, "GPs call for paracetamol ban" *GP*, June 19, 1992, p. 4.

[12] Ibuprofen has been shown to cause kidney failure in elderly persons. See Meek, "Ibuprofen Link to Kidney Problems Spurs New Caution" *The Scotsman*, April 18, 1990, p. 3.

[13] See Colin-Jones, Langman, Lawson and Vessey, "Postmarketing surveillance of the safety of cimetidine: 12 month mortality report" (1983) *B.M.J.*, 286, p. 1713.

[14] The brand names of drugs will generally be used throughout this book. The name which is given in brackets is a drug's generic title.

[15] See p. [45] below, in relation to silicone implants.

[16] *The Thalidomide Children and the Law*, Report by the *Sunday Times* (London, Andre Deutsch, 1973) Preface, p. 7.

most notorious of the injuries caused by thalidomide are "phocomely" and "amely" (incomplete development, and absence of the limbs). A study conducted in the 1940s had found one case of shortened or missing limbs in four million births. During the 1960s thalidomide had been taken by so many women that virtually every paediatric clinic in Germany had at least one child born in this way[17]; in Hamburg alone there were 50 phocomelia births in one year.[18]

Thalidomide was marketed in Britain by Distillers Co. (Biochemicals) Ltd as a treatment for morning-sickness. Distillers advertised the drug as one which could "be given with complete safety to pregnant women and nursing mothers without adverse effect on mother or child".[19] In December 1961 a British doctor wrote to *The Lancet*, noting that there appeared to be an increasing number of limb malformation in children whose mothers had been taking thalidomide during pregnancy.[20]

Of the 430 British children who were injured by thalidomide, 62 of them attempted to sue Distillers. An out of court settlement was reached in 1968 but a second legal action was started in 1971. This resulted in a lump sum of £3.5 million being offered to all the claimants by the company. Public pressure forced Distillers to increase this, ultimately to £20 million. Most of this money was placed in a trust fund. It is expected that this fund will be exhausted within the next 15 years and the thalidomide victims, many of whom now have their own families, have recently succeeded in persuading Guinness, Distiller's successor company, to provide more compensation.[21]

(B) DIETHYLSTILBESTROL (DES)

Described as "America's Thalidomide", Diethylstilbestrol is a synthetically produced oestrogen which was first synthesised in Britain in 1937.[22]

---

[17] Teff and Munro, *Thalidomide: The Legal Aftermath* (Farnborough, Hants, Saxon House, 1976) p. 5.

[18] Knightley, *Suffer the Children: The Story of Thalidomide* (London, Andre Deutsch, 1979) p. 97.

[19] Dworkin, "Pearson: Implications for Severely-Handicapped Children and Products Liability", Part V, Chap. 3, in Allen, Bourne and Holyoak, *Accident Compensation after Pearson* (London, Sweet & Maxwell, 1979).

[20] McBride, "Thalidomide and congenital abnormalities" (1961) *The Lancet*, p. 1358.

[21] See Waterhouse, "Thalidomide victims given £3.75m bail-out" *The Independent*, May 4, 1995, p. 2.

[22] See (1981) *B.M.J.*, 282, p. 1536.

5

In 1947 the American Food and Drug Administration (FDA) licensed the drug for the prevention of early miscarriage. It seems, however, that DES may actually have *increased* the likelihood of complications in pregnancy. It was also responsible for causing a rare form of vaginal and cervical cancer in the daughters of women who took the drug during pregnancy.[23] It is suspected of having increased the incidence of genital tract abnormalities in the male off-spring of these women,[24] and to be responsible for an increased risk of breast cancer in the women themselves.[25]

Three to four million women in the United States of America ingested DES and between 20,000 and 100,000 babies were exposed to the effects of this drug each year for 20 years.[26] It has also been taken by about 8,000 British women and a DES Action Group has been established to co-ordinate their claims for compensation.

It is normally essential for a plaintiff in a product liability suit to establish that the defendant was the manufacturer responsible for producing the drug which is alleged to have caused injury. When DES was first synthesised in 1937 no patent was applied for and as a result more than 300 companies have produced this drug. It has therefore been very difficult for a plaintiff to establish that the DES which was prescribed to her mother 15 to 20 years previously was manufactured by a particular pharmaceutical company.[27] Legal Aid was granted in England to allow this to be investigated. Unfortunately, many of the doctors who prescribed the drug have since died and their records and those of pharmacists and drug companies have been lost or destroyed.

(C) INTRAUTERINE DEVICES

About 7 per cent of British women currently use intrauterine contraceptive devices. This has however been a prominent area of product liability, particularly in the United States.

---

[23] Herbst, Ulfelder and Poskanzer, "Adenocarcinoma of the vagina: association of maternal stilbestrol therapy with tumor appearance in young women" (1971) *New England Journal of Medicine*, 284, p. 878.

[24] See *Doe v. Eli Lilly & Co.* (No. 82–3515, U.S. Dist. Ct., D.D.C. 1985).

[25] See Dutton, *Worse than the Disease: Pitfalls of Medical Progress* (Cambridge University Press, 1988) p. 87.

[26] *ibid.* pp. 56–57.

[27] This is explored in Chap. 9, below.

i. The Dalkon Shield. The Dalkon Shield became one of the most litigated products in pharmaceutical history; it was described as "a deadly depth charge in [women's] wombs, ready to explode at any time".[28] It was manufactured in America by A.H. Robins Co., which began selling the Shield in 1971 and continued doing so until the mid 1970s.[29] Within that time 4.5 million Shields had been inserted in American women and the device had been marketed in 80 countries. It has been estimated that about one in 20 women became pregnant while using this contraceptive device. The Shield is alleged to have caused pelvic inflammatory disease (an infection which damages the reproductive capacity of many women), and to have caused spontaneous miscarriages and ectopic pregnancies in others.

Robins suspended sales of this IUD on June 28, 1974 after the American Food and Drug Administration expressed concern over the incidence of spontaneous septic abortions in Shield users. The Shield caused 200 such miscarriages within its first four years on the market.[30] By 1985 Robins had paid out about $368 million in compensation and it was calculated that it would require to pay out more than $1 billion to meet future liabilities. The company declared bankruptcy in 1986, by which time it had paid out $21 million in legal expenses.[31] Judge Miles W. Lord charged the Robins executives that:

> "[N]one of you has faced up to the fact that more than nine thousand women have made claims that they gave up part of their womanhood so that your company might prosper. It is alleged that others gave their lives so you might so prosper. And there stands behind them legions more who have been injured but who have not sought relief in the courts of this land ... The only conceivable reasons you have not recalled this product are that it would hurt your balance sheet and alert women who already have been harmed that you may be liable for their injuries."[32]

In Britain almost 9,000 women have attempted to claim compensation

---

[28] *Per* Judge Miles Lord; see Mintz, *At Any Cost: Corporate Greed, Women, and the Dalkon Shield* (New York, Pantheon Books, 1985) p. 267.
[29] For a history of the development of the Shield see Pendergast and Hirsh, "The Dalkon Shield in Perspective" (1986) *Medicine and Law*, 5, 35.
[30] *ibid.* p. 37.
[31] For litigation associated with this device see *In re A H Robins Co.*, 406 F.Supp. 540; 419 F.Supp. 710 (1976), 438 F.Supp. 942 (1977); 453 F.Supp. 108 (1978); 505 F.Supp. 211 (1981); 570 F.Supp. 1480 (1983).
[32] See Mintz, *op. cit.* pp. 265–267.

from the Robins Company. Although Robins had set up a trust fund of £1.5 billion it had offered some women as little as £440.

ii. Other IUDs. The Dalkon Shield is not the only intrauterine device to have been associated with serious side effects. In 1985 an American woman who required to have a hysterectomy as a result of using the Lippes Loop IUD was awarded $563,000.[33] The Coper-7 IUD also came under attack and has now been withdrawn from the market by GD Searle, its manufacturers. It has been suggested that this IUD was targeted at a less than suitable market (young, nulliparous women)[34] and that the information leaflets provided to doctors failed to describe the risks of infection in an appropriate manner. Pretl and Osborne have stated:

"Although in the estimation of many gynaecologists, the IUD when properly used and monitored may be the contraceptive of logical choice for many women, the industry's mishandling of testing and marketing has prompted litigation as a result of which virtually no market exists in the United States today for any IUD."[35]

(D) VACCINES

Although there are no compulsory vaccination programmes in Britain, the Department of Health does recommend that children be immunised against diphtheria, tetanus, poliomyelitis, tuberculosis, measles and whooping cough (pertussis), and that female children be vaccinated against rubella. In 1963 the government established a Joint Committee on Vaccination and Immunisation to advise the Health Ministers of any medical aspects of these immunisation procedures. Critics of childhood immunisation programmes have argued that a rise in childhood asthma and allergies could be due to the fact that vaccinations cause a lower general

---

[33] *Beyette v. Ortho Pharmaceuticals Corporation* Case No. 82–71670 E.D. Mich. 1985.
[34] That is, women who have not had children.
[35] Pretl and Osborne, "Trends in U.S. Drug Product Liability—the Plaintiff's Perspective" Chap. 9 in Howells, ed., *Product Liability, Insurance and the Pharmaceutical Industry: an Anglo-American Perspective* (Manchester University Press, 1991) p. 114.

8

immunity. Some doctors have also suggested that the natural immunity achieved from actually catching the disease is greater than that attained from immunisation.

Whooping cough is a common infection of the respiratory tract. It can cause breathing difficulties in children, as well as complications such as pneumonia and bronchitis. Convulsions leading to a loss of consciousness and, in rare cases, epilepsy or permanent brain damage, have also been associated with pertussis. Children who are not immunised run a risk of contracting whooping cough which is greater than one in six.[36]

Many parents came to believe that the pertussis vaccine could itself cause similar, serious side effects, and the Association of Parents of Vaccine Damaged Children (APVDC) was formed in the early 1970s. Many members of the medical profession were also of this opinion. Following the first allegations that the whooping cough vaccine could induce brain damage, immunisation rates fell by one third. These rates have since increased to 73 per cent but this means that more than one in five British children are still not being immunised.

Pertussis is not the only vaccine which has been linked to iatrogenic injury. The immunisation against rubella can cause arthritis in between 9 and 14 per cent of females.[37] The safety of the vaccine used to protect children from measles has also been questioned; paralysis and seizures have been alleged to have resulted from this vaccine[38] and this vaccine has been linked to the development of inflammatory bowel diseases, including Crohn's disease.[39] Two vaccines (Pluserix-MMR and Immravax) were withdrawn by the government in September 1992 after it was found that they could cause meningitis.

Concerns over vaccine injury led the Pearson Commission to recommend a system of State compensation for vaccine induced injury in children,[40] which in turn led to the Vaccine Damage Payments Act 1979.[41]

---

[36] "Whooping cough: taking a risk?" in *Mims Magazine*, May 15, 1992, p. 14.

[37] See "Joint problems and MMR vaccination" *Medical Monitor*, May 8, 1992, p. 34. It should however be borne in mind that the rubella infection itself can cause arthritis in up to a third of women, as well as endangering the unborn foetuses of pregnant women.

[38] See Rogers, "Parents seek measles jab recompense" *The Sunday Times*, October 1, 1995.

[39] Hunt, "Study links measles vaccine to increase in bowel disease" *The Independent*, April 28, 1995.

[40] See Chaps. 25–27 of the Pearson Report, *Royal Commission on Civil Liability and Compensation for Personal Injury*, Cmnd. 7054, 1978.

[41] The operation of this Act is described in Chap. 12, below.

JABS (Justice, Awareness and Basic Support) is a self-help group which continues to campaign for compensation for persons injured by vaccinations. More than 450 families have contacted the group.

3. Recent Drug Litigation

(A) THE BENZODIAZEPINES

The benzodiazepines are a group of chemically related hypnotics, sedatives, anxiolytics (anxiety reducing drugs) and anticonvulsants. At one time benzodiazepines were among the top five drugs prescribed in most Western countries and 16 million NHS prescriptions were issued for this group of drugs in Britain in 1992, at a cost of £14 million.[42] According to Parish:

"Throughout the seventies and into the eighties millions of prescriptions for benzodiazepine tablets and capsules were issued to patients. Some doctors applied little or no control over their supply, and many patients were kept on benzodiazepine anti-anxiety drugs for years on end, often for a disorder that did not need treating with such drugs in the first place. Unfortunately, some of these patients became dependent on their benzodiazepines."[43]

One person in six can become addicted to these tranquillisers after taking a normal dose for six months, and one person in three may be addicted after a year. According to the Council for Involuntary Tranquilliser Addiction (CITA) there are about three million people in Britain who are addicted to sleeping pills and tranquillisers, some of whom may have been taking their medication for 30 years. It is ironic that the benzodiazepines were introduced as a safer alternative when the addictive nature of barbiturates was discovered.[44]

In 1988 several hundred patients began to attempt to obtain compensation from the manufacturers of these tranquillisers, claiming that the latter had not warned the medical profession of the dangers of addiction. It was

---

[42] Sweeney, "Should you be on Drugs?" *The Times*, March 29, 1994.

[43] Parish, *Medical Treatments. The Benefits and Risks* (London, Penguin Books, 1991) p. 607.

[44] For an excellent discussion of this see Medawar, *Power and Dependence: Social Audit on the Safety of Medicines* (Social Audit Ltd, Bath Press, 1992).

also alleged that some doctors had not passed on to their patients those warnings which were provided. Among the benzodiazepine group of drugs particular attention was focused on Ativan, Valium, Librium and Halcion.[45]

i. Ativan (lorazepam).   Ativan is one of the best known benzodiazepines. Wyeth Laboratories, its manufacturer, faced suit by hundreds of persons who had become addicted to that drug. They alleged, *inter alia*, that the manufacturer ought to have warned doctors that this tranquilliser should only be prescribed for a limited duration. In July 1990 the Scottish Legal Aid Board approved applications for Legal Aid in six cases and in April 1991 a test case was started and 2,000,000 pages of documents from Wyeth were recovered by the pursuer.[46] This case was sisted to await the outcome of similar claims in England. One million people are still regularly taking Ativan, although it is now prescribed only in "exceptional" circumstances and for short periods.

ii. Librium (chlordiazepoxide) and Valium (diazepam).   Most of the people who are now in a position of dependence on these drugs will have been first prescribed them many years ago; Librium came on the market in 1960 and Valium in 1963. Valium is among the 20 best selling drugs in the world. More than 1,000 people formed a co-ordinated action committee to sue the manufacturers of these drugs.

iii. Halcion (triazolam).   Dr Graham Dukes, formerly a doctor with the World Health Organisation, has called the Halcion affair "one of the worldwide drug scandals of the century". This tranquilliser was alleged to cause dramatic mood changes and violent behaviour. It was manufactured by the Upjohn Company and was its second best-selling drug, with annual sales of about £143 million. In the United States Mrs Ilo Grundberg succeeded in obtaining damages from Upjohn.[47] She had been charged with the murder of her 83 year old mother but the charges were withdrawn after a Utah court accepted evidence from two psychiatrists who testified

---

[45] See, however, Fitzsimons, "Hidden dangers of new tranquillisers" *The Sunday Observer*, March 27, 1988 in which BuSpar, a supposedly safer drug than Valium or Ativan, comes under attack.

[46] *McInally v. John Wyeth Ltd* 1992 S.L.T. 344.

[47] *Grundberg v. Upjohn Co.* (C.D. Utah, 1991) 137 F.R.D. 372.

that Mrs Grundberg had been "involuntarily intoxicated" due to her consumption of Halcion at the time of the killing. She then sued the company for causing her to kill her mother. The civil case settled out of court and the amount of damages remains undisclosed, but it has been suggested that the figure could be $6–8 million. In May 1992 the FDA concluded its investigation into Halcion's safety. It decided not to ban the drug but ordered Upjohn to provide stronger warning information to patients as to its potential side effects.

There were 402 reports of adverse reactions to Halcion made to the British Committee on Safety of Medicines between 1978 and 1991 and the Department of Health finally decided to ban this drug in October 1991. It has been estimated that 600,000 people were using Halcion at the time of its banning, and that in excess of two million prescriptions were written for it in 1989. Upjohn has been informed by the licensing authority that its revocation of Halcion's licence is permanent.

The only personal injury suits which are now proceeding against Wyeth, Roche and Upjohn in relation to Ativan, Valium and Halcion, respectively, are being privately funded, since Legal Aid has been withdrawn in respect of all three actions.[48]

(B) HUMAN INSULIN

More than 400 diabetics considered taking legal action on the basis of the alleged side effects of some human insulins, such as Humulin. The Law Societies of England and Scotland both established action groups to co-ordinate their claims.[49] The change from animal to human insulin was alleged to have caused severe adverse reactions including sudden blackouts. More than 80 per cent of Britain's 200,000 insulin takers had been prescribed human insulin in preference to animal insulin.[50] The British Diabetic Association distributed a questionnaire to patients, asking whether they had been adversely affected by the change in insulin. About half of all respondents felt that their condition had deteriorated on human insulin.[51]

---

[48] See Chap. 10, below.
[49] McKeone, "Plaintiffs proliferate in insulin action" (1991) L.S.G., 88:31, p. 7.
[50] McKeone, "Solicitors prepare for lengthy battle on human insulin" (1991) L.S.G., 88:29, p.4.
[51] Pickup, "Human insulin" (1989) B.M.J., 299, p. 991. See also "Transferring diabetic patients to human insulin", (1989) The Lancet, p. 762.

Many doctors switched their patients from animal to human insulin because of rumours that the former type of insulin might not be available for very much longer. Insulin manufacturers have now given assurances that they will continue to make beef and porcine insulin. The lack of warning of hypoglycaemia was not the only side effect which was alleged for human insulin; some diabetics claimed that it caused them to develop multiple sclerosis. It was also suggested that the use of human insulin caused an increase in the number of deaths in young diabetics.[52] It was claimed that the manufacturer's own scientists knew that there could be problems with Humulin:

"It acted faster to reduce blood sugar and the symptoms it produced were so different that patients might not realise their blood sugar was getting dangerously low."[53]

A study by Teuscher and Berger had supported this[54] but their findings have been accused of "bias in patient selection" and therefore "inconclusive".[55] More recently, a study of patients who had previously reported loss of awareness with human insulin concluded that ". . . the use of human insulin carries no specific risk of altered awareness of hypoglycaemia."[56] The steering committees in both England and Scotland were unable to find medical experts willing to support these claims (many doctors who specialise in diabetes had been hired as potential expert witnesses by the drug companies), and have now been disbanded.

(c) MYODIL

Manufactured by Glaxo, Myodil was a yellow dye which was injected into the spinal cavity prior to X-ray. It was alleged to have caused arachnoiditis—inflammation of the membranes covering the nerve roots

---

[52] Gale, "Hypoglycaemia and human insulin" (1989) *The Lancet*, p. 1264.
[53] "Synthetic Insulin Scare", Channel 4 news, October 11, 1989, *per* Andrew Veitch (transcript).
[54] "Hypoglycaemia unawareness in diabetics transferred from beef/porcine to human insulin" (1987) *The Lancet*, ii, p. 382.
[55] Hepburn and Frier, "Hypoglycaemic unawareness and human insulin" (1989) *The Lancet*, p. 1394.
[56] Patrick, Bodmer *et al.*, "Human insulin and awareness of acute hypoglycaemic symptoms in insulin-dependent diabetes" (1991) *The Lancet*, p. 528 at p. 531.

within the spinal cord. There is no known cure for this condition. Myodil had been used in Britain since 1944 despite the fact that a large number of medical papers had been published from the 1950s onwards, linking its use to the later development of arachnoiditis. It was withdrawn in Sweden in the 1950s following the publication of these papers but remained in use in Britain until voluntarily withdrawn by Glaxo in 1987. Safer dyes have been available since 1977.

It had been estimated that the risk to a patient of developing arachnoiditis following a Myodil X-ray was 2 or 3 per cent. Such a risk might be thought to be acceptable since few medical procedures are entirely risk free. It must be remembered, however, that Myodil was only a diagnostic tool; in itself, it did not alleviate the back pain of patients on whom it was used. In fact, it has transpired that some of the people who were injected with this dye had nothing wrong with their backs. More than 3,600 patients alleged that the company was negligent in its testing of the dye and that it continued to manufacture Myodil when it became aware, or after it *ought* to have become aware, of the risks the dye posed. The Myodil cases were settled by Glaxo on July 31, 1995 for an *ex gratia* payment of £7 million; the company has not accepted liability.[57]

(D) OPREN (BENOXAPROFEN)

Opren was a non-steroidal anti-inflammatory drug (NSAID) used in the treatment of arthritis. When first promoted by its Swiss manufacturer, Eli Lilly, Opren was hailed as a "wonder drug" and soon the British Health Service was spending £9 million each year on this one drug. The first benoxaprofen death was reported in the *British Medical Journal* in January 1982. In the following month its manufacturer received two reports of fatal cholestatic jaundice and by August of that year 10 more fatalities had been noted in the medical literature. The drug proved to be particularly lethal to the elderly and 61 people died before the British CSM suspended the drug's licence.[58] 3,500 side effects were reported in total and some of Opren's

---

[57] See "Back pain sufferers win £7m payout" *The Times*, August 1, 1995, p. 7, and Hall, "Medical dye row is settled for £7m" *The Independent*, August 1, 1995, p. 5. It has been estimated that each claimant will have received £16,431.

[58] For a criticism of the CSM's behaviour in relation to the decisions to license, and later withdraw Opren, see Chap. 4 of Abraham, *Science, Politics and the Pharmaceutical Industry* (London, UCL Press, 1995).

non-fatal adverse effects, such as phototoxicity, (an acute and painful sensitivity to sunlight) were unique to that drug. It was marketed in the United States at Oraflex in April 1982 but was withdrawn within four months due to the British fatalities. It has now been withdrawn worldwide by the company.

In December 1987 many of the British plaintiffs agreed to accept an out-of-court settlement with Eli Lilly in which claimants would receive a share of £2.275 million. The maximum amount any individual will have received under this scheme is likely to have been between £7,000 and £8,000. The average claimant will have received only £2,000 or £3,000. This is in contrast to the situation in the United States of America, where one plaintiff alone was awarded $6 million against the company.[59]

(E) ORAL CONTRACEPTIVES

Several women who allege that they have been injured by oral contraceptives are contemplating suing the manufacturers of these products. The women have suffered from pulmonary embolisms, which is a recognised risk of the Pill. They are claiming that the manufacturers ought to have provided clearer warnings of these risks.[60] Concern has also arisen over the increased risks of thrombosis associated with certain makes of the Pill, known as "mini Pills".[61]

4. Types of Defect

Defective pharmaceutical products may be divided into three broad categories: manufacturing defects, design defects, or defects which arise in the marketing of the product. Manufacturing defects are caused by errors which occur in the production process and may be manifest in a single item or batch of items, only. This type of defect will include any foreign body which may have contaminated the product. An example of a pharmaceut-

---

[59] *Borom v. Eli Lilly & Co.* (1983), reported in Patterson, ed., *Drugs in Litigation: Damage Awards Involving Prescription and Nonprescription Drugs* (Virginia, The Michie Company, 1992) p. 49.

[60] See Aitkenhead, "A hard pill to swallow" *The Independent*, May 1, 1995, p. 21; and Ferguson, "An Ill for every Pill" (1995) *N.L.J.*, 145 p. 836 on.

[61] Laurance, "Doctors urge women on 'unsafe' Pill not to panic" *The Times*, October 20, 1995.

ical which suffered from a manufacturing defect occurred in the American case of *Gottsdanker v. Cutter Laboratories*.[62] It was alleged that the vaccine which had been administered to the plaintiffs had been contaminated in the manufacturing process with live polio virus, resulting in them developing polio. Similarly, in *Abbott Laboratories v. Lapp*[63] a serum had been contaminated during manufacture by streptococci and staphylococci bacteria. A more recent example is the case of *Best v. Wellcome Foundation*[64] in which the Irish Supreme Court held that a particular batch of pertussis vaccine was more potent than it ought to have been.[65] Manufacturing defects are rarely encountered in pharmaceutical products due to the strict controls which government agencies like the British Committee on Safety of Medicines and the American Food and Drug Administration exercise over their production.[66]

The second form of defect is the "design defect". This will occur even though the product was manufactured as intended. In essence, such a product should not have been marketed at all. Such a defect will of course be present in all examples of the product, and may therefore result in multiple injuries. Pharmaceutical products have been described as an area which is "particularly prone to design problems",[67] and a prominent illustration of this is the Dalkon Shield intrauterine device.[68] The problem with this device lay in its "tail string", a length of fibre used in facilitating its removal. Most IUDs have tail strings which are monofilaments so that any bacteria which make their way on to the end of the string will not proceed to infect the rest of it. The Dalkon Shield had a tail string of 200 to 450 filaments; this meant that bacteria could be drawn into the wearer's womb. The controversy concerning salbutamol inhalers, used by asthmatics, is an example of an alleged design defect in respect of a pharmaceutical product's *container*.[69]

The final category is the "marketing defect", which consists of a failure to furnish adequate warnings about the dangers of the product, or to

---

[62] 182 Cal.App.2d 602; 6 Cal.Rptr. 320 (1960).

[63] 78 F.2d 170 (7th Cir. 1935).

[64] [1992] I.L.R.M. 609.

[65] See p. [46], below.

[66] The British regulatory process is explored in Chap. 2, below.

[67] Griffiths, "Defectiveness in EEC Product Liability" (1987) *Journal of Business Law*, p. 222.

[68] See p. [7], above.

[69] See Hunt, "Asthma deaths could be linked to inhaler flaw" *The Independent*, September 28, 1993.

produce adequate guidance concerning a product's use. Instructions for use should include any necessary warnings as to the consequences of failure to follow those directions. This is the most common "defect" which is alleged in respect of pharmaceutical products. Examples of this include the allegations concerning the benzodiazepines, Myodil and certain oral contraceptives.

5. Assessing the Risks

It has been estimated that about one in 20 of all hospital admissions are due to problems with medicines[70] and that up to 20 per cent of cases of acute renal failure resulting in dialysis or transplantation are caused by pharmaceutical drugs.[71] According to Hawkins:

> "Adverse effects of drug therapy are thought to affect between ten and eighteen per cent of patients admitted to hospital and may account for one in forty consultations in general practice."[72]

Assessing the risks and benefits of pharmaceutical drugs can be problematic, since the potential benefits may be different for different individuals; for example, a strong pain killer could be used for a mild, transient condition, or for a highly painful and/or terminal illness. Even where two people with the same illness are treated with the same drug, the risks may be greater for one than the other due to personal idiosyncrasies.

It is difficult to determine the level of risk which persons are prepared to accept from their medical treatments. As Burstall has noted:

> "The lay public is not forgiving where damage through drugs is concerned. The risks of surgery are generally very much greater than those of pharmaceutical treatment, but they are accepted. To take medicine is thought to be essentially risk-free. That this attitude is irrational is beside the point: it exists."[73]

---

[70] See "Are Drugs Safe?", Chap. 3 of Bryan, *Drugs For All?* (Harmondsworth, Penguin Books, 1986) p. 37.
[71] See Cove-Smith, "Drugs that Damage the Kidney" *MIMS Magazine*, July 1, 1986, p. 42.
[72] Hawkins, *Mishap or Malpractice?* (Oxford, Medical Defence Union, Blackwell Scientific Publishing, 1985) p. 121.
[73] *op. cit.* p. 37.

He has argued that even in cases such as the Opren disaster the rate of side effects was low, being a one in 25,000 chance of death, per patient per year.[74] Drawing on Office of Population Censuses and Surveys, Burstall calculated that in a 10 year period 2,870 out of every 10,000 people aged between 65 and 75 will die. The number dying from Opren would be four more, giving an increase of 0.14 per cent. He concludes that this "is not an impressive level of danger, especially when one considers the undoubted benefits of the product".[75]

Dr Brian Strom, a leading pharmacoepidemiologist, has suggested that there are many factors which affect a patient's willness to accept the risks of adverse reactions associated with a particular drug therapy.[76] Two very important criteria used by patients in their assessment of risk are severity and reversibility; people are clearly less willing to run the risk of more serious reactions and ones whose harm is permanent. Should a drug have a risk of causing an illness such as cancer, a patient's reluctance to take that risk is obviously increased. Much will also depend on the illness for which a patient is being treated and, understandably, people find even slight risks to be less acceptable if the condition being treated is not in itself a serious one. Strom suggests that the time at which any adverse reaction is liable to manifest itself is also relevant. Hence it appears that people are more likely to accept the risks of adverse reactions which are delayed in their effect than they are to accept the risk of immediate harm. As already noted, adverse reactions may be subdivided into those which commonly occur, are dose-related, and tend to be less serious, and those more serious reactions which are less easily predicted, non dose-related and potentially very serious. As one might except, patients are more inclined to accept the risk of experiencing the first of these types of reaction.

Strom provides a comparative study of the risks involved in various activities. This reveals that although it is estimated that 4.3 oral contraceptive users between the ages of 25 and 34 will die each year per 100,000 women exposed to the Pill, about the same number of people will die while engaging in cave exploration (4.5) and the number of deaths caused by powerboat racing or motorcycling is much higher, at 80 and 100 per

---

[74] *ibid.* p. 51.
[75] *ibid.*
[76] See Strom, "When Should One Perform Pharmacoepidemiologic Studies?" Chap. 5 in Strom, ed., *Pharmacoepidemiology* (Chichester, John Wiley & Sons Ltd, 2nd ed., 1994) from p. 62.

100,000, respectively. Figures are also given for the number of suicides (11.2) and homicides (7.5) per 100,000 people per year.[77]

It may be argued that Strom's example of a contraceptive drug is not a particularly good one, since there is a greater element of genuine choice in a patient's decision to accept this "therapy" than is the case with many other medicines. Contraceptives can be distinguished from the majority of pharmaceutical products in that their use is frequently not therapeutic. If Strom is using the contraceptive drug as an example of the risks typically offered by a pharmaceutical product then one should be wary of relying too much on his figures. Many of the other activities which he lists are pastimes which a person may or may not decide to participate in. He mentions scuba diving and hang gliding, along with cave exploration and sport parachuting. Balancing and pleasure derived from one's hobbies as against the risks associated with those hobbies is rather different from comparing the risks of adverse drug reactions with the pain or discomfort associated with the underlying illness or disease condition. In the latter situation, one has to chose between the lesser of two evils.

Furthermore, figures for deaths by homicide (estimated to be 7.5 per 100,000, as mentioned above), being struck by lightning (0.05) or by a tornado (0.2) are of little value for comparison with drug risks, since each person will consider that he or she is as unlikely as the next person to be injured in these ways, and that there is little which can be done to minimise such risks. Being exposed to the risks of a particular drug is quite different. One has the option of taking the drug and exposing oneself to the risk, or not, and it is an *additional* risk to those which we face in the course of daily life. One often hears in relation to drug risks that "we live with risks every day, you are at risk when you get out of bed in the morning, and when you cross the road". This is of little comfort to the potential patient, however, since these background risks are present for each one of us, and there is little we can do to avoid them completely.

6. Compensation

This chapter has described some of the more notorious examples of pharmaceutical product injury, yet none of these cases has resulted in a

---

[77] *ibid.* at 64.

successful suit against a pharmaceutical manufacturer in a British court. In relation to thalidomide, Opren and Myodil the plaintiffs were ultimately offered out of court settlements, and cases involving prednisolone were settled by its manufacturer shortly before they were due to be tried.[78] In contrast to this, large awards have been won by plaintiffs in the United States of America in suits concerning, for example, Diethylstilbestrol, the Dalkon Shield and Halcion. We have already noted the vast difference in the size of awards achieved by British Opren victims, compared to their American counterparts. Subsequent chapters describe some of the more important legal obstacles which prevent British plaintiffs from succeeding in their suits.

---

[78] For a detailed critique of out of court settlements in the field of personal injuries, generally, see Genn, *Hard Bargaining: Out of Court Settlement in Personal Injury Actions* (Oxford, Clarendon Press, 1987).

Chapter 2

Government Regulation

"[T]he history of drug regulation parallels the history of major adverse drug reaction 'disasters.' Each change in pharmaceutical law was a political reaction to an epidemic of adverse drug reactions."[1]

1. Introduction

Following the thalidomide disaster the pharmaceutical industry became subject to a very high degree of government regulation. As Burstall has pointed out:

"Even countries which have strong commitment to unfettered free enterprise, such as the USA, maintain strict official controls over the introduction of new medicines to the national market."[2]

This chapter describes the different stages of a drug's development, and outlines the British regulatory process.

---

[1] Strom, "What is Pharmacoepidemiology?" Chap. 1 in Strom, ed., *Pharmacoepidemiology* (Chichester, John Wiley & Sons, 2nd edition, 1994) p. 3.
[2] Burstall, *1992 and the Regulation of the Pharmaceutical Industry* (London, IEA Health and Welfare Unit, 1990) p. 3.

2. Drug Development

The search for a new drug begins with the discovery stage, with thousands of chemical compounds being synthesised and tested for pharmacological activity. Those which show promise at the discovery stage are then tested on animals for acute, subchronic and chronic toxicity; that is, by a single dose, a ten day dose, and administration for six months, respectively. Where the compound is likely to be used for long-term treatments, these tests can take about two years and involve approximately 400 rodents.[3] Tests for carcinogenicity and, if the product is intended for use by pregnant women, for teratogenicity (pre-natal injury) may also be carried out, and this may take up to five years. Compounds which are successful are used in human clinical trials.

There are three stages of trials in humans. Phase I trials are commonly conducted on healthy volunteers and are designed to find out basic information, such as the metabolism of the drug in humans and identification of dose-related adverse reactions. These trials should reveal any extremely common adverse reactions which have not been discovered during animal testing. Research subjects are usually monitored 24 hours a day. In Phase II trials a small group of about 40 to 50 patients (persons for whom such a drug might be prescribed, once marketed) are given the drug, and are closely monitored. Phase II studies aim to gather data as to the efficacy of the drug and to refine the therapeutic dose.

Phase III involves the administration of the drug to larger groups of potential patients. Once the drug is marketed, Phase IV trials monitor the use of the drug in practice.[4] If all the tests are successful the company will then apply for a licence to market the drug. It has been estimated that for every 9000 to 10,000 compounds which are synthesised, only one will ultimately reach the market.[5]

---

[3] Neal, *Keeping Cures from Patients: The Perverse Effects of Pharmaceutical Regulation* (The Social Affairs Unit, 1995) p. 13.
[4] See Bryan, *Drugs for All?* (Penguin, 1986) p. 56.
[5] Gad, *Safety Assessment for Pharmaceuticals* (Van Nostrand Rheinhold, 1995) p. 2; and Burstall, *op. cit.* p. 14.

3. The History of Regulation

The potential of pharmaceutical products to cause harm has long been recognised; in 1747 a Select Committee of the House of Commons heard evidence of the poor quality of drugs, the incompetence of pharmacists and the lack of power of the authorities to order drugs which were found to have been adulterated to be destroyed.[6] It was not, however, until the middle of the nineteenth century that there were legal restrictions governing the sale of drugs. Until 1843, when the Pharmaceutical Society of Great Britain was granted a charter of incorporation, any person could claim to be a pharmacist or chemist.[7]

In 1914 a House of Commons Select Committee on Patent Medicines reported that, with the exception of mixtures which contained scheduled poisons, the law was powerless to prevent anyone from obtaining any drug, or preparing any compound. Nor were there any laws which prohibited the advertising of these preparations, even where extravagant claims were made as to their curative powers.[8]

As a result, the Committee recommended that a manufacturer should be required to provide an account of the composition of its "medication", along with any therapeutic claims being made about the compound. This would be assessed by a special committee, which could authorise the marketing of such preparations. It is unfortunate that these recommendations were not acted upon until the 1960s, and that it took the thalidomide tragedy to galvanise the government into action.

Three years after the thalidomide tragedy the Sainsbury Committee was established to consider the relationship between the NHS and the Pharmaceutical Industry.[9] This Committee considered that about two-thirds of all drugs which were on the market at the time were therapeutically effective. The remaining one-third was described as "undesirable".

[6] Report from the Select Committee on Examination of Drugs, to Prevent Adulteration (1747) Journals (H.C.) 25, 592.
[7] The Pharmacy Act 1852 empowered the Society to set examinations and issue certificates. Only members of the Society could lawfully describe themselves as "pharmaceutical chemists".
[8] Report of the Select Committee on Patent Medicines (1914), 414, ix, I p. ix.
[9] Report of the Committee of Enquiry into the Relationship of the Pharmaceutical Industry with the National Health Service, 1965–1967, London, H.M.S.O. 1967.

4. European Controls

Many of the British regulations are based on European directives. According to the European Commission itself "... the pharmaceutical industry is the sector most extensively covered by Community legislation."[10] This began with Directive 65/65,[11] which provided that no medicinal product could be placed on the market in a Member State unless it had received authorisation from the competent authority in that state.[12] The competent authority for Britain is the "licensing authority", the operation of which is described, below. A European Medicines Evaluation Agency (EMEA) was established in 1993.[13] The EMEA has two sub-committees, the Committee for Veterinary Medicinal Products (CVMP) and the Committee for Proprietary Medicinal Products (CPMP).[14] Member States must ensure that a medicinal product is withdrawn from the market if it is shown to be harmful under normal conditions of use, has no therapeutic efficacy or that its qualitative or quantitative composition is not as declared.[15] The provisions of existing Directives were extended in 1989 such that blood products, vaccines, sera, toxins and allergens are now within the ambit of the regulatory process.[16]

Most Member States consult the CPMP before withdrawing a drug from their home market. Since January 1995 authorisation of a product by the CPMP will be valid in all Member States. It is too soon to assess the impact of this, but it seems likely that companies will generally opt for the centralised procedure in future, since this will be cheaper than applying for a separate licence from each Member State.

---

[10] Background Report: The European Medicines Evaluation Agency, ISEC/B23/94, December 1994.

[11] See 1965 J.O. 22/65.

[12] See also the Medicines for Human Use (Marketing Authorisations Etc,) Regs. (S.I. 1994 No. 3144).

[13] See Reg. 2309/93, and Jones, "European Drug Regulatory Integration" Chap. 13 of Goldberg and Dodds-Smith, eds., *Pharmaceutical Medicine and the Law* (London, RCPL, 1991).

[14] See Dir. 75/318.

[15] Dir. 75/319 [1975] O.J. L147/13.

[16] See Dir. 89/341; 89/342; and 89/391.

5. The Medicines Act 1968

The 1968 Act establishes general policies in relation to the manufacture, testing and marketing of pharmaceutical products, the details of which are fleshed out by numerous statutory instruments.[17] Given that the Misrepresentation Act 1967 and the Trade Descriptions Act 1968 were passed shortly before this, it has been suggested that the Medicines Act was part of a "consumer movement" aimed at decreasing the consumer's "vulnerability in the face of dubious marketing techniques".[18]

The Act established a licensing authority,[19] and empowered it to appoint a Medicines Commission.[20] In turn, the Commission set up a number of committees, including the Committee on Safety of Medicines (CSM).[21] The CSM provides the licensing authority with advice with respect to the safety, quality and efficacy of medical products. The licensing authority was authorised by the 1968 Act to make regulations governing the manufacture, testing and marketing of drugs. Regulations also control their labelling, advertising and packaging.[22] It is a criminal offence to sell, distribute, import or export any medicinal product without a product licence[23] and no medicinal product can be manufactured without a manufacturer's licence.[24] Detailed as the regulations are, they do not provide a complete picture of the extent of government control since they are supplemented by "administrative directions", published in the Medicines Act Information Letters (MAIL). The Medicines Control Agency (MCA), which is an executive agency of the Department of Health, took over responsibility for all drug licensing and inspection in 1989.

---

[17] The 1968 Act followed a Government White Paper, "*Forthcoming Legislation On The Safety, Quality and Description of Drugs and Medicines*" 1967, Cmnd. 3395.

[18] Teff, "Regulation under the Medicines Act 1968: A Continuing Prescription for Health" (1984) *Modern Law Review*, 47, p. 303 , at pp. 306–307.

[19] s.6. The relevant Secretaries of State and Health and Agriculture Ministers who make up the licensing authority are defined in s.1(1).

[20] s.2(1). See also the Medicines Commission and Committees Regulation 1970, (S.I. 1970 No. 746).

[21] By virtue of s.4 of the Act. See also the Medicines (Committee on Safety of Medicines) Order (S.I. 1970 No. 1257). Its predecessor was the Committee on Safety of Drugs, which was the first adverse reaction reporting system in the world.

[22] See p. [39], below.

[23] s.7.

[24] s.8(2). ss.9 and 10 provide exceptions to this for doctors, dentists, veterinary surgeons and pharmacists.

(A) PRODUCT LICENCES

In determining whether or not to grant a licence for a new drug the licensing authority must consider its safety, efficacy and quality.[25] A product licence lasts for five years, after which a manufacturer will require to submit an application for its renewal.[26] A company may not alter its method of manufacture, route of administration or recommended therapeutic uses for a drug unless it has first obtained authorisation from the licensing authority. Licensing applications require to be supported by scientific evidence, which in practice can amount to "as many as 250 or more volumes, each containing two or three hundred pages of text or tables".[27]

If the authority decides not to accept a submission from a pharmaceutical company in respect of a new drug, it must advise the company of its reasons for rejecting the application, and does so by means of a "section 21(1)" letter. The company may appeal against this decision, and in doing so need only address the points queried in that letter.

Marketing authorisation is required for all new products, including those which are the generic equivalent of an existing product. Fresh authorisation is required if an existing product is to be marketed for a new application. It is the regulatory authorities which decide on the classification of a new product—whether it can be marketed to the general public, whether it can only be sold under the supervision of a pharmacist, or whether it requires to be acquired by a doctor's prescription. More than half of all applications for a product licence are refused[28] and it takes almost two years, on average, for an application for a new chemical entity to be processed.

An insight into the licensing processes occurred in 1989 when the CSM was taken to court by a disgruntled pharmaceutical company. Organon, the manufacturers of Bolvidon (an antidepressant), wanted to lead

---

[25] s.19.
[26] s.24(1).
[27] Fowler, "Careers in Drug Regulatory Authorities" Chap. 23 of Stonier, *Discovering New Medicines: Careers in Pharmaceutical Research and Development* (John Wiley & Sons, 1994) p. 242.
[28] See Collier, "Licensing and Provision of Medicines in the United Kingdom: an Appraisal" (1985) *The Lancet*, pp. 377–381; and the study of United Kingdom product licence applications by Rawlins and Jeffreys, (1991) *B.M.J.*, pp. 223–225, giving a rejection rate of 60 per cent for licence applications.

evidence before the CSM that its drug was safer than others. The company claimed that Bolvidon had a lower toxicity than other anti-depressants, hence was less likely to be fatal if an overdose was taken.[29] The CSM had ruled that the safety or otherwise of a drug in an overdose situation was not relevant in assessing its safety, and refused to allow the evidence to be heard.

This was overturned by the Divisional Court and ultimately by the Court of Appeal.[30] The latter held that, in assessing the risks and benefits of a drug, account could be taken of the risks attaching to misuse of the drug.[31] Mustill L.J. held that the object of the Medicines Act 1968 was to promote public health and safety, and that the Act should be construed in a way which was favourable to the attainment of that object. He further held that the licensing authority was entitled to take into account the risks associated with other drugs for the same purpose.[32] It would seem to follow from this that the CSM would be entitled to recommend the removal of a drug from the market, purely on the basis that there exists another drug which, after comparison of the risks and benefits of the two drugs have been made, is regarded as being safer.

(B) LEAFLETS AND LABELLING

Section 85 allows regulations to be made in respect of the labelling of containers and packaging. The purpose of such regulations is to ensure that drugs are "correctly described and readily identifiable" and that "any appropriate warning or other appropriate information or instruction is given".[33] Section 86 applies to leaflets. A leaflet need not be supplied with a product if all relevant information can be contained in the packaging itself. As a result of a recent European Directive all drugs, whether obtained with or without a prescription, must include the following information[34]:

---

[29] Lincoln, "Court acts to stop mianserin curb" *GP*, February 3, 1989, p.3.
[30] See *The Guardian*, Law Report, March 6, 1989.
[31] See *R. v. DHSS and others, ex p Organon Laboratories* [1990] 2 CMLR 49 [1996] C.O.D. 272.
[32] By virtue of s.28(3)(g).
[33] s.85(2)(a) and (b).
[34] See Dir. 92/27/EEC (L113/8), which was implemented in Britain by the Medicines (Labelling) Amendment Regulations (S.I. 1992 No. 3273) and the Medicines (Leaflets) Amendment Regulations (S.I. 1992 No. 3274).

(a) the name of the product, its active ingredients, pharmaceutical form, pharmo-therapeutic group, the manufacturer's name and address, and details of the holder of the marketing authorisation;

(b) the therapeutic indications for the product;

(c) any information which is necessary before taking the product. This includes information on precautions for use and any contraindications;

(e) all necessary and usual instructions for proper use;

(f) a description of the side effects which can occur under normal use and, if necessary, the action to be taken, as well as an express invitation to communicate any undesirable effect which is not mentioned in the leaflet, to the patient's pharmacist or doctor;

(g) warning and storage precautions, and the expiry date as indicated on the label.

The information must be clearly legible and understandable. It must be indelible and in the language of the country in which the product is being sold. Member States are free to require manufacturers to include additional information, such as the price. These provisions apply to all new drugs put in circulation after January 1, 1994 and to existing products when their licences come up for renewal. Contravention of these labelling requirements is a criminal offence.[35]

(C) THE PROVISION OF INFORMATION TO DOCTORS

Pharmaceutical manufacturers are required to provide doctors with information about prescription drugs.[36] A manufacturer may not send advertisements or make any representations about its product to a member of the medical profession unless it has sent the doctor a copy of the product's data sheet within the preceding 15 months.[37] These data sheets may be consulted by doctors when they are deciding which particular drug to prescribe and must include details of any risks and contra-indications. Doctors may also refer to other sources of information such as the *Monthly Index of Medical Specialities* (MIMS) *or the British National Formulary* (BNF).

---

[35] By s.86(2).
[36] s.96 of the Medicines Act 1968.
[37] Medicines (Data Sheet) Regs. (S.I. 1972 No. 2076).

MIMS does not give detailed information about contra-indications and side effects, and is therefore of less use than the Data Sheets.

(D) POST-MARKETING CONTROLS

The regulation of the pharmaceutical industry does not cease once a product is marketed. Standards of Good Manufacturing Practice (GMP) are agreed between the licensing authority and the pharmaceutical industry, and members of the Medicines Inspectorate of the MCA visit the premises of manufacturers and wholesale dealers "to examine in detail how companies' products are made, controlled, stored and distributed".[38] It is also a licensing condition that a company has adequate procedures for prompt recall of its products, should this become necessary.[39]

6. The Detection of Adverse Reactions

(A) THE MANUFACTURER'S DUTY TO REPORT

Drug companies must report any adverse reactions discovered during their clinical trials.[40] All adverse reactions must be reported, whether major or minor. Any reaction which occurs during a clinical trial held in another country must also be reported. One condition of the granting of a new product licence is that the manufacturer has a system for detecting adverse reactions which are discovered once the drug is marketed.[41] A manufacturer must maintain a record of each adverse reaction which is reported to

---

[38] Fowler, *op. cit.* p. 243.

[39] See the Medicines (Standard Provisions for Licences and Certificates) Regs. (S.I. 1971 No. 972), para. 6 of Pt. I, of Sched. 1, as amended by the Medicines (Standard Provisions for Licences and Certificates) Amendment Regs. (S.I. 1992 No. 2846.) This implements Dir. 91/356/EEC by requiring the holder of a manufacturer's licence to maintain an effective system for product recall.

[40] Sched. 1, Pt. II, reg. 3(2), para. 2.

[41] See the Medicines (Standard Provisions for Licences and Certificates) Regs. (S.I. 1971 No. 972).

it. Such reactions must be reported within a month of receipt. Reactions which are fatal, sufficiently severe to interfere with a patient's normal activities, or which are unusual must be reported, as must any reaction which may be an example of possible drug interaction, or which involves congenital abnormalities, endocrine disturbances, fertility effects, haemorrhaging, jaundice (however mild), ophthalmic signs or symptoms, severe CNS effects, severe skin reactions after an injection or topical application, and reactions in pregnant women.

It has been estimated that the CSM receives approximately 20,000 ADR reports each year.[42] It also receives copies of the "Death entry" supplied by the Office of Population Census and Surveys, which provides the information which is contained in death certificates.[43] In November 1991 it was announced that the Medical Control Agency had developed "the world's fastest and most sophisticated system for monitoring adverse drug reactions".[44] The Adverse Drug Reactions On-line Information Tracking system (ADROIT) is able to process reports of adverse reactions in days, rather than in weeks. These reports come from doctors, dentists and coroners. About 70 per cent of reports come from GPs, 15 per cent from hospital doctors, and the remainder are reported mainly by the pharmaceutical companies themselves.

(B) THE "YELLOW CARD" SCHEME

Referred to as "the cornerstone of drug safety monitoring",[45] the Yellow Card Scheme is used for the spontaneous reporting of Adverse Drug Reactions by doctors. This system was established by Sir Derrick Dunlop, then chairman of the Committee on Safety of Drugs (later, the CSM) in 1964. He asked doctors to report "any untoward condition in a patient which might be the result of drug treatment".[46] The cards are now included as part of doctors' prescription pads.

---

[42] See (1991) *P.L.I.*, p. 175.
[43] Griffin and Weber, "Voluntary systems of adverse reaction reporting—Part I" (1985) *Adv. Drug React. Ac. Pois. Rev.* 4, pp. 213–230, at p. 217.
[44] *P.L.I., op. cit.*
[45] Talbot, "Spontaneous reporting", Chap. 4 in *Drug Safety: A Shared Responsibility* (Glaxo Group Research, Churchill Livingstone, 1991) p. 38.
[46] Balfour, "How to report suspected adverse drug reactions (ADRs)" Chap. 8 in *Drug Safety: A Shared Responsibility, op cit.*, p. 77.

The success stories of the Yellow Card system include the discovery that jaundice could be caused by halothane,[47] thrombo-embolism by oestrogens, and liver damage by ibufenac.[48] In relation to halothane, it has been argued that:

> "the unravelling of the reported association between halothane and jaundice was a masterly use of adverse reaction data derived from the yellow cards."[49]

Other successes have linked Aldomet (methyldopa) with hepatitis, and Hypovase (prazosin) with a loss of consciousness.[50]

The CSM publishes *Current Problems* every three months, advising pharmacists, doctors and dentists of potential danger areas. If it is felt that doctors need to be advised of a particular adverse reaction more quickly than this then a "Dear Doctor" letter may be used.

7. Limitations on the Detection of Adverse Reactions

(A) LIMITATIONS OF PRE-MARKETING TESTS

In practice, it is far from easy to discover any but the most common adverse reactions during the clinical trial stage. Such trials are, to some extent, a crude form of identifying adverse reactions, for a number of reasons.

i. The Number of Participants. The number of persons who are actually exposed to the drug during such trials is very small. Many popular types of drug, such as those for arthritis or hypertension, may have been tested on one or two thousand people at most, yet will be prescribed for ten times that number in their first year of marketing.[51] Bryan suggests that "those

---

[47] Inman and Mushin, "Jaundice after repeated exposure to halothane. An analysis of reports to the Committee on Safety of Medicines" (1974) *B.M.J.*, pp. 5–10; and Inman and Mushin, "Jaundice after halothane: a further report" (1978) *B.M.J.*, p. 1455.

[48] Stephens, *The Detection of New Adverse Drug Reactions* (Basingstoke, The MacMillan Press, 3rd ed., 1992) p. 89. Ibufenac was voluntarily withdrawn.

[49] Griffin and Weber, "Voluntary systems of adverse reaction reporting—Pt. I" (1985) *Adv. Drug React. Ac. Pois. Rev.* 4, pp. 213–230, at p. 228.

[50] *ibid.* p. 227.

[51] Bryan, *op. cit.* p. 58.

10,000 people are participating in ... delayed clinical trials".[52] Even if a new drug has been given to 3,000 people in pre-marketing tests, a side-effect which occurs in one in a thousand cases is unlikely to have been detected in such a small number of people.[53] As Burstall has noted:

> "Most of the major withdrawals of products from national and international markets have been prompted by adverse reaction instances of between one in 5,000 treated patients and one in 10,000. It is highly unlikely that these would have been picked up in the course of normal clinical testing."[54]

ii. The Time Period. It is not only the number of test subjects which limits the efficacy of such studies; the period during which these people are taking the drug is very much shorter than the time-span over which many of these drugs would be taken in practice. The CSM has stressed that even post-marketing clinical trials are no substitute for the experience doctors gain by using a new drug in daily practice.[55] Furthermore, the Committee recognises that to require manufacturers to conduct longer trials on a greater number of people would simply delay the marketing of new drugs, and would deprive patients of treatments which could potentially be very beneficial.[56]

iii. The Characteristics of Participants. A further limitation which is commonly noted is that the characteristics of the people who are given the test drug in the clinical trial situation are frequently dissimilar to the type of person who may be prescribed the drug after marketing. The drug in question will have been given, not to a sample of patients who are suffering from the condition the drug is designed to treat, nor even to a random sample of the population, but to a very select group of people. Test subjects tend to be young and healthy since such people are "unlikely to suffer a sudden deterioration in health for reasons unrelated to the administration of the drug under study".[57] Elderly persons, pregnant women or women of child-bearing age, patients with impaired hepatic, cardiovascular or renal

---

[52] *ibid.*
[53] See Burstall, *op. cit.* at p. 56.
[54] *ibid.*
[55] "Safety of New Drugs", Notes and News, (1986) *The Lancet* i, p. 337.
[56] *ibid.*
[57] *Safety Requirements for the First Use of New Drugs and Diagnostic Agents in Man* (C.I.O.M.S., Geneva, 1983) p. 40.

functions and children may often be excluded for ethical reasons. However, these may be the very groups of people for whom the drug will ultimately be prescribed, and who may be most vulnerable to the side effects of certain drugs.[58]

This problem was highlighted by the injuries associated with Opren. The licensing authority introduced new clinical trial rules following the Opren tradgedy, to ensure that a new medicine which is intended for use primarily in the elderly be tested on elderly persons, prior to marketing.[59] In summary:

"... because of the relatively small size and generally homogenous populations in the usual pre-marketing clinical trials, those trials cannot be expected to detect reliably adverse effects occurring at rates less than one per thousand exposures".[60]

Many very serious adverse events occur more rarely than this. For example, the risk of developing aplastic anaemia from Chloramphenicol is one in 6,000, and the risks of suffering myocardial infarction or deep vein thrombosis from oral contraceptives is one in 10,000.[61]

It may not, therefore, be possible to avoid future injuries from pharmaceutical drugs and devices simply by tightening up the regulatory process, and demanding more stringent pre-marketing tests. In fact, it has been suggested that some of the tests performed on new drugs "are done more to satisfy regulatory requirements than from any substantial evidence that they are necessary in a scientific sense".[62] This suggests that current licensing requirements may actually be hindering the development of new drugs, without improving their safety. A similar point is made by Burstall:

"The demands of regulatory bodies have not been the sole cause of the fall in new active substances to reach the world market, but they have been a major contributory factor."[63]

---

[58] See Roden, "An introduction to drug safety surveillance" Chap. 1 of *Drug Safety: A Shared Responsibility, op. cit.* p. 2.
[59] "Are Drugs Safe?", Chap. 3 of Bryan, *op. cit.* p. 52.
[61] See Freeman, "They test drugs don't they?" Chap. 2 of *Drug Safety: A Shared Responsibility, op. cit.* p. 21. Recent studies have suggested that the risk of thrombosis from the "mini Pill" may be higher than this, at 30 in 100,000 (*The Times*, October 20, 1995, p. 1.)
[62] C.I.O.M.S., *op. cit.* p. 11.
[63] *op. cit.* p. 47.

(B) Limitations of the Yellow Card Scheme

It has been estimated that 3,500 people died in the 1960s due to excessive use of pressurised aerosols by asthmatics,[64] yet only six doctors considered the possibility that any of these deaths might be due to the drug treatment regime. In the 1970s, Inman discovered 44 cases of aplastic anaemia in patients who had been prescribed phenylbutazone and oxyphenbutazone, yet the CSM had been notified of only five of those cases.[65] Similarly, the CSM interviewed 53 doctors whose patients had been taking oral contraceptives when they died. Only two of those doctors had reported this to the CSM.[66] Practolol was a beta-blocker which caused serious ear, eye and intestinal damage,[67] yet only one adverse reaction was notified to the CSM in the four years following its initial marketing. The drug had been given to more than 100,000 patients during that period, and it has been estimated that "scores of deaths and hundreds of serious injuries" occurred during that time.[68] Once doctors became aware of the potential for eye injury, over 200 Yellow Cards were sent to the CSM within a few weeks, some of these being retrospective reports.[69]

In 1986 a working party which had been set up by the CSM concluded that the Yellow Card system was inadequate at monitoring new drugs where they were going to be used for long periods.[70] Opren's licence was not suspended until more than 3,500 adverse reaction reports had been received and 61 people had died.[71] There are a number of reasons for the low incidence of Yellow Card reports.

i. Failure to Report by Patients.   Patients who suffer from a side effect of a drug may not report this to their doctors. Stephens has suggested various

---

[64] Inman and Adelstein, "Rise and fall of asthma mortality in England and Wales in relation to use of pressurised aerosols" (1969) *The Lancet*, p. 279.

[65] Inman, "Study of fatal bone marrow depression with special reference to phenylbutazone and oxyphenbutazone" (1977) *B.M.J.*, p. 1500.

[66] Inman and Vessey, "Investigation of deaths from pulmonary, coronary and cerebral thrombosis in women of childbearing age" (1968) *B.M.J.*, 2, p. 193.

[67] Wright, "Untoward effects associated with practolol administration: oculomucocutaneous syndrome" (1975) *B.M.J.*, 1, p. 595.

[68] See Crawford, *Kill or Cure? The Role of the Pharmaceutical Industry in Society* (London, ARC Print, 1988) p. 5.

[69] *ibid.* p. 5.

[70] "Safety of New Drugs", Notes and News, (1986) *The Lancet* p. 337.

[71] Teff, *op. cit.* p. 304, n. 5.

reasons for this.[72] Among these are the fact that they may not associate the symptoms which they are experiencing with consumption of the drug, or may surmise that there is a connection between the two, but feel that it is something which has to be endured. Alternatively, patients may feel unable to continue taking the treatment due to the side effects, but may not tell their doctors that they are no longer taking the medication. Even patients who complete their course of treatment may be reluctant to report suspected side effects to their doctors, for fear of being labelled as neurotic.

ii. Failure to Report by Doctors. Even where patients do report adverse reactions, the incidence of under-reporting by the medical profession is notorious. The CSM's own figures suggest that more than 80 per cent of doctors never report any adverse reactions,[73] and that, at most, only a tenth of all reactions are reported.[74] An evaluation of the reports submitted to the CSM between 1972 and 1980 found that of 122,000 doctors who were eligible to make such reports, only 16 per cent did so.[75]

Inman has suggested that the lack of British reports is due to what he describes as the "seven deadly sins". These are: complacency, a mistaken belief that only safe drugs are allowed on the market; fear of litigation; guilt, because the treatment prescribed by the doctor may have harmed the patient; ambition to collect and publish a personal series of cases; ignorance of how to report; diffidence about reporting mere suspicions; and lethargy.[76] Inman's second "deadly sin", the perceived threat of litigation, is a mistaken one. At its inception in 1964, the then Chairman of the Committee on Safety of Drugs undertook that:

> "all reports or replies that the Committee receive from doctors will be treated with complete professional confidence by the Committee and their staff. The Health Ministers have given an undertaking that the information supplied will

---

[72] *op cit.* p. 3.

[73] Scrip, April 1985. Griffin and Weber have estimated that 80 per cent of doctors did not report any suspected adverse reactions in the period 1972–80; see "Voluntary system of adverse reaction reporting—Parts I and II" (1985) *Adv. Drug React. Ac. Pois. Rev.*, 4, pp. 213–230, and (1986) 5, p. 1.

[74] *ibid.*

[75] Speira, Griffin, Weber, Glen-Bott and Twomey, "Demography of the U.K. adverse reaction register of spontaneous reports" (1984) *Health Trends,* 16, p. 49.

[76] Inman, *Monitoring for Drug Safety* (Lancaster, MTP Press, 2nd ed., 1986) p. 37. See also Talbot, "Spontaneous Reporting" Chap. 4 of *Drug Safety: A Shared Responsibility, op. cit.,* p. 39.

never be used for disciplinary purposes or for enquiries about prescribing costs."[77]

This under-reporting means that it is meaningless to say that a certain fraction of cases experience adverse reactions. The numerator (*i.e.* the total number of adverse reactions) is not ascertained with any degree of accuracy. Furthermore, the denominator (*i.e.* the total quantity of any particular drug which has been taken) is also less than certain, although a random sample of prescriptions processed by the Prescription Pricing Authority (in England and Wales) can serve as a rough guide.

A survey conducted in 1986 found that only 15 per cent of doctors felt that the Yellow Card system worked well, and needed no improvement.[78] Commenting on this, the editor of the *British Medical Journal* has suggested that doctors might be more willing to refer suspected adverse reactions if they were to be paid a fee for doing so.[79] This was tried in the Republic of Ireland; doctors were paid IR£3 for each completed Yellow Card. During the six weeks for which payments were made 150 reports were received. Once the fee was withdrawn, this dropped to 30 reports.[80]

8. Improved Post-Marketing Systems

In 1983 the CSM established a working party to explore methods of improving the collection of information on drug safety. Following the first report of the working party the Subcommittee on Safety, Efficacy and Adverse Drug Reactions was set up. The group has attempted to encourage GPs to report more suspected adverse reactions to the CSM, and has

---

[77] *ibid.* p. 16. Despite this under-reporting, a study of reporting rates in 15 countries in 1982 placed the U.K. in a group of six countries with the highest reporting rates. See Griffin and Weber, "Voluntary systems of adverse reaction reporting" (1986) *Adv. Drug React. Acute Poisoning Rev.* 1, p. 23.

[78] Walker *et al*, "The attitude of GPs to monitoring and reporting adverse drug reactions" (1986) *Pharmaceutical Medicine* I, 195–203 and Walker *et al*, "The under-reporting of adverse drug reactions seen in general practice" (1986) *Pharmaceutical Medicine* I, 205–212. See also Sinclair, "CSM: An inefficient user of yellow card system and a slave to political diktat—fact or fiction?" *Doctor*, May 22, 1986, p. 8.

[79] Langman, "Did the drug do it?" (1986) *B.M.J.*, pp. 219–220.

[80] Feely, Moriarty and O'Connor, "Stimulating reporting of adverse drug reactions by using a fee" (1990) *B.M.J.*, p. 22.

developed a system whereby the CSM keeps GPs appraised of recent developments by drawing their attention to areas of concern in the *British Medical Journal*. In 1983, doctors were asked to report any suspected adverse reactions to "any therapeutic agent" which is defined to include drugs, vaccines, blood products, X-ray contrast media, dental or surgical materials, IUDs absorbable sutures and contact lens fluids. In respect of new drugs, doctors were requested to advise the CSM of *any* adverse or unexpected event, even if minor.[81] The guidelines specifically advise that a doctor should report such findings, "despite uncertainty in the doctor's mind about a causal relationship" between the drug and the reaction.

Inman initiated a novel form of post-marketing surveillance in Southampton. His Drug Safety Research Unit engages in Prescription Event Monitoring (PEM), in which copies of the first 10,000 prescriptions written in England under the National Health Service for a new drug are sent to the DSRU, which then sends a questionnaire about adverse events to each doctor who wrote one of these prescriptions.[82] This enjoys a higher response rate than the Yellow Card Scheme, since it actively seeks information from the doctor—by 1986 there were 18,000 GPs involved in the "Green Card" scheme operated by Inman, as opposed to the 2,000 doctors who regularly send their Yellow Cards to the CSM.[83] It is able to concentrate on only a few drugs at any one time but, despite this limitation, the scheme has produced some significant results.[84]

9. Risks and Benefits

The Committee on Safety of Medicines attempts to perform a delicate balancing act. It aims to safeguard the public by attempting to ensure that

---

[81] *Current Problems*, No. 12, (1983).

[82] Inman, "Prescription Event Monitoring" (1984) *Acta. Med. Scand.* [Suppl] 683, p. 119. See also Inman, "Postmarketing surveillance of adverse drug reactions in general practice. II. Prescription-event monitoring at the University of Southampton" (1981) *B.M.J.* 282, p. 1216; and "Prescription-event monitoring" (1982) *B.M.J.*, 285, p. 809.

[83] Sinclair, *op. cit.*

[84] See "Deafness with Entalopril and Prescription Event Monitoring" (1987) *The Lancet*, p. 872; and "Erythromycin Estolate and Jaundice" (1983) *B.M.J.*, p. 1954, both by Inman and Rawson. In a similar Scottish system, prescription details from Tayside Region are considered along with Morbidity Returns from hospitals in Scotland, see Macdonald and McDevitt, "The Tayside Medicines Monitoring Unit (MEMO)" Chap. 18 of Strom, *op. cit.*, p. 245 on.

harmful drugs do not reach the market place, and that any which do so are quickly detected and withdrawn from use. At the same time, it must try not to deprive the public of the great benefits which may be derived from a particular drug by having too cumbersome a licensing process, or by withdrawing a drug without clear evidence that its benefits are outweighed by its risks.

It is clearly not realistic to expect current pre-marketing tests to detect any but the most common adverse reactions. If more stringent procedures were introduced, involving many more people in clinical trials over longer periods, this would increase the cost of drug development and greatly delay the marketing of new, and possibly highly beneficial, drugs. Under present regulations, certain very useful drugs such as aspirin, penicillin and paracetamol, would have been refused licences on account of their adverse reactions.[85]

While more could be done to improve *post*-marketing detection methods, thereby limiting the amount of harm which a drug may cause, this inevitably means that some patients will have been injured, in the interim. A question also remains as to how the licensing authority should most appropriately respond once it becomes aware of an adverse reaction. It may decide that the safest course is to withdraw the product's licence but, except in the most extreme of cases where the benefits themselves are questionable and are greatly outweighed by the risks, this deprives those patients who had benefitted from the drug.[86]

An example of this is the decision to withdraw the licence for Halcion after the drug had been on the market for 13 years. While those who suffered its side effects wondered why it took so long to be withdrawn from the British market, given that the first adverse reports had been received in 1979, and the drug had been withdrawn in the Netherlands, the thousands of people who took the drug without apparently suffering from any of its side effects questioned why it had to be withdrawn at all.[87] One pharmacologist called the CSM's decision "a farce". Pointing out that tricyclics, another class of drugs used in the treatment of depression, cause 40 deaths in every one million prescriptions, he argued: "There's nobody

---

[85] Neal, *Keeping Cures from Patients: The Perverse Effects of Pharmaceutical Regulation* (The Social Affairs Unit, 1995) p. 10.

[86] Diethylstilbestrol and the Dalkon Shield are examples of pharmaceutical products which offered little benefit. See Chap. 1, above.

[87] Webb, "Sleeping pill ban puzzles doctors" *New Scientist*, October 12, 1991, p. 13.

dead with Halcion. What is it the government knows that I don't know?"[88] There was a similar outcry in 1986 when the CSM decided that aspirin was no longer suitable for children under 12 years of age, due to reports which linked the drug to the development of Reye's Syndrome.[89]

The alternative to withdrawing a drug's licence is to issue more stringent warning information; this was the response of the American FDA to both the Halcion and aspirin side effects. The inclusion of precautions for use or contraindications may result in the doctor or patient choosing an alternative therapy. Such information will at least alert the patient to the prospect of side effects and make it more likely that appropriate action will be taken if symptoms appear. An example of this is the warning that drowsiness may be caused by certain anti-histamines. This may lead the patient to opt for a different drug (or choose to do without any drugs) or to avoid activities like operating machinery or driving, which could be dangerous should the side effect materialise.

In certain cases, however, warning information can do little more than alert patients to the fact that they may be one of the unfortunate few who will be harmed by the drug, leaving them to determine whether or not to take that risk. As one author has noted:

"... it must be accepted that drugs may cause adverse reactions. A drug can consequently—in spite of the fact that it can cause serious side effects—be registered and released for public use by the authorities. This is because the positive effects of the drug are much greater than the negative. For this reason it must be accepted that a few people will suffer injury so that many more people will be cured."[90]

In response, it may be suggested that the many people who will be cured ought to bear the cost of compensating the few who will suffer injury.[91]

---

[88] ibid.

[89] "Aspirin is banned for children under age 12" (1986) GP, June 13, p. 1. "Reye's syndrome is a rare but devastating encephalopathy, occurring typically after a feverish illness such as flu. Half the victims die and 10 per cent of the survivors have brain damage." (ibid.) See also "Bitter Pill" (1986) Doctor, July 3, p. 11.

[90] Oldertz, "Compensation for Personal Injuries—the Swedish Patient and Pharma Insurance" Chap. 2 of Mann and Havard, eds., No Fault Compensation in Medicine (London, Royal Society of Medicine Services, 1989) p. 18.

[91] This argument is considered more fully in Chap. 12, below.

10. Conclusions

There can be little doubt that the regulatory regime established by the licensing authority is a valuable safeguard in preventing drug injuries. It attempts to prevent manufacturing defects, to detect design defects at an early stage, and to ensure that suitable warning information of known risks is provided, thus minimising "marketing defects".[92] It currently takes up to 12 years to market a new drug, and costs on average £200 million.[93] While it is apparent that the process is not infallible, to attempt to make it so would increase the time and expenditure involved, which would have a detrimental effect on the development of new and potentially beneficial drugs. Inevitably, some people will be injured by adverse reactions which the regulatory process has failed to detect. The legal hurdles faced by such individuals are explored in chapters 3 to 10.

---

[92] See p. [16], below.
[93] ABPI Press Release, October 30, 1995.

Chapter 3

The Common Law Liability of the Manufacturer

1. Introduction

In Britain the law governing liability for injuries caused by pharmaceutical products is not a separate body of law. Such products are not, generally, afforded any special treatment and the legal liability of a manufacturer of a drug is, in theory, similar to that of any other producer.[1] One notable aspect of litigation involving pharmaceutical products is the limited role of contractual remedies. While a person who purchases drugs via a private prescription may have contractual rights, these would be against the pharmacist who supplies the product, not its manufacturer. Prior to the passing of the Consumer Protection Act 1987, therefore, an injured party's civil law remedies were primarily based on the tort of negligence.

A party who wishes to sue a manufacturer under tort for injuries allegedly resulting from the use or consumption of one of the latter's products will require to show that the manufacturer owed that party a duty of care, that the duty of care was breached, and that the breach caused the injuries complained of. It is not possible for a person who acts in the course of a business to exclude or restrict liability for negligence where this results in death or personal injury.[2]

---

[1] One peculiarity in the realm of pharmaceutical product liability is the compensation system established by the Vaccine Damage Payments Act 1979. This is described in Chap. 12, below.
[2] The Unfair Contract Terms Act 1977 (c. 50) s.2(1).

2. The Duty of Care

It is clear that a manufacturer owes a duty of care to the ultimate consumer of its products.[3] Reasonable care must be taken to safeguard all persons who are foreseeable as being likely to be injured by these products.[4]

(A) THE UNBORN PLAINTIFF

Doubts as to whether manufacturers owed a duty of care to an unborn plaintiff was one of the reasons for the British families of the thalidomide victims accepting a negotiated settlement. Their leading counsel had advised them that the difficulty of establishing that such a duty of care existed meant that the chances of winning the case were "significantly less than evens".[5]

It is now clear that a duty of care is owed to the unborn child. In Scotland this is by virtue of the Common Law.[6] The issue arose in the case of *Hamilton v. Fife Health Board*[7] in which the court required to determine if a child who died due to ante-natal injuries was a person who had died "in consequence of personal injuries sustained by him", for the purposes of the Damages (Scotland) Act 1976. Lord Prosser had dismissed the parents' claim for compensation under this Act, holding that the child had not suffered "personal injuries" since it was a foetus, rather than a legal person, when these injuries were sustained.[8] Lord Morton of Shuna had reached the opposite conclusion in the case of *McWilliams v. Lord Advocate*.[9] When the *Hamilton* case was reclaimed, however, it was held that the parents of the dead child did have a valid cause of action. Lord McCluskey stated:

---

[3] See *Donoghue v. Stevenson* [1932] A.C. 562.
[4] The duty of care has been held to cover defective containers and packaging: *Hill v. James Crowe (Cases) Ltd* [1978] 1 All E.R. 812, and has been extended to passers-by: *Stennett v. Hancock and Peters* [1939] 2 All E.R. 578.
[5] See *The Sunday Times: The Thalidomide Children and the Law* (London, Andre Deutsch, 1973) p. 15.
[6] See *Liability for Antenatal Injury*, Scot. Law Com. No. 30, (1973) Cmnd. 5371.
[7] [1993] 4 Med.L.R. 201; 1993 S.L.T. 624; 1993 S.C.L.R. 408.
[8] See 1992 S.L.T. 1026.
[9] 1992 S.L.T. 1045; 1992 S.C.L.R. 954. See Norrie, "Liability for Injuries Caused Before Birth" 1992 S.L.T.(Notes) 65; and McCall Smith, "When is a foetus a person and when is it not?" *The Times*, March 30, 1993.

"... I see no reason to restrict 'personal' in the phrase 'personal injuries' so that it means injuries suffered by one on whom the law has conferred legal personality for certain purposes."[10]

In England the position has been clarified by the Congenital Disabilities (Civil Liability) Act 1976. It should be noted, however, that under this Act the claim of a child injured pre-natally is derivative; it is dependent on a duty of care having been owed to the child's parent by the defendant. It is also contingent on the child having been born alive. Recent cases such as *Burton v. Islington Health Authority*[11] and *De Martell v. Merton & Sutton Health Authority*[12] suggest that the victims of thalidomide would have succeeded in establishing that a duty of care was owed by the drug's manufacturers at Common Law.[13]

Proving that pre-natal injuries were caused by a pharmaceutical product can be particularly difficult. As one author has put it:

"Human development in the womb carries a substantial risk of death or abnormality ... Three to six per cent of children born have malformations ... For most of these disasters there is no one to blame."[14]

Thalidomide and diethylstilbestrol (DES) are notorious examples of drugs which can cause birth defects. Another example is Accutane (isotretinoin). About 600 babies may have been handicapped as a result of the use of this acne treatment by their mothers during pregnancy.[15]

(B) The Third-Generation Plaintiff

The position of a third-generation plaintiff of a drug disaster was at issue in the American case of *Enright v. Eli Lilly & Co.*[16] The plaintiff in that case

---

[10] *op. cit.* p. 629. It may also be argued that the injuries are "sustained" so far as Scots law is concerned, when the injured child is born.

[11] [1993] Q.B.D. 204; [1992] 3 W.L.R. 637; [1992] 3 All E.R. 833; [1993] 4 Med.L.R. 8.

[12] [1991] 2 Med.L.R. 209.

[13] See Ferguson, "Pharmaceutical Products Liability: 30 Years of Law Reform?" (1992) *Juridical Review,* **3**, p. 226 at p. 239.

[14] Patterson, ed., *Drugs in Litigation: Damage Awards Involving Prescription and Nonprescription Drugs* (Virginia, The Michie Company, 1992) at pp. 278–279.

[15] See Parish, *Medical Treatments: The Benefits and Risks* (London, Penguin Books, 1991) p. 1012.

[16] 77 N.Y. 2d 377, 570 N.E. 2d 198 (1991).

was a nine-year-old girl who suffered from cerebral palsy. The child claimed that her condition had resulted from her *grandmother's* ingestion of DES in 1959. Her grandmother had taken the drug during pregnancy and it was alleged that this had caused deformities in the reproductive system of her daughter, the plaintiff's mother, and that this in turn had caused the plaintiff's handicap. One of the judges argued that the girl ought to have the same right of suit as her mother:

> "... [she] is one of a class of thousands of persons who have allegedly suffered devastating abnormalities and injuries resulting from [the] defendants' marketing of DES ... Is there any basis in the law or social policy or any principled reason in justice and fairness for holding that she—unlike other members of the class—should not be permitted to prove her case?"[17]

This approach did not find favour with the other six judges of the New York Court of Appeal, which held that a third-generation DES injury claim could not be taken. It stressed the need to confine manufacturers' product liability to "manageable limits", and decided that this could be achieved by limiting a right of action to "those who ingested the drug or were exposed to it *in utero*".[18]

The Court relied on previous authorities in which it had been held that no cause of action lay where injuries were alleged to have been sustained as a result of a tort committed prior to the plaintiff's conception.[19] The decision in *Enright* was followed by the Ohio Supreme Court in *Grover v. Eli Lilly & Co.*[20] In a different context, the Court of Appeals of Oklahoma has pointed out that such an approach would mean that "an infant suffering personal injury from a defective food product, manufactured before his conception, would be without remedy".[21]

The position in relation to pre-conception injuries in England is clear; the Congenital Disabilities (Civil Liability) Act 1976 expressly provides a cause of action where a person has been injured due to an "occurrence" which affected his or her mother or father prior to the child's conception.[22]

---

[17] See Brahams, "Diethylstilboestrol: [*sic*] Third-Generation Injury Claims" (1991) *Medico-Legal Journal*, **59**, p. 126 at p. 127.
[18] *ibid.*
[19] *Albala v. City of New York*, 429 N.E. 2d 786 (N.Y. 1981).
[20] 591 N.E. 2d 696 (Ohio 1992).
[21] *Jorgensen v. Meade Johnson Laboratories* C.A.-10 Okla. 1973 483 F.2d 237.
[22] s.1(2)(a).

It is possible that the Scottish courts would also grant a remedy for a person who sustained injuries in such circumstances, but in practice the difficulty of establishing causation in such a case is likely to be an insurmountable hurdle in either jurisdiction.[23]

3. Failure to Test

A pharmaceutical product manufacturer which fails to conduct appropriate tests on its drugs or devices prior to marketing is likely to be considered negligent. This arose in the American case of *Bichler v. Eli Lilly & Co.*[24] in which the plaintiff alleged that the manufacturer of Diethylstilbestrol had been negligent in failing to test the drug on pregnant mice. The company admitted in court that it was aware of the threat of cancer posed by DES, and that it knew that the drug was capable of crossing the placental barrier.[25]

Similarly, in December 1991 a Californian jury held that Dow Corning, the primary manufacturer of silicone breast implants, required to compensate a woman whose implant had ruptured, and awarded her $7.3 million in compensation.[26] According to one report the company's internal memos indicated that it may have been over hasty in marketing the implants and may not have tested them adequately prior to marketing.[27] The company did seem to lack a sound base of knowledge about its own product, it was unable to say how often the implants rupture, what the consequences of such a rupture might be, or how long the implants could be expected to last.[28]

One way of establishing that a defendant manufacturer has failed to exercise reasonable care in its testing procedures is to show that it has not

---

[23] Causation issues are explored in Chap. 9, below.

[24] 436 N.E. 2d 182, (N.Y.C.A., 1982).

[25] *ibid.* at 189. See also the case of *Parke-Davis & Co. v. Stromsodt*, 411 F.2d 1390 (8th Cir. 1969).

[26] *Hopkins v. Dow Corning* (unreported, but see (1992) *P.L.I.*, 14:1, p. 5). See also Sharpe, "Breast implants: are they really safe?" (1992) *Mims Magazine*, April 15, p. 22 at p. 28.

[27] Schwartz and Kaplan, "Dow Corning under Fire" (1992) *Newsweek*, January 27, p. 39.

[28] Cowley, Springen and Hager, "Calling a Halt to the Big Business of Silicone Implants" (1992) *Newsweek*, January 20, p. 52. The deadline for women who wished to register for a share in an *ex gratia* fund established by the manufacturers of these implants was December 1, 1994.

complied with the standards of its own industry. But what if those standards have been complied with? Does this preclude a plaintiff from arguing that the standards ought to have been higher? The issue is particularly difficult where the testing procedures have been established by a government body. This was considered by the Irish courts in the recent case of *Best v. Wellcome Foundation*.[29] At issue was whether the defendant had breached its duty of care in allowing a batch of pertussis vaccine to be released, despite the fact that this particular batch had failed one of the tests used to monitor the vaccine's toxicity. The test in question, known as the "mouse weight gain test", was controversial, and was not one which the company was legally required to undertake at the time.[30] The defendant therefore argued that it had not been negligent in disregarding the results and relying instead on other and, in the company's view, more reliable, tests.

The Irish Supreme Court held that a manufacturer of vaccines was under a duty to exercise all reasonable care in order to avoid exposing the recipients of its products to harm or danger. Significantly, the Court held that merely to comply with the mandatory requirements imposed by national health authorities would not necessarily constitute a sufficient degree of care. Such requirements established minimum standards, only.[31] It is impossible to know whether a similar approach would be adopted by the British courts, but it is suggested that the *Best* case is likely to be followed.

4. Failure to Warn

Part of a manufacturer's duty of care to the ultimate consumer of its goods includes the provision of adequate information and relevant warnings. Failure to supply appropriate warning information may amount to negligence at Common Law if a manufacturer knew or ought to have known of any latent dangers, inherent in its products. This general proposition is illustrated by the case of *Vacwell Engineering v. BDH Chemicals*

---

[29] [1992] I.L.R.M. 609.
[30] The plaintiff had been vaccinated on November 17, 1969.
[31] On June 3, 1992 the Irish Supreme Court approved an award of £2.75 million against the Wellcome Company, for causing the plaintiff's brain damage.

Ltd,[32] in which the defendants were found liable for injuries caused when ampoules of boron tribromide which they had supplied to the plaintiffs exploded, killing a scientist. The explosive nature of this chemical had been explored in scientific journals. It ignited when mixed with water, and it was held that the defendant manufacturer should therefore have been aware of this, and ought to have provided more adequate warning information to the plaintiffs.[33]

Mention has already been made of the suits which had been raised against drug manufacturers in respect of tranquilliser addiction.[34] Patients who attempted to sue for Ativan addiction claimed that its manufacturer, Wyeth, knew by the late 1970s that there was a risk that patients might become addicted to this drug, yet did not warn patients until 1988. According to Fitzsimons there was:

"... a mass of evidence showing that the medical profession and the drug companies knew many years ago that there were major problems with these drugs, but did not act in their patients' interests to limit the damage they were likely to cause."[35]

As already noted, the withdrawal of legal aid has meant that few of these cases are continuing. For those that do remain, however, it may not be easy for plaintiffs to succeed in suing the manufacturers for these alleged failures to warn. As we have seen, a recent European Directive on Labelling and Leaflets has provided that from January 1, 1994 both prescription and non-prescription drugs must contain detailed information leaflets.[36] This provision was not in force at the time at which these tranquillisers were prescribed, and it seems that prior to these European requirements manufacturers were under no duty to provide information concerning prescription drug risks directly to patients. Rather, the manufacturer's duty was to convey warning information to an intermediary, namely the doctor.[37] While the position cannot be stated with absolute certainty due to the dearth of reported cases involving personal injury suits against the

---

[32] [1971] 1 Q.B. 111; [1970] 3 W.L.R. 67; [1969] 3 All E.R. 1681.
[33] See also *Baker v. Hopkins* [1959] 1 W.L.R. 966; [1959] 3 All E.R. 225.
[34] See p. [10], above.
[35] Fitzsimons, "Minister rebuffs tranquilliser victims" *The Sunday Observer*, April 3, 1988, p. 1.
[36] See pp. 27–28, above.
[37] See Ferguson, "Liability for Pharmaceutical Products: A Critique of the Learned Intermediary Rule" (1992) *Oxf.J.L.S.*, 12:1, pp. 59–82.

pharmaceutical industry, this proposition has the support of several commentators.[38]

The operation of this "learned intermediary" rule in relation to other products is illustrated by the case of *Holmes v. Ashford*.[39] The defendants manufactured a hair dye and included a warning that the dye could be harmful to certain skin types. They recommended that a test be carried out on each customer before the dye was used. The hairdresser made no test and did not warn the plaintiff of the dangers. The latter contracted dermatitis from the dye. Despite the fact that no warning had reached the customer, she failed in her attempt to sue the manufacturers; the Court of Appeal held that the warning to the hairdresser constituted sufficient compliance by the manufacturers with their duty of care.[40] According to Tucker L.J.:

> "... hairdressers may be expected to interpose their judgment and reason whether they are going to use a hair dye or not. In my view, if [the manufacturers] give a warning which, if read by a hairdresser, is sufficient to intimate *to him* the potential dangers of the substance with which he is going to deal, that is all that can be expected of them. I think it would be unreasonable and impossible to expect that they should give warning in such form that it must come to the knowledge of the particular customer who is going to be treated ... The most that can be expected of the manufacturers of goods of this kind is to see that *the hairdresser* is sufficiently warned."[41]

In the field of prescription drugs, Miller and Lovell have noted that:

> "Many cases will turn on the question whether the manufacturers' duty has been discharged by *warning a responsible intermediary* rather than the plaintiff himself ... Similar considerations would apply where the danger is from side-effects associated with the taking of a particular drug which is available only on

---

[38] See, for example, Clark, *Product Liability* (London, Sweet & Maxwell, 1989) p. 88; Forte, "Medical Products Liability" in McLean, ed., *Legal Issues in Medicine* (Aldershot, Gower, 1981) p. 67 at p. 72; Buckley, *The Modern Law of Negligence* (London, Butterworths, 1988) p. 337.

[39] [1950] 2 All E.R. 76.

[40] See also *Watson v. Buckley, Osborne Garrett and Co.* [1940] 1 All E.R. 174, and *Kubach v. Hollands* [1937] 3 All E.R. 907.

[41] *op. cit.* p. 80, emphases added.

prescription. Inquiry would then concentrate on the adequacy of warnings *to the medical profession* to enable it to achieve an informed balancing of risks."[42]

Hence it is argued that prior to the recent provisions on leaflets, the doctor, like the hairdresser, acted as an intermediary between the manufacturer and the ultimate consumer. By analogy with *Holmes v. Ashford*, doctors were deemed to have the relevant information about the product, were able to use their skill and judgment to determine which drug product was suitable to the needs of their patients, and were therefore relied upon to communicate appropriate warning information.

A similar "learned intermediary" rule operates in the United States of America.[43] The rule has been justified as follows:

"Prescription drugs are likely to be complex medicines, esoteric in formula and varied in effect. As a medical expert, the prescribing physician can take into account the propensities of the drug, as well as the susceptibilities of his patient. His is the task of weighing the benefits of any medication against its potential dangers. The choice he makes is an informed one, an individualized medical judgement bottomed on a knowledge of both patient and palliative. Pharmaceutical companies then, who must warn ultimate purchasers of dangers inherent in patent drugs sold over the counter, in selling prescription drugs are required to warn only the prescribing physician, who acts as a 'learned intermediary' between manufacturer and consumer."[44]

The doctor is therefore considered to be a person with knowledge both of the properties of the medication, and the relevant characteristics of the patient.[45] It is this which makes the physician "learned". This duty on the part of the medical profession to provide warning information is explored in chapter 4.

---

[42] *Product Liability* (London, Butterworths, 1977) p. 245, emphases added.

[43] The term "learned intermediary" was first used by an American court in respect of prescription drugs in the case of *Sterling Drugs Incorporated v. Cornish* 370 F.2d 82 (8th Cir. 1966). See also *Lindsay v. Ortho Pharmaceutical Corporation* 637 F.2d 87 (2d Cir. 1980); *Mahr v. GD Searle & Co.* 390 N.E. 2d 1214 (Ill. App. 1979); *Salmon v. Parke-Davis & Co.* 520 F.2d 1359 (4th Cir. 1975) and *Schenebeck v. Sterling Drugs Incorporated* 423 F.2d 919 (8th Cir. 1970). More recent cases have affirmed the doctrine: see *Hurley v. Lederle Laboratories* 851 F.2d 1536, (5th Cir. 1988) and *Ashman v. Smith Kline & French Lab Co.* 702 F.Supp. 1401 (1988).

[44] *Reyes v. Wyeth Laboratories* 498 F.2d 1264 (5th Cir.); 419 U.S. 1096 (1974) at 1276.

[45] A similar rule has been held to operate in Canada: see *Buchan v. Ortho Pharmaceutical (Canada) Ltd* (1986) 32 B.L.R. 285 (Ont. C.A.).

Where patient package leaflets are provided, the courts may be required to decide whether the information therein is adequate. In determining whether a product's hazards have been sufficiently warned against one must consider the exact wording of the warning and the circumstances surrounding the use of the product. As Waddams has noted:

> "There can be no hard and fast rule. The only test is whether the label, taking into account the size and colour of type as well as the design of the label as a whole and the particular words used is, in all the circumstances, sufficient to bring home to a reasonable user the true extent of the risk and of the precautions required."[46]

The information leaflets provided with pharmaceutical drugs and devices differ from those which accompany other products, since the former have the approval of a government regulatory body. One might therefore imagine that a court would be reluctant to criticise this information. This issue arose in the American case of *MacDonald v. Ortho Pharmaceutical Corporation*.[47] A Patient Package Insert supplied with an oral contraceptive had warned that the drug could cause "abnormal blood clotting which can be fatal", and that this could occur in "vital organs such as the brain".[48] The plaintiff suffered a permanently disabling stroke as a result of taking the Pill and argued that she had not realised that the reference to "abnormal blood clotting" meant that there was a risk of consumers having a stroke. She also testified that she would not have taken the drug if an express warning of this had been provided. The plaintiff was aged 30 when she suffered the stroke, and this case has been criticised on the basis that the risk to a woman of that age who was taking oral contraceptives was very small.[49] Nevertheless, the court held that the jury was entitled to find that this warning was insufficient, since the absence of a reference to the word "stroke" had:

> "unduly minimized the warning's impact or failed to make the nature of the risk reasonably comprehensible to the average consumer."[50]

---

[46] Waddams, *Products Liability* (Toronto, The Carswell Co. Ltd, 1974) pp. 48–49.

[47] 475 N.E. 2d 65 (Mass. 1985); see also *Hamilton v. Hardy* 549 P.2d 1099.

[48] *ibid.* p. 67 n. 4.

[49] Flannagan suggested a figure of 1.5 in 100,000 users. See: "Products Liability: The Continued Viability of the Learned Intermediary Rule as it Applies to Product Warnings for Prescription Drugs" (1986) *University of Richmond Law Review*, 20, 405 at 422.

[50] *op. cit.* p. 141.

The court held that these warnings were not adequate, despite the fact that the wording had complied with the requirements of the Food and Drug Administration.[51]

A similar decision was reached in the case of *Brochu v. Ortho Pharmaceutical Corporation*;[52] the information about the risks of injury which was provided in the patient package insert was held to be inadequate, despite the fact that the wording had been approved by the FDA. In *Wooderson v. Ortho Pharmaceutical Corporation*[53] the FDA had discouraged the manufacturer of a particular oral contraceptive from adding a warning as to the risks of haemolytic uraemic syndrome. The FDA were not satisfied with the result of a British study which suggested that there was a link between the drug and this syndrome. Eventually, studies in the United States confirmed the British findings and a new warning was added to the American products. In *Wooderson*, the plaintiff received a multimillion dollar sum in compensation when she developed this syndrome at a time during which this was not warned against in the United States. She also obtained an award of punitive damages, the jury obviously taking the view that the pill manufacturer *ought* to have copied the British warnings despite the fact that it had been advised against the incorporation of such a warning by the FDA.

Discussing *Brochu* and *Wooderson*, one author has argued that these cases have established the jury, rather than the FDA, "as the final arbiter of whether and how a medicine should be marketed".[54] This approach is summed up in the case of *Chambers v. GD Searle & Co.*[55] in which it was noted that "approval by the FDA of the language involved [in a package insert] is not necessarily conclusive on the adequacy of the warnings".[56]

Licensing bodies are concerned that doctors and patients are not warned about every extremely rare risk, for fear of an "information overload". The conclusion that a manufacturer may have complied with all government

---

[51] See also *Skill v. Martinez* 91 F.R.D. 498 (D.N.J. 1981); *Feldman v. Lederle Laboratories* 97 N.J. 429; 479 A.2d 374 (1984) and *Stephens v. GD Searle & Co.* 602 F.Supp. 379 (E.D. Mich. 1985).

[52] 642 F.2d 652 (1st Cir. 1981).

[53] 235 Kan. 387, 681 P.2d 1038 (1984).

[54] "A Question of Competence: The Judicial Role in the Regulation of Pharmaceuticals" (1990) *Harvard Law Review*, 103, p. 773 at p. 779.

[55] 441 F.Supp. 377 (1975); 567 F.2d 269 (1977).

[56] *ibid.* at 378. See also Epstein, "Legal Liability for Medical Innovation" (1987) *Cardozo Law Review*, 8, p. 1139.

regulations yet still be found liable is not, therefore, a reasonable one, unless it can be shown that the defendant had acquired further information on side effects or contraindications but had failed to notify the licensing authorities of this. In the event of such a failure, although the existing warnings may be in accordance with licensing requirements, the manufacturer's behaviour in not disclosing the new risk information to the relevant authorities may be held to amount to negligence.[57]

The lack of cases involving pharmaceutical products which have reached the trial stage in this country makes it difficult to determine the approach which a British court is likely to take in assessing the adequacy of warning information. The Association of the British Pharmaceutical Industry has made it clear that its members do not regard approval by the licensing authority as reducing their legal responsibility for their products.[58] This is rightly so, since the authority is itself dependent on each company supplying adequate and accurate information and keeping it informed if any new reactions are discovered. It may be argued, however, that a drug information leaflet or label which has the approval of the licensing authority ought to be regarded as adequate in law. A drug company should only be liable for failing to supply further or clearer warning information if it has withheld risk information from these government bodies.[59] In practice, it seems unlikely that a British court would hold that a drug's warning information was inadequate where the leaflet or label in question was authorised by the CSM, and accurately reflected the knowledge which was available to the company.

It has been suggested that people rarely pay sufficient attention to warning information.[60] Most of the research which has been done on the effect of warnings has concentrated on everyday or household objects, such as hammers, lawnmowers and car seat-belts, and it is arguable that a patient taking a pharmaceutical product for the first time might be more inclined to treat warning information with greater care. Whether any attention is paid to information leaflets once the patient has become accustomed to

---

[57] See *Toole v. Richardson-Merrell Incorporated*, 60 Cal. Rpt. 398 (1967).

[58] *Pearson Commission Report, Royal Commission on Civil Liability and Compensation for Personal Injury*, Cmnd. 7054, 1978, para. 1260.

[59] See also Gilhooley, "Innovative Drugs, Products Liability, Regulatory Compliance, and Patient Choice" (1994) 24 *Seton Hall Law Review*, pp. 1481–1506, arguing for a "compliance" defence.

[60] Robinson and Brickle, "Warning labels: science and the law" (1992) *N.L.J.*, 142, p. 83.

using a particular drug is more debatable. These concerns highlight the need for greater education of patients, that is, for the provision of more, rather than less, information about their medicines.

5. Duration of the Duty of Care

One issue of importance to a manufacturer is the duration of its duty of care; does it continue after a product has been marketed? In *Donoghue v. Stevenson* itself Lord Macmillan argued that:

> "where a manufacturer has parted with his product and it has passed into other hands it may well be exposed to vicissitudes which may render it defective or noxious, for which the manufacturer could not in any view be held to be to blame. It may be a good general rule to regard responsibility as ceasing when control ceases."[61]

It is likely that this would now be given a narrow interpretation; although a manufacturer may not be liable to the ultimate consumer if a third party has tampered with the product once it has left the manufacturer's control, it is at least arguable that it nevertheless owes a continuing duty of care to the consumer.

One American author has advocated that pharmaceutical product manufacturers should undertake their own post-marketing studies, even if this has not been made a licence requirement by the Food and Drug Administration. He argues:

> "One often hears the phrase 'What you don't know won't hurt you.' However, in pharmacoepidemiology this view is shortsighted and, in fact, very wrong ... even if the drug did cause the adverse outcome in question, a manufacturer certainly can document that it was performing state-of-the-art studies to attempt to detect whatever toxic effects the drug had. In addition, such studies could make easier the defense of totally groundless suits in which a drug is blamed for producing adverse reactions it does not cause."[62]

---

[61] *ibid.* p. 622.
[62] Strom, "When Should One Perform Pharmacoepidemiologic Studies?" Chap. 5 of Strom, ed., *Pharmacoepidemiology* (Chichester, John Wiley & Sons Ltd, 2nd ed., 1994) p. 60.

Although there do not appear to be British cases which consider the duration of the duty of care for pharmaceutical products, the issue was considered in relation to chemicals in the case of *Wright v. Dunlop Rubber Co. Ltd.*[63] The plaintiff had been employed by Dunlop since 1946 and developed cancer of the bladder in 1966. Dunlop used Nonox-S, an anti-oxidant, which was supplied by ICI. Dunlop brought ICI into the action, as second defendants. The latter had become aware of the carcinogenic potential of Nonox-S by 1945 but did not warn Dunlop's employees nor cease supplying this chemical, despite its dangers, until 1949. The court stated that the manufacturer's duty:

"... is not necessarily confined to the period before the product is first produced or put on the market. Thus, if, when a product is first marketed, there is no reason to suppose that it is carcinogenic, but thereafter information shows, or gives reason to suspect, that it may be carcinogenic, the manufacturer has failed in his duty if he has failed to do whatever may have been reasonable in the circumstances in keeping up to date with knowledge of such developments and acting with whatever promptness fairly reflects the nature of the information and the seriousness of the possible consequences."[64]

The court held that it was ICI's duty:

"... to take all reasonable steps to satisfy themselves that [Nonox-S] was safe: 'safe' in the sense that there was no substantial risk of any substantial injury to health on the part of persons who were likely to use it ..."[65]

This suggests that a manufacturer's duty of care continues even after its products have been marketed. This does seem to be the position in Canada. In relation to pharmaceutical products, in particular, it was stated in the case of *Buchan v. Ortho Pharmaceutical (Canada) Ltd*[66] that:

"A manufacturer of prescription drugs occupies the position of an expert in the field; this requires that it be under a continuing duty to keep abreast of scientific developments pertaining to its product through research, adverse reaction reports, scientific literature and other available methods."[67]

---

[63] (1972) 13 K.I.R. 255 C.A.
[64] *ibid.* p. 272.
[65] *ibid.*
[66] (1986) 25 D.L.R. (4th) 658, 54 O.R. (2d) 92 (Ont. C.A.).
[67] *ibid.* at 678 (D.L.R.) or 112 (O.R.).

The manufacturer in *Wright v. Dunlop Rubber Co. Ltd* was found to have been negligent for not acting on a *suspicion* that its product was causing injury. Since the warnings and information which a drug manufacturer provides with its products are dictated to a large extent by government regulatory bodies, it is perhaps unlikely that a pharmaceutical product manufacturer would be expected to warn of adverse reactions of which there was only a "mere suspicion".

As already noted, the British licensing authority will not issue a product licence to a company unless the latter satisfies them that it has an adequate recall programme.[68] In addition, a wholesale distributor of pharmaceutical products will not be granted authorisation unless it has formulated emergency plans for prompt product recall.[69] The American FDA has similar powers to order a manufacturer to recall its products should they prove to be defective. It has used this power to order Shiley Incorporated to recall 5,700 of its Bjork-Shiley heart valves. The company were also required to contact all cardiologists and cardiovascular surgeons practising in the United States and ask them to monitor carefully patients in whom this type of valve had been implanted.[70]

6. Statutes of Limitation

Most legal systems have enacted limitations legislation, which provides that certain types of civil actions must be raised within a particular period, otherwise they become "time-barred". This is designed to ensure that a defendant does not carry the risk of suit for an indefinite period, and to encourage potential plaintiffs to commence litigation sooner rather than later, when the documentary evidence is more easily attainable, and memories are keener. As Spahn has pointed out:

"Statutes of limitations represent the legislature's balance between two competing interests: (1) allowing plaintiffs to pursue meritorious claims; and (2)

---

[68] See p. [29], above.
[69] See Dir. 92/25/EEC (L113/1).
[70] Sanbar, in Wecht, ed., *Legal Medicine 1986* (New York, London, Praeger, 1986) p. 91.

providing potential defendants [with] the expectation that those claims will be pursued within a reasonable time—before the trail of evidence cools."[71]

Under English Law the general rule is that time limits–start to run as soon as the injury or loss occurs. The Limitation Act 1980 provides that actions in tort or arising from contract must generally be commenced within six years[72] but the time period is three years if such actions involve personal injury.[73] At common law this rule operated strictly such that the time limit ran from the date of injury, despite the fact that the injured party may have been unaware of the injury, and even in cases where it would not have been possible for the injured party to have discovered that he or she had been injured. In the case of *Cartledge v. Jopling & Sons Ltd*[74] Lord Reid stated that:

". . . a cause of action accrues as soon as a wrongful act has caused personal injury beyond what can be regarded as negligible, even when that injury is unknown to and cannot be discovered by the sufferer."[75]

This case led to statutory provisions designed to mitigate the harshness of the rule.[76] Under that legislation, plaintiffs had to commence proceedings within 12 months of the date on which they became aware, or could reasonably be expected to have become aware, of their injury. This period was ultimately extended to three years. The current limitation period in England now commences from the date at which a plaintiff knew, or *ought* to have known, of the following:

1. that the injury was significant (that is, that it was known to be sufficiently serious to justify proceedings);
2. that this injury was at least partly attributable to the act or omissions of the defendant, and that this may have been negligent;
3. the identity of the defendant.[77]

---

[71] Spahn, "The Statute of Limitations Defense" in Vinson and Slaughter, eds., *Products Liability: Pharmaceutical Drug Cases* (Colorado, Shephard's/McGraw-Hill Inc, 1988) p. 85. See also the dictum of Lord Edmund-Davies in *Birkett v. James* [1978] A.C. 297 at 331.

[72] ss.2 and 5, respectively.

[73] s.11(1).

[74] [1963] A.C. 758; [1963] 2 W.L.R. 210; [1963] 1 All E.R. 341.

[75] [1963] 1 All E.R. 341 at 343.

[76] See the Limitation Act 1963, which was based on the recommendations in the Davies Report: *Report of the Committee on Limitation of Actions in Cases of Personal Injury*, Cmnd 1829 (1962).

[77] s.14(1).

The injured parties in the landmark cases of *Donoghue v. Stevenson*[78] and its American equivalent, *Greenman v. Yuba Power Products Incorporated*[79] were in a position to investigate the possibility of raising an action from an early stage. This can be contrasted with the situation of persons who sustain injury due to the side effect of a drug. In respect of the first two criteria required by the 1980 Act, in many situations such victims may not even be aware that they have sustained injury, and any physical signs which are apparent may be mistakenly attributed to underlying illness or disease processes, rather than to the treatment.

The current English legislation gives the courts a discretion to allow claims to be taken after the three year period, even if the delay is not attributable to lack of knowledge concerning a material fact.[80] The Limitation Act 1980 provides six guidelines to assist a court in its exercise of this discretion. These are:

1. the length of and reasons for the plaintiff's delay;
2. the extent to which the cogency of evidence adduced by either party may be affected by the delay;
3. the defendant's conduct after the cause of action arose, including his response to requests by the plaintiff for information or inspection for the purpose of ascertaining relevant facts;
4. duration of any disability of the plaintiff after the cause of action arose;
5. the promptitude and reasonableness of the plaintiff's conduct once he knew that there might be a cause of action;
6. the steps taken by the plaintiff to obtain expert advice and the nature of the advice he received.[81]

Justice Hidden was not prepared to use this discretion in the recent Opren litigation. Many claimants had settled their actions in December 1987,[82] but a further 250 people issued writs against Eli Lilly between March and May of 1988. Nine of this latter group were selected as test cases. Many of them had been assured by their doctors that any side-effects

---

[78] 1932 S.C., H.L., 31; [1932] A.C. 562.

[79] 59 Cal. 2d 57; 27 Cal.Rptr. 697 (1963).

[80] Limitation Act 1980, s.33. See *Hartley v. Birmingham City District Council* [1992] 1 W.L.R. 968; [1992] 2 All E.R. 213. In the case of *Brookes v. J.P. Coates Ltd* [1984] 1 All E.R. 702 an action was allowed to commence, despite a 15-year delay.

[81] s.33(3).

[82] See p. [15], above.

which they were experiencing were transitory and would end once they stopped taking Opren. Most had therefore delayed court action in the hope that their symptoms would eventually disappear. Despite this, Hidden J. held in the case of *Nash v. Eli Lilly and Others* that eight of the nine test actions were time-barred.[83] This was, however, reversed on appeal.[84]

It is important to note that constructive knowledge may be sufficient to start the time limitation periods running—the section refers to knowledge which a plaintiff had, *or ought to have had.* A person is therefore expected to have acquired knowledge of any facts which were observable or ascertainable, and this includes knowledge which a person could be expected to have acquired with the help of medical or other appropriate expert advice which it was reasonable for him to seek.[85] In *Nash v. Eli Lilly* the Court of Appeal held that for the purposes of section 14 of the 1980 Act plaintiffs must have actual knowledge; they must have known that the nature of their injuries justified the taking of preliminary steps for the initiation of court proceedings against the person who caused those injuries. Where the plaintiffs' beliefs require to be confirmed by experts, these beliefs do not become knowledge until such confirmations are obtained. Similarly, in *Davis v. City and Hackney Health Authority*[86] the plaintiff's mother had been injected with Ovametrin, during her labour in 1963. It was held by Jowitt J. that the plaintiff did not know that this injection could be the cause of his injury until he acquired an expert's report in 1986.

A three year time limit also operates in Scotland in actions for personal injuries. This is by virtue of section 17 of the Prescription and Limitation (Scotland) Act 1973.[87] Time starts to run against a pursuer from the date on which the latter's injuries were sustained, or, if later, from the date on which the pursuer became aware of certain facts. These criteria are similar to those of the English legislation.[88] Prior to the Prescription and

---

[83] [1991] 2 Med.L.R. 169; *The Times* February 13, 1991. See also *Berger v. Eli Lilly & Co.* [1992] 3 Med.L.R. 233.

[84] See [1993] 1 W.L.R. 782; [1993] 4 All E.R. 383; [1992] 3 Med.L.R. 353.

[85] s.14(3)(f).

[86] [1991] 2 Med.L.R. 366; *The Times*, January 27, 1989.

[87] As amended by the Prescription and Limitation (Scotland) Act 1984.

[88] The Scottish criteria are as follows: that the injuries were sufficiently serious to justify the bringing of an action; that the injuries were at least partly attributable to an act or omission; and that the defender was a person to whose acts or omissions the injuries were attributable. (s.17(2)).

Limitation (Scotland) Act 1984 it had been held in a number of cases that a lack of knowledge of the wrongdoer's identity was not a factor which prevented time limits from running against the injured party.[89] This was in contrast to the position in England.[90]

We have already noted that English law gives the courts a discretion to extend the three year period, in certain circumstances. A similar discretionary power is available to a Scottish court, "if it seems to it equitable" to extend the period.[91] The courts have stressed that this power should be used sparingly[92] but have exercised the discretion in a number of cases.[93] Where the court chooses to exercise its discretion, the subsequent hearing of the case should not be before a jury.[94] The Scottish courts have made it clear that there is no real difference in approach between the Scottish legislation and section 33 of the English Limitation Act 1980.[95]

7. Conclusions

It is clear from the above discussion that members of the pharmaceutical industry owe duties of care which are similar to those who manufacture other products. It may, however, be very difficult for a plaintiff to determine whether a pharmaceutical company has adequately tested its drugs, or whether any alternative precautions could have been taken. In

---

[89] See *Kerr v. J.A. Stewart (Plant) Ltd*, 1975 S.L.T. 138; 1976 S.L.T. 255; and *Love v. Haran Sealant Services Ltd*, 1979 S.C. 279; 1979 S.L.T. 89.

[90] See *Clark v. Forbes Stuart (Thames Street) Ltd* [1964] 1 W.L.R. 836; [1964] 2 All E.R. 282. The Scottish position has been changed by the insertion of a new s.17(2)(b) into the 1973 Act.

[91] s.19A of the Prescription and Limitation (Scotland) Act 1973, as amended by the Prescription and Limitation (Scotland) Act 1984. See *Donner v. Melville Dundas & Whitson Ltd*, 1990 S.L.T. 186; 1989 S.C.L.R. 587; *Nicol v. British Steel Corporation (General Steels) Ltd*, 1992 S.L.T. 141; *Clark v. McLean*, 1993 S.L.T. 492; and *Percy v. Glenburnie Securities Ltd*, 1993 S.L.T. (Sh.Ct.) 78.

[92] See *Whyte v. Walker*, 1983 S.L.T. 441, and *Carson v. Howard Doris*, 1981 S.C. 278; 1981 S.L.T. 273.

[93] See, for example, *Comber v. Greater Glasgow Health Board and Others*, 1989 S.C.L.R. 515; 1989 S.L.T. 639, in which the pursuer's action was allowed to proceed, despite a delay of almost six years.

[94] s.19(4). For a detailed description of the Scottish legislation see Walker, *The Law of Prescription and Limitation of Actions in Scotland* (Edinburgh, W. Green & Son Ltd, 4th ed., 1990).

[95] See *McLaren v. Harland and Wolff*, 1991 S.L.T. 85, *per* Lord Milligan at 88, and *Elliot v. J. & C. Finnie*, 1989 S.L.T. 208, *per* Lord Coulsfield at 211 (affirmed at 1989 S.L.T. 605).

general, a defendant is only liable for failing to prevent injuries which it foresaw, or ought to have foreseen. If an adverse drug reaction has not been discovered during pre-market testing, and these tests have been performed without negligence, then it is likely that any side effect which manifests itself thereafter will be regarded as "unforeseeable".

The evidence on which it is decided to issue a licence to a new drug is not made available to the public,[96] nor are detailed reasons given for the decision to withdraw a drug.[97] Indeed, it is a criminal offence under the Medicines Act 1968 for officials to disclose such information.[98] Citizens of the United States of America have much greater access to the information on which drug regulatory bodies make their decisions than their British counterparts; the American Food and Drug Administration is required to publish information detailing the tests and studies done on a new drug, and the reasoning which led to approval of the drug.

Furthermore, as Dodds-Smith has argued, the very existence of a government licensing system may:

> "... make it more difficult for claimants to prove negligence, given that the regulatory authorities and their expert committees have been satisfied by the research data available and have been satisfied that criteria of quality, safety and efficacy have been met."[99]

It is not simply that the secrecy which surrounds the testing and manufacturing of drugs may make it difficult for injured parties to uncover a company's negligence; it is apparent from our discussion of the testing processes in chapter 2 that a drug which causes serious adverse reactions may be marketed *without their having been any negligence* on the part of its manufacturer.

While this book is concerned mainly with the legal liability of the

---

[96] See ss.19 and 20 of the Medicines Act 1968.

[97] The withdrawal of Halcion by the CSM in October 1991 raised many questions as to the need for secrecy. "The side-effects of secrecy" *The Scotsman*, October 3, 1991, p. 1, (and p. [38], above).

[98] By s.118. The ABPI has, however, announced that from January 1, 1996 the public will be able to ask a pharmaceutical company for a summary of the data which it supplied to the licensing authority. This will include information on side effects, and details of the scientific basis on which the approval for the medicine was sought. (*Pharmaceutical Industry Takes Action to Offer Patients More Information on Medicines*, ABPI Press Release, October 30, 1995.)

[99] Dodds-Smith, "The Impact of Product Liability on Pharmaceutical Companies" (unpublished paper given at the Fulbright Colloquium, Keele University, September 18–19, 1989).

manufacturers of pharmaceutical products, a plaintiff may contemplate suing some other party or body. The following chapter explores the Common Law liability of members of the medical profession, and chapters 5 and 6 consider the liability of pharmacists and government licensing bodies, respectively.

Chapter 4

The Common Law Liability of the Doctor

1. Introduction

A doctor may be held liable for acts or omissions, such as negligence in the performance of a surgical procedure, or a failure to diagnose correctly, neither of which necessarily involves the use of a pharmaceutical drug or device.[1] This chapter will therefore concentrate on those areas of liability which are most relevant to pharmaceutical products. Hospital doctors and nurses administer drugs directly to patients; annually the NHS Hospital Service spends £300 million on drugs.[2] Few pharmaceutical products are actually provided by general practitioners. It is more common for a doctor to write a prescription, and for the drug to be supplied by a pharmacist and self-administered by the patient. A doctor may, however, supply drugs in an emergency, and may insert or remove an intrauterine device, or administer a vaccine or other injection, on a routine basis.[3] Rural doctors may also do their own dispensing, and this accounts for six per cent of all prescriptions.[4]

---

[1] For a more detailed discussion of the potential liability of members of the medical profession see Jones, *Medical Negilgence* (London, Sweet & Maxwell, 1991); Power and Harris, *Medical Negligence* (London, Butterworths, 1990) and Nelson-Jones and Burton, *Medical Negligence Case Law* (London, Fourmat Publishing, 1990).

[2] Cook, Doyle and Jabbari, *Pharmaceuticals, Biotechnology and the Law* (Hants, Macmillan Publishers Ltd, 1991) at p. 10.

[3] s.58(3) of the Medicines Act 1968 allows doctors to supply prescription-only medical products to their patients, without providing a prescription.

[4] Cook, Doyle and Jabbari, *op. cit.*

2. Contract Law

Medical consultations may take place under the National Health Service, or on a private basis. In the latter, patients or their insurance companies pay for their doctors' services, and there will be contractual relations between the parties. The exact nature of the obligations owed by a doctor to such a patient will be dependent on the wording of their particular contract. A doctor who undertakes that a patient will "definitely be cured" will be in breach of contract if this eventuality does not result. It will, of course, be very rare indeed for a member of the medical profession to make such a claim.[5]

In most cases the patient will be receiving treatment under the National Health Service, and it is generally considered that this does not result in any contractual relationship between doctor and patient under English law.[6] The doctrine of consideration requires there to be an exchange of benefits between the parties before a contract will arise, and no money passes directly from a patient to an NHS doctor for the latter's services.[7] Some authors have, however, pointed out that a doctor's remuneration increases when a patient allows his or her name to be added to that doctor's patient list,[8] and have argued that this could amount to the necessary consideration.[9] This may not be correct; the case of *Appleby v. Sleep*[10] makes it clear that payment to a third party for the provision of services to a patient does

---

[5] See however *Thake v. Maurice* [1986] 1 All E.R. 479 and *Eyre v. Measday* [1986] 1 All E.R. 488.

[6] See para. 1313 of the *Report of the Royal Commission on Civil Liability and Compensation for Personal Injury* (The Pearson Report, Cmnd. 7054, 1978); Deutsch and Schreiber, eds., *Medical Responsibility in Western Europe* (Berlin, New York, Springer-Verlag, 1985) p. 134 and pp. 571–572; Dias and Markesinis, *Tort Law* (Oxford, Clarendon Press, 2nd ed., 1989) p. 154; Oughton, *Consumer Law: Text, Cases & Materials* (London, Blackstone Press, 1991) p. 309, para. 10.2; and Bell, "The Doctor and the Supply of Goods and Services Act 1982" (1984) *Legal Studies*, 4, 175.

[7] s.2 of the Supply of Goods and Services Act 1982 (c. 29) also requires there to be consideration for a contract for the supply of services.

[8] Doctors' remunerations are governed by s.29(4) of the National Health Service Act 1977 (c. 49), as amended by s.29(5)(b) of the Health Services Act 1980 (c. 53), and by s.19(3) of the National Health Service (Scotland) Act 1978 (c. 29).

[9] See Jackson and Powell, *Professional Negligence* (London, Sweet & Maxwell, 3rd ed., 1992) p. 448, para. 6.03.

[10] [1968] 2 All E.R. 265. See p. [80], below.

not, of itself, create a contract between that patient and the supplier of those services.

The doctrine of consideration does not apply in Scots law.[11] One author has suggested that "where patients call in a doctor participating in the National Health Service these facts may raise a contract between them."[12] The same author has, however, noted elsewhere that the situation is "questionably contractual". He writes:

"... formerly if a person consulted a physician he impliedly made a contract with him ... but today if a person registered under the National Health Service consults the doctor with whom he is registered the relationship is questionably contractual. If the doctor fails to see him, or treats him negligently, has the patient any remedy on the ground of breach of contract? ... the contention that the relationship is contractual has to face many difficulties, such as when and how was the contract made? What are its terms?"[13]

The author concludes that the rights and duties existing in such relationships are "probably *statutory* rather than contractual."[14] Doctors are required by statute to treat their patients, and it has been held that where services are provided under a statutory obligation this will not result in any contractual relationship.[15]

Might a Scottish patient have a *ius quaesitum tertio*, based on the contract of employment which exists between the doctor and the health authority? In the English case of *Roy v. Kensington and Chelsea and Westminster Family Practitioner Committee*[16] it was held that the relationship between general practitioners and their family practitioner committees was not contractual. The position in Scots law is likely to be similar, hence such a *ius quaesitum tertio* for the patient will not arise. Blackie accepts that Scots law recognises the actionability of seriously intended promises but argues that, as far as the doctor/patient relationship is concerned, this is "of theoretical interest

---

[11] For the essentials of a valid contract in Scots law, see Walker, *The Law of Contracts and Related Obligations in Scotland* (London, Butterworths, 2nd ed., 1985) p. 40, para. 3.13. See also Woolman, *An Introduction to the Scots Law of Contract* (Edinburgh, W. Green & Son Ltd, 1987).
[12] Walker, *The Law of Delict in Scotland* (Edinburgh, W. Green & Son Ltd, 2nd ed., 1981) p. 1057.
[13] Walker, *The Law of Contracts and Related Obligations in Scotland, op. cit.* p. 12, para. 1.32.
[14] *ibid.* emphasis added.
[15] *Pfizer Corporation v. Minister of Health* [1965] A.C. 512, discussed at p. 79, below.
[16] [1992] 1 All E.R. 705, *per* Lord Bridge at 709.

only, since [the existence of such contracts] must be proved by writing or admitted on oath by the promisor."[17]

In the private medicine sphere, where a contract does exist, Giesen has suggested that a patient who is injured by a pharmaceutical product may have a claim under sale of goods legislation, for breach of an implied term as to the fitness or quality of the product.[18] He bases his argument on the case of *Dodd and Dodd v. Wilson and McWilliam*[19] in which veterinary surgeons were sued when the toxoid which they had injected into the plaintiffs' cattle was found to have been defective. The vets were held strictly liable in contract. However, the contract between a doctor and a paying patient is not generally regarded as being a contract of *sale*, but rather, is for the provision of goods and services. The Supply of Goods and Services Act 1982 implies into such contracts a condition that the goods supplied will be of satisfactory quality and fit for their usual purpose. It should be noted that this condition will only relate to goods which are *supplied*. A doctor who uses a needle to inject drugs into a patient will therefore not be held strictly liable in contract should the needle itself prove to be defective, injuring the patient.[20] In such a situation the doctor *has* supplied the substance which is being injected, hence may be liable under the 1982 Act should the drug itself not be of satisfactory quality. Section 13 of the Supply of Goods and Services Act 1982 implies into contracts for the supply of services that the service will be performed with reasonable care and skill. This is the same standard as the Common Law duty of care which is imposed in the tort of negligence.[21]

3. Tort Law

Doctors owe a duty of care to their patients. The test of reasonable care in relation to medical practice was described in the case of *Bolam v. Friern Hospital Management Committee*[22] as being:

---

[17] In Deutsch and Schreiber, *Medical Responsibility in Western Europe* (Berlin, New York, Springer-Verlag, 1985) p. 572.
[18] Giesen, *International Medical Malpractice Law: A Comparative Study of Civil Liability Arising From Medical Care* (Dordrecht, Martinus Nijhoff Publishers, 1988) p. 21.
[19] [1946] 2 All E.R. 691.
[20] This occurred in the case of *Brazier v. Ministry of Defence* [1965] 1 Lloyds Rep. 26.
[21] See *Edgar v. Lamont* 1914 S.C. 277.
[22] [1957] 1 W.L.R. 582.

"... the standard of the ordinary skilled man excercising and professing to have that special skill. A man need not possess the highest expert skill; it is well established law that it is sufficient if he exercises the ordinary skill of an ordinary competent man exercising that particular art."[23]

In relation to pharmaceutical products, a doctor may be liable for a patient's injury if this were caused by negligence in the selection[24] or use of a product, or in the writing of a prescription.[25] It has been estimated that about two per cent of British prescriptions cannot be dispensed because they are illegible, or require the pharmacist to clarify them with the physician.[26]

The Department of Health produces guidelines on good clinical practice for general practitioners. In relation to the pertussis vaccine for example, the guidelines specified that this vaccine should not be given to a child who had a history of neurological illness, either in the family or personally; who suffered from a febrile illness at the time of vaccination, or who had suffered a serious neurological reaction to a previous immunisation. It may be negligence for a doctor to deviate from guidelines such as these without good reason.[27] It was alleged in the litigation concerning pertussis that these guidelines *had* been breached by some doctors.

So far as "defective products" are concerned, a doctor who supplies or administers such a product is unlikely to be found liable in negligence since the exercise of reasonable care is unlikely to reveal that a drug has a manufacturing defect, or has been defectively designed. The issue of

---

[23] *ibid.* at 586, *per* McNair J. The *Bolam* test has been applied in many subsequent decisions, including the cases of *Sidaway v. Governors of the Bethlam Royal Hospital and the Maudsley Hospital and Others* [1985] 1 A.C. 871; 643 and *Maynard v. West Midlands Area Health Authority* [1984] 1 W.L.R. 634; [1985] 1 All E.R. 635. See also the Scottish case of *Hunter v. Hanley* 1955 S.C. 200; 1955 S.L.T. 213.

[24] See *Robinson v. Post Office* [1974] 2 All E.R. 737, C.A., and the American case of *Cobbs v. Grant* 104 Cal. Rptr. 505, 515 (1972).

[25] See the case of *Prendergast v. Sam & Dee Ltd* [1989] 1 M.L.R. 36 in which the plaintiff sustained permanent brain damage as a result of his doctor's negligence in not writing the prescription more clearly. The case is discussed in more detail at p. 82, below.

[26] Hunter, "Pharmacists urge sole right to dispensing" *Doctor*, February 19, 1987. According to the ABPI about 60 per cent of adverse reactions are due to "inappropriate prescribing". See Medawar, *Power and Dependence: Social Audit on the Safety of Medicines* (London, Social Audit Ltd, Bath Press, 1992) p. 228.

[27] See also the case of *Sharangdhar Prasad v. General Medical Council* [1987] 1 W.L.R. 1697, in which a general practitioner was found guilty of serious professional misconduct and struck off the medical register for "repeatedly and unnecessarily" vaccinating his patients.

"marketing defects" is of more relevance, since the duty of care which doctors owe to their patients includes a duty to provide appropriate information about the drugs which they use or prescribe. The doctor's responsibility to provide adequate warning information is the corollary of a patient's right to be free from interference to which he or she has not consented, hence the issues of failure to warn and consent to treatment are intimately related.

4. Failure to Warn

The law views the individual as a self-determining moral agent and, in general, no interference is acceptable without a person's acquiescence. The civil law holds that no wrong is done to one who consents. Any interference with a person without that person's consent may found an action in tort.[28] An illustration of this in relation to pharmaceutical products is provided by the case of *Barbara v. Home Office*,[29] in which the plaintiff was arrested by the police and forcibly injected with a tranquilliser. He claimed damages for trespass to the person and was awarded £600 in compensation.

Consent to medical treatment need not be in writing, and it has been held that a patient who held up an arm to be vaccinated could not complain thereafter of a lack of consent.[30] In relation to prescription drugs, it is arguable that the patient consents to treatment by accepting the prescription from the physician. Ideally, the doctor should have spent some time prior to this outlining to the patient the diagnosis, proposed treatment, and any important hazards associated with that treatment. In medical cases we are not, generally, faced with a complete lack of consent. The more common problem occurs where a patient purports to consent yet has not been advised of a particular risk, which then materialises, causing harm. This raises the issue of "informed consent".[31]

---

[28] See *Devi v. West Midlands Regional Health Authority* [1980] Scottish Current Law Year Book 687.
[29] (1984) *New.L.J.*, 134, p. 888.
[30] *O'Brien v. Cunard Steamship Co.* (1891) 28 N.E. 266.
[31] For a more detailed account of the informed consent issue see McLean, "The Right to Consent to Medical Treatment" Chap. 8 of Campbell, Goldberg *et al*, eds., *Human Rights: From Rhetoric to Reality* (Oxford, Blackwell, 1986) and Brooke & Barton, "Consent to Treatment" Chap. 12 of Power and Harris, *Medical Negligence* (London, Butterworths, 2nd ed., 1994).

In an ideal world the doctor could be relied upon to ensure that the patient is given relevant warnings and risk information. The reality is likely to fall far short of this; not infrequently, patients leave their doctors' surgeries without knowing what has been prescribed for them. It is clear that there would have been minimal discussion of any risks associated with the medication in such cases.

Mention has already been made of the suits which had at one time been considered in respect of the alleged side effects of human insulin. A number of these diabetics claimed that their doctors did not inform them that they were being switched from animal to human insulin. This was alleged to have occurred in the case of Colin Jack, who later died as a result of a serious hypoglycaemic attack.[32] In an editorial in the *British Medical Journal* in October 1989 Dr John Pickup cautioned that doctors should:

" . . . be aware of the risk of altered control, explain this risk to their patients (as well as the reasons for any changeover), and closely monitor the patient in the subsequent weeks. It is particularly necessary to warn patients of the danger of hypoglycaemia while driving and remind them of the need for checking blood glucose concentrations before the journey and at about two hourly intervals during long periods of driving. Doctors should take any adverse effects seriously and even be ready to change the patient back to animal insulin if necessary."[33]

In the light of recent concerns as to the effects of human insulin, it may be negligent for a doctor to switch a patient to human insulin without first discussing the possible implications of this. The more difficult question is whether doctors were negligent in not discussing such matters with patients in 1989, when Colin Jack died. Colin's mother had collected the prescription for her son. According to Mrs Olive Jack:

"The chemist said I should take [the prescription] back because he didn't stock animal [insulin] any more. I left it with the doctor's receptionist and, when I picked it up later, [the doctor] had added the word 'human' to it."[34]

If this is correct, then the doctor did not decide to change Colin's treatment until after the prescription had been written. Had Colin, then, consented to

---

[32] See Shannon, "The cure that went wrong" *The Sunday Times Magazine*, May 31, 1992, p. 57 at p. 58.
[33] Pickup, "Human Insulin" (1989) *B.M.J.*, 299, p. 991 at p. 993.
[34] Shannon, *op. cit.*, p. 58.

this change in his treatment regime? At first sight it might be thought that a civil action for battery might lie against the doctor if there had been treatment without the patient's consent. However, even if a court was prepared to hold that Colin Jack did not consent to the treatment, this would not amount to a battery since this requires the defendant to have "touched" the plaintiff without the latter's consent, and this physical element was not present in this case.[35] Furthermore, it seems likely that a court would hold that when Mr Jack realised that he had been prescribed something different, but decided nevertheless to take the new kind of insulin, he *did* consent to the change in treatment.

The issue would thereafter focus on whether the patient's consent could be described as "informed". Any suit based on a lack of informed consent will generally require to be based on the tort of negligence, rather than trespass or battery.[36] Examination of the relevant case law suggests that the British courts do not require very much information or explanation to be given by doctors before their patients will be considered to have validly consented to a course of treatment.

The leading case here is *Sidaway v. Governors of the Bethlam Royal Hospital and the Maudsley Hospital and Others.*[37] The plaintiff suffered chronic pain in her right shoulder and neck, and an operation was advised by her neurosurgeon. The operation had an inherent risk of damage to the nerve root and to the spinal cord. The surgeon advised Mrs Sidaway as to the possibility of damage to the nerve root, but did not mention the risk to the spinal cord. The latter was assessed as a less than one per cent risk of damage, but the potential injury could be very serious. As a result of the operation the plaintiff did indeed sustain injury to her spinal cord and was rendered severely disabled as a result. Mrs Sidaway then attempted to sue her Area Health Authority, citing her neurosurgeon's failure to advise her of this risk and claiming that she would have decided against the operation had she been more fully informed.[38]

The court at first instance found as a fact that Mrs Sidaway would not

---

[35] See Brazier, *Medicine, Patients and the Law* (Penguin Books, 2nd ed., 1992) p. 75: "A patient who, for example, agreed to take a drug orally, *having been totally misled as to the nature of the drug* could not sue in battery." (Emphasis added).

[36] See *Chatterton v. Gerson* [1981] 1 All E.R. 257; and *Hills v. Potter* [1983] 3 All E.R. 716.

[37] [1985] 1 A.C. 871; [1985] 2 W.L.R. 480; [1985] 1 All E.R. 643 H.L.

[38] The neurosurgeon had died prior to Mrs Sidaway's case coming to court, hence the court had difficulty in ascertaining the facts.

have agreed to the operation had she known of the risk of spinal cord injury. That is, the court accepted that the plaintiff had established a casual link between the surgeon's omission and her injury. Despite this, the case was decided in favour of the defendants on the basis that there had been no breach of duty by the surgeon, and this decision was affirmed by the Court of Appeal. According to Sir John Donaldson, Master of the Rolls:

> "What information should be disclosed and how and when it should be disclosed is very much a matter for professional judgment, to be exercised in the context of the doctor's relationship with a particular patient in particular circumstances."[39]

A "prudent patient" test is used by some American courts to determine the level of information which patients ought to be given. This is an objective test, by which the courts endeavour to ascertain what a "reasonable person" would require to know in the circumstances, and how such a patient would have reacted had he or she been appraised of the relevant risk information. The prudent patient test was rejected in *Sidaway* and it was suggested that this hypothetical patient was, in reality, a "fairly rare bird".[40]

This decision of the Court of Appeal was upheld by the House of Lords and the case of *Bolam v. Friern Hospital Management Committee*[41] was applied; a doctor is not to be considered to have been negligent if he or she has acted in accordance with a practice which is accepted as proper by a responsible body of medical practitioners. In failing to disclose the spinal cord risk, Mrs Sidaway's surgeon had adopted a practice which was common at that time.[42]

The *Sidaway* case involved a surgical operation rather than drug therapy,

---

[39] [1984] Q.B. 493, at 512. This emphasis on the "professional judgement" of the medical practitioner is also shown by the case of *Hatcher v. Black, The Times*, July 2, 1954, in which Lord Denning stated, albeit *obiter*, that a doctor may in certain circumstances be justified in lying to a patient about the risks involved in a course of treatment. The plaintiff's voice was damaged as a result of an operation to her throat. She had specifically asked her surgeon whether such an injury was a possibility, and he had assured her that there was no risk. In the *Sidaway* case, Lord Bridge of Harwich opined that a doctor who is asked a direct question must answer truthfully ([1985] 1 All E.R. 643, at 661).

[40] *ibid.*

[41] [1957] 1 W.L.R. 582; [1957] 2 All E.R. 118.

[42] The *Sidaway* decision has aroused a great deal of comment. See Kennedy, "The Patient on the Clapham Omnibus" (1984) *M.L.R.*, 47, p. 454; Brahams, "Consent to Treatment—How Informed is Informed Consent?" (1984) *Medico-Legal Journal* 52, p. 77; "What Should A Doctor Tell?" (1984) *B.M.J.*, 289, p. 325; Brahams, "'Informed Consent'—the Thin End of

but the issue of informed consent to treatment is the same in either situation. The case of *Blyth v. Bloomsbury Area Health Authority*[43] involved the contraceptive injection, Depo-Provera. It was held that a doctor is under no obligation to give a patient full details about a particular drug therapy, but need only give a "reasonable amount" of information, depending on the circumstances. Kerr L.J. emphasised that what a patient required to be told could not be divorced from the *Bolam* test.[44] This involves a consideration of what the hypothetical "reasonable doctor" would have done in the circumstances, which in turn depends on the behaviour of doctors generally, and their state of knowledge about the side effects of any particular drug.

The principle of "therapeutic privilege" recognises that in some cases, warnings or risk information ought to be withheld from patients, on the basis that it would be detrimental to their physical or mental health should such details be revealed. However, therapeutic privilege should only be invoked where there is a real danger that the information would harm the patient. It may be contended that the great majority of patients are capable of assimilating risk information and deciding for themselves whether to undertake a particular risk, thus a decision to withhold such information should be made only in the most extreme of circumstances.

Where the court feels that information has been omitted which the "reasonable doctor" would have provided, then the defendant may be liable if a patient is harmed as a result. In the case of *Dwyer v. Roderick and Jackson and Cross Chemists Banbury Ltd*[45] a doctor prescribed Migril without warning his patient that she should not exceed a certain number of capsules per day. Due to this negligence, the woman's feet became gangrenous.[46] The information was required to allow the patient to take her medication safely, and this is therefore rather different from cases where the warning which has not been given concerns the inherent risk of an adverse reaction.

The latter situation occurred in a more recent case, in which a woman sued her doctor for failing to warn her about the side effects associated with

---

the Wedge" (1985) *N.L.J.*, 135, p. 201, and p. 215; Finch, "Caution on Consent" *GP Magazine* February 3, 1984, p. 22; Finch, "Right and Proper Information" *GP Magazine* March 9, 1984, p. 23; and Jackson and Powell, *Professional Negligence* (London, Sweet & Maxwell, 3rd ed., 1992) pp. 519–521.

[43] [1993] 4 Med. L.R. 151.

[44] *ibid.* 157.

[45] Unreported, but see (1982) *Pharm. Journal* 205.

[46] She was awarded £100,000 in damages.

Loniten, a treatment for hypertension.[47] She had complained of excessive facial hair growth for two and a half years. The patient's appearance returned to normal within a year, once the problem was investigated and her dosage gradually reduced. She had experienced great distress as a result of these changes in her appearance and argued that her doctor ought to have warned her about these adverse effects. The drug's data sheet, compiled by its manufacturers, had warned: "Hypertrichosis occurs in most patients treated with Loniten, and *all patients should be warned of this possibility before starting therapy.*" The case was settled when the plaintiff accepted £1,500 in damages.

Injured patients who claim that they received insufficient warning information also have to prove that they would not have accepted the drug treatment had they been aware of the risks it posed. This is illustrated by the Scottish case of *Goorkani v. Tayside Health Board.*[48] The pursuer had lost the sight in one of his eyes and his doctor prescribed Chlorambucil to prevent the other eye from deteriorating. The doctor failed to warn Mr Goorkani that there was a risk of infertility associated with Chlorambucil. While this omission on the part of the doctor was a breach of his duty of care, the court found that the pursuer had not shown that he would have refused to consent to the treatment if he been made aware of the risks it posed. The pursuer's damages were accordingly limited to £2,500 for the distress caused by the manner in which he became aware of the possibility that he had been rendered infertile.

The incidence of drug injury might be reduced if doctors and patients were more aware of the hazards associated with pharmaceutical products. Opren was described in newspaper reports as heralding a "new era" in the treatment of arthritis, and many patients arrived at their doctors' surgeries clutching newspaper cuttings and demanding that their medication be changed to this new "wonder drug". One doctor complained to the *British Medical Journal* at the time:

"For the last few weeks we have had to tell our patients gently that it is too early

---

[47] See Herxheimer and Young, "A Prescriber's Duty of Care" (1990) *N.L.J.* 859.
[48] [1991] 3 Med.L.R.; 1991 S.L.T.(Notes) 94.

to know whether the new drug is better suited to their condition than their existing treatment."[49]

As we have seen, the doctor was right to be hesitant. Reflecting on the Opren tragedy, the editor of the *British Medical Journal* argued thus:

"... the crucial need is for doctors to think more carefully before prescribing a new or newish drug ... If the new preparation really does seem to have advantages that outweigh the risks implicit in its novelty, then the prescribing doctor must accept that his decision should carry with it an obligation to be alert for all 'events', to record them, and to report all possible adverse drug reactions to the CSM."[50]

There may be less pharmaceutical product injury if members of the medical profession were more hesitant in the prescribing of new drugs, and were more careful to check for potential contra-indications before prescribing established therapies.

5. Conclusions

It is clear that persons who are injured by prescription pharmaceutical products will find it difficult to mount a successful suit against their doctors. The law of contract offers plaintiffs the best remedies since it imposes strict liability in respect of the quality of products. As we have seen, unlike private patients, those who receive NHS treatment are unlikely to be able to rely on any contractual remedies. Injured plaintiffs will have to rely, therefore, on the tort of negligence,[51] but the insistence of the courts that members of the medical profession are negligent only where they deviate from a practice which is accepted as proper by the medical profession itself means that it will not be easy for a plaintiff to persuade a court that there has been a breach of the duty of care.

---

[49] See Dr Bernard Caplan's letter, (1980) *B.M.J.*, 281, p. 1493. In an editorial in the same journal two years later, it was argued that the Opren affair showed the "dangers of current marketing policies by pharmaceutical companies." See "Benoxaprofen" (1982) *B.M.J.*, p. 459.

[50] "Benoxaprofen" (1982) *B.M.J.* p. 459.

[51] The potential liability of doctors under the Consumer Protection Act 1987 is discussed in Chap. 7, below.

In relation to the duty to furnish adequate warnings, we have already noted that recent European regulations now require pharmaceutical *manufacturers* to provide detailed product information to the ultimate consumer.[52] While this may lessen the risk of drug injury, it may also allow doctors to argue that they omitted to provide more detailed warnings since they were relying on the patient receiving appropriate information from the manufacturer, once the prescription was filled. Even if this argument is not accepted, plaintiffs may experience great difficulty in establishing that their doctors were at fault, due to the courts' attitude to the principle of informed consent.

---

[52] See p. [27], above.

Chapter 5

The Common Law Liability of the Pharmacist

1. Introduction

There are about 12,000 retail pharamacies in this country.[1] As with members of the medical profession, a pharmacist's liability for injuries caused by a pharmaceutical drug or device will vary according to whether the product was obtained without a prescription, or acquired by means of a National Health or private prescription.

2. Non-Prescription Products

About 20 per cent of the United Kingdom drug market is for non-prescription drugs.[2] Sales of such drugs in 1994 amounted to £1,200 million.[3] These are, typically, cough and cold remedies, indigestion tablets, food supplements, pills for minor headaches, etc. Non-prescription products generally offer less risks of adverse reaction. Where injury does occur, the injured party may have a contractual remedy against the pharmacist. Such contracts are governed by the Sale of Goods Act 1979.

[1] Cook, Doyle and Jabbari, *Pharmaceuticals, Biotechnology and the Law* (Hants, Macmillan Publishers Ltd, 1991) at p. 10.
[2] Hancher, *Regulating for Competition: Government, Law, and the Pharmaceutical Industry in the United Kingdom and France* (Oxford, Clarendon Press, 1990) p. 72.
[3] Annual Report 1995, Proprietary Association of Great Britain.

Section 61(1) of that Act defines "goods" as including "all personal chattels other than things in action and money". In Scotland, goods are "all corporeal moveables except money". Pharmaceutical products are clearly within these definitions. It has been held that the "goods" include the container and packaging in which the products are supplied,[4] any instructions which have been provided,[5] and even any foreign matter erroneously included.[6] In relation to a pharmaceutical product any assessment of the goods may therefore include the provision, or otherwise, or a child-proof container, as well as the patient information leaflets.

The 1979 Act implies certain terms into all contracts of sale, hence the goods sold must be of satisfactory quality and reasonably fit for any purpose made clear to the seller by the purchaser[7]; a chemist who sells a cough mixture, suitable for a person with catarrh, will therefore be in breach of contract if the purchaser requested a mixture to suppress a cough. However, a pharmacist will not be liable under contract where any reaction suffered by the plaintiff was due to some idiosyncratic condition of the customer, which was not disclosed.[8]

A pharmacist who makes an inaccurate representation about a non-prescription product, such as "these pills are safe for you to use, even although you are pregnant" or "this medicine will cure your cough", may be liable for breach of contract. This kind of statement must be contrasted with what is referred to as "puffery" or sales talk. If the pharmacist says "this is a great cough mixture" that will be regarded as mere sales talk and the pharmacist is unlikely to be held liable should the claim be less than accurate.

These provisions in the Sale of Goods Act cannot be contracted out of, as regards consumer contracts.[9] While these terms do not apply to defects which have been specifically drawn to the buyer's attention,[10] it would be most unusual for a pharmacist to attempt to sell a drug which was known to be flawed in some way, and indeed this may constitute an offence under the Medicines Act 1968.[11]

---

[4] *Geddling v. Marsh* [1920] 1 K.B. 668.
[5] *Wormell v. RHM Agriculture (East) Ltd* [1986] 1 All E.R. 769.
[6] *Wilson and Another v. Rickett Cockerell & Co. Ltd* [1954] 1 Q.B. 598.
[7] See the 1979 Act, as amended.
[8] See *Griffiths v. Peter Conway Ltd* [1939] 1 All E.R. 685.
[9] See the relevant provisions of the Unfair Contract Terms Act 1977.
[10] s.14(2c)(a).
[11] See ss.63 and 64.

Liability under these sections is "strict" in that the purchaser does not require to prove that the injury arose as a result of any negligence on the part of the seller.[12] Likewise, any lack of fault cannot be founded on by the seller as a defence.[13]

A patient may also have remedies under the law of tort for injuries resulting from the negligence of a pharmacist in selling a non-prescription drug. A pharmacist who neglected to store certain medications appropriately, for example, to ensure that products were kept refrigerated, or sold before their "sell-by" date, could be sued if a customer were harmed as a result.

3. Prescription Products

Prescription drugs account for 80 per cent of the sales of the pharmaceutical industry[14] and the vast majority of cases in which injury is alleged to have occurred involve drugs which are available only on prescription. Although doctors may occasionally dispense prescriptions themselves it has been estimated that 93 per cent of NHS prescriptions are dispensed by a pharmacist.[15]

The legal position of a person injured by a National Health Service prescription drug is less than clear but it is thought that there is no contract between the dispenser of the drug and the patient. The legal nature of the transaction between pharmacist and patient where the latter is supplied with a NHS prescription drug was considered by the House of Lords in the case of *Pfizer Corporation v. Minister of Health*.[16] The Sale of Goods Act 1979 defines a sale as being a contract for a monetary consideration, called the price.[17] Lord Reid emphasised in the *Pfizer* case that the charge for the prescription:

"is not in any true sense the price: the drug may cost much more [than the

---

[12] See *Wren v. Holt* [1903] 1 K.B. 610.
[13] See *Frost v. Aylesbury Dairy Co. Ltd* [1905] 1 K.B. 608 and *Ashington Piggeries Ltd v. Christopher Hill Ltd* [1972] A.C. 441.
[14] See Marsh, "Prescribing All the Way to the Bank" *New Scientist*, November 18, 1989, p. 54.
[15] Galloway, "Pharmacists prescribe a wider role" *Doctor*, May 30, 1991, p. 55.
[16] [1965] 2 W.L.R. 387; [1965] A.C. 512; [1965] 1 All E.R. 450.
[17] s.2(1).

prescription fee] and the chemist has a right under his contract with the authority to receive the balance from them."[18]

It would seem, then, that there is no contract of sale between a pharmacist and an NHS patient. Lord Reid concluded:

"Sale is a consensual contract requiring agreement express or implied. In the present case there appears to me to be no need for any agreement. The patient has a statutory right to demand the drug on payment of [the prescription charge.] The hospital has a statutory obligation to supply it on such payment. And if the prescription is presented to a chemist he appears to be bound by his contract with the appropriate authority to supply the drug on receipt of such payment. There is no need for any agreement between the patient and either the hospital or the chemist . . . It appears to me that any resemblance between this transaction and a true sale is only superficial."[19]

Pfizer's case related to a drug obtained from a hospital dispensary by an out-patient. It was followed in the case of *Appleby v. Sleep*[20] in which a woman took a National Health Service prescription to her local pharmacy. She was supplied with a bottle of pendural syrup and later found a lump of glass in the medicine. Following *Pfizer's* case it was accepted that there was no contract of sale between the pharmacist and the customer.[21]

It might be thought that the true nature of the relationship between pharmacist and customer was one of contract for the supply of goods and services, rather than a contract of sale. If this were the case the Supply of Goods and Services Act 1982 would apply in England, and similar terms would be implied into the contract by Scots Common Law.[22]

The distinction between a contract for services and a sale contract is often drawn where the provider of the goods is acting in a professional

---

[18] *op. cit.* p. 455.
[19] *ibid.*
[20] [1968] 2 All E.R. 265.
[21] See the dictum of Lord Parker, *ibid.* at 269. The question at issue was whether there could be said to have been a sale by the chemist to the NHS Executive Council. It was held, however, that the relationship between these parties was that of a contract for services, and that the pharmacist was paid for such services.
[22] See, for example, *Brett v. Williamson*, 1980 S.L.T. (Sh.Ct.) 56; *Dickson v. The Hygienic Institute*, 1910 S.C. 352; 1910 S.L.T. 111; *Macintosh v. Nelson*, 1984 S.L.T. (Sh.Ct.) 82.

capacity, hence pharmacists may be deemed to be performing a service, not merely selling goods to the public. Section 18 of the 1982 Act defines goods as including "all personal chattels . . . other than things in action and money". This wording is very similar to that of section 61(1) of the Sale of Goods Act 1979 and would appear to cover pharmaceutical drugs and devices. However, it seems to be the case that there is *no* contract between a NHS customer and a pharmacist, not even a contract for the supply of services. This is indicated by Lord Reid's insistence in the *Pfizer* case that there was no need for *any* agreement between the patient and the chemist.[23] Lord Upjohn stated that "the patient had a statutory right to demand the drug and the transaction accordingly is one which is *sui generis*, it is the creature of statute".[24] Thus there is no contractual relationship between the parties, and the implied terms of the 1982 Act will not apply.

The position in Scotland would seem to be similar. Woolman writes:

"Some matters seem to defy the offer and acceptance approach. Take chemist's prescriptions. They are difficult to analyse because the customer can be said to be exercising a statutory right to pharmaceuticals under the relevant provisions relating to the National Health Service, rather than entering into a contract."[25]

In contrast to this, there will be a contract where a drug is procured under a private prescription, or an over-the-counter medication is purchased. In relation to non-prescription drugs the contract is one of sale; in relation to a private prescription, the contract is for the supply of goods and services.

It is less than satisfactory that a person who is injured by a drug which is acquired without a prescription or by means of a private prescription will have remedies under the law of contract which are denied to a patient who is supplied with an identical drug under an NHS prescription. Many drugs are available with or without a prescription. Since a person injured by a product obtained by means of a NHS prescription will have no remedies under contract, any proceedings against the pharmacist will therefore require to be based in tort.[26]

A pharmacist owes a duty to take reasonable care in filling prescriptions

---

[23] *op. cit.* at 455.

[24] *op. cit.* at 466.

[25] *op. cit.* p. 31.

[26] A pharmacist's liability under the Consumer Protection Act is explored in Chap. 7, below.

and a pharmacist who dispenses the wrong drug or device, through negligence, will be liable for any injury caused thereby. In the case of *Prendergast v. Sam & Dee Ltd*[27] £139,147 compensation was awarded to the plaintiff. Mr Prendergast had presented his pharmacist with a prescription for Amoxil, which he had been prescribed for a chest infection. The pharmacist mis-read the prescription and supplied Daonil, a drug used in the treatment of diabetes. The plaintiff suffered permanent brain damage as a result. In holding both the doctor and the pharmacist liable for negligence, the court stated that the latter had not been paying sufficient attention to what he was doing. He should have realised that if the prescription had been for Daonil, it was being prescribed in the wrong quantity and dosage, and should also have noticed that the customer did not claim exemption from the prescription fees, despite the fact that diabetics are not required to pay such charges. As well as prescribing the wrong drug, there have been cases in which a pharmacist has supplied the correct drug, but in the wrong dosage.[28]

4. Failure to Warn

Some American courts have held that a pharmacist who sells a non-prescription drug has a duty to warn the customer of possible side effects. In one unreported case in North Carolina the plaintiff bought some antihistamine tablets for an allergy. The pharmacist did not provide the customer with any warning information. In particular, he did not point out the propensity of this antihistamine to cause drowsiness. The customer was involved in a car accident as a result of feeling sleepy and attempted to sue the pharmacist for negligence. It is not known whether the case succeeded on its facts, but the action for $875,000 in damages was held to be competent. The position is likely to be similar in Britain if it is reasonably foreseeable that injury could result from a pharmacist's failure to take reasonable care. It seems likely, however, that the pharmacist would now

---

[27] [1989] 1 M.L.R. 36. See also Dale and Appelbe, *Pharmacy Law and Ethics* (London, Pharmaceutical Press, 4th ed., 1989) p. 220.

[28] See the American cases of *Watkin v. Jacobs Pharmacy* 48 Ga.App. 38, 171 S.E. 830 (1933) and *Marx v. Shultz* 175 N.W. 182 (Mich. 1919).

be able to rely on the warning information which was provided by the manufacturer.

In relation to prescription products, mention has already been made of the case of *Dwyer v. Roderick and Jackson*[29] in which a pharmacist was found liable jointly with the prescribing doctor for providing capsules of Migril.[30] The pharmacist had failed to tell the patient that she should take care not to exceed a certain number of capsules per day. The patient suffered gangrene as a result, and required surgery to both feet. The court found that the pharmacist was 45 per cent to blame and stressed that a pharmacist owes a duty to customers to ensure that all drugs are properly prescribed; he should have noticed the error and checked the prescription with the doctor. Commenting on this case, Bryan states that a "precedent has therefore been set and pharmacists can expect to be held responsible in future for errors which slip through their hands".[31]

It should be noted, however, that in *Dwyer v. Roderick and Jackson* the pharmacist was found liable for failing to spot a patent error in the writing of the prescription; the case is not authority for the proposition that a pharmacist is under *a general duty* to advise consumers of any risks or contraindications associated with a prescription medicine. The duty to warn and inform a patient belongs to the manufacturer, or to members of the medical profession in their capacity as "learned intermediaries".[32]

5. Conclusions

Contractual remedies against pharmacists are only available in respect of non-prescription drugs or private prescriptions, hence the majority of injured plaintiffs must rely on the tort of negligence. Whilst there are a number of ways in which a customer may be injured as a result of a pharmacist's acts or omissions, a court will not brand such behaviour as negligence unless the defendant has acted in a manner which falls below the standard of the "reasonable pharmacists".

---

[29] (1983) 127 S.J., 806; (1983) 80, *L.S.G.*, 3003, C.A.
[30] See p. [72], above.
[31] Bryan, *Drugs for All?* (Harmondsworth, Penguin Books Ltd, 1986) p. 163.
[32] See p. [48], above.

The traditional role of pharmacists was very different from the functions which they perform today. In the past, pharmacists were involved in the actual compounding or manufacturing of drugs, while today the advent of prepacked medication means that there is little for them to do beyond matching the details on the prescription with the appropriate pack. As a result of the growing feeling of frustration that their job is being de-skilled, there have been calls from within the pharmaceutical profession for the adoption of a wider role in the provision of health care.[33] Many pharmacists would like to operate screening processes for coronary heart disease, diabetes, raised levels of cholesterol, and even for the detection of AIDS.[34] As Sutters and Nathan have pointed out:

"With an estimated 6 [million] members of the public visiting a community pharmacy each day in the U.K., the potential for the pharmacist in diagnosis of minor conditions and treatment or referral to the GP for POMs [Prescription Only Medicines] is enormous."[35]

It seems likely that pharmacists will become more involved in future in advising patients as to the risks and contraindications of their medications. Some pharmacies are now compiling computer records of all prescriptions filled for a particular patient. A pharmacy which operates a computer prescription system, and advises customers that particular warnings *will* be given, undertakes a specific duty of care to its customers, and will be liable if it fails to provide such warnings. In short, the greater the responsibility which pharmacists assume for their customers, the greater their potential legal liability becomes. This illustrates the tension which exists between society's desire to improve health care facilities, and the need to provide a remedy for a person who is injured by the provision of these services.

---

[33] Sutters and Nathan, "Can the Pharmaceutical Industry promote collaboration between community pharmacists and general practitioners?" (1993) *The Pharmaceutical Journal*, 250:6734, 546.

[34] Galloway, "Pharmacists prescribe a wider role" *Doctor*, May 30, 1991, p. 55.

[35] *op. cit.* p. 548.

Chapter 6

Suing the Licensing Authorities

1. Introduction

It is unclear whether a person who has been injured by a pharmaceutical product can sue a government regulatory body, if its officers or employees have acted negligently. Actions have been raised against the Committee on Safety of Medicines and the licensing authority in a number of recent cases. In the Opren litigation, for example, the suit against the CSM was based on the advice that body gave to the licensing authority, and the action against the latter was based on its statutory functions. Do such bodies owe a duty of care to individual patients who may sustain injury due to an official's negligence in licensing a particular pharmaceutical product? Or is a duty of care owed only to the general public, but not to individuals?

2. Common Law Duty

The categories of persons who may find themselves under a duty of care are not fixed.[1] As one author has argued:

"... the function of the concept of duty of care is simply to define the boundaries

---

[1] See *Candler v. Crane, Christmas & Co.* [1951] 2 K.B. 164, at 192.

of liability for damage caused by negligent conduct by reference to what are commonly called 'policy considerations'."[2]

In *Anns v. Merton London Borough Council*[3] Lord Wilberforce proposed a two-fold test:

". . . in order to establish that a duty of care arises in a particular situation, it is not necessary to bring the facts of that situation within those of previous situations in which a duty of care has been held to exist. Rather the question has to be approached in two stages. First one has to ask whether, as between the alleged wrongdoer and the person who has suffered damage there is a sufficient relationship of proximity or neighbourhood such that, in the reasonable contemplation of the former, carelessness on his part may be likely to cause damage to the latter—in which case a prima facie duty of care arises. Secondly, if the first question is answered affirmatively, it is necessary to consider whether there are any considerations which ought to negative, or to reduce or limit the scope of the duty or the class of person to whom it is owed or the damages to which a breach of it may give rise . . ."[4]

This case has been criticised in a number of subsequent cases, such as *Peabody Donation Fund Governors v. Sir Lindsay Parkinson & Co. Ltd,*[5] *Shire of Sutherland v. Heyman*[6] and *Leigh and Sillivan Ltd v. Aliakmon Shipping Co. Ltd*[7] In the *Peabody* case Lord Keith cautioned that a duty of care should not be imposed unless it was "just and reasonable" to do so.[8] More recently, in *Curran v. Northern Ireland Co-ownership Housing Association Ltd*[9] Lord Bridge warned against extending the *Anns* principle, such that:

". . . although under no statutory duty, a statutory body may be held to owe a common law duty of care to exercise its statutory powers to control the activities

---

[2] Cane, *Atiyah's Accidents, Compensation and the Law* (London, Butterworths, 5th ed., 1993) at p. 61.
[3] [1978] A.C. 728.
[4] *ibid.* at 751–2.
[5] [1985] A.C. 210; [1985] 3 All E.R. 529.
[6] [1985] 157 C.L.R. 424.
[7] [1986] A.C. 785. For a discussion of these cases see Logie, "Rethinking Negligence", (1988) S.L.T. 185.
[8] *op. cit.* at 534.
[9] [1987] 2 All E.R. 13.

of third parties in such a way as to save harmless those who may be adversely affected by those activities if they are not effectively controlled."[10]

Anns was over-ruled by the case of *Murphy v. Brentwood District Council*.[11] Both cases concerned liability for pure economic loss, rather than personal injury.[12] The principle in *Anns* has been attacked on so many occasions that it is unlikely to be followed in future.[13] It is therefore difficult to ascertain whether the courts would be prepared to hold that government bodies such as the CSM owe a Common Law duty of care to persons who consume pharmaceutical drugs.

3. Breach of Statutory Duty

The question of when a statute is to be held to provide a cause of action for a breach of duty was considered by the House of Lords in the case of *Cutler v. Wandsworth Stadium Ltd*.[14] Lord Simonds said this:

"I do not propose to try to formulate any rules by reference to which such a question can infallibly be answered. The only rule which in all circumstances is valid is that the answer must depend on a consideration of the whole Act and the circumstances, including the pre-existing law, in which it was enacted. But that there are indications which point with more or less force to the one answer or the other is clear from authorities which . . . will have great weight with the House. For instance, if a statutory duty is prescribed but no remedy by way of penalty or otherwise for its breach is imposed, it can be assumed that a right of civil action accrues to the person who is damnified by the breach. For, if it were not so, the statute would be but a pious aspiration."[15]

According to Vaughan Williams L.J. in the early case of *Groves v. Wimborne*:[16]

---

[10] *ibid.* at 18.
[11] [1990] 3 W.L.R. 414 H.L.
[12] See also p. [90], below.
[13] For a detailed discussion see Cane, *Tort Law and Economic Interests* (Oxford, Clarendon Press, 1991), Appendix.
[14] [1949] A.C. 398; [1949] 1 All E.R. 544.
[15] *ibid.* at 407.
[16] [1898] 2 Q.B. 402.

"... where a statute provides for the performance by certain persons of a particular duty, and some one belonging to a class of persons *for whose benefit and protection the statute imposes the duty* is injured by failure to perform it, prima facie, ... an action by the person so injured will lie against the person who has so failed to perform the duty."[17]

One might imagine that the provisions of the Medicines Act 1968 and regulations made thereunder are for the benefit of persons who are prescribed drugs, or who receive treatment which involves the administration or use of pharmaceutical products. But does this duty confer a right of action? According to section 133(2) of the 1968 Act:

"the provisions of this Act shall not be construed as—
   (a) conferring a right of action in any civil proceedings ... in respect of any contravention of this Act or of any regulations or order made under this Act, or
   (b) affecting any restriction imposed by or under any other enactment, whether contained in a public general Act or in a local or private Act, or
   (c) derogating from any right of action or other remedy (whether civil or criminal) in proceedings instituted otherwise than under this Act."

In other words, while the Act does not itself create a right of action against the licensing authority or any of its committees, it does not exclude any action which may have existed at Common Law, prior to its passing. The position under the National Health Act 1977 must also be considered. It does not explicitly provide for a remedy for any breach of the duties imposed on the Secretary of State, and in the case of *R. v. Secretary of State for Social Services and West Midlands RHA, ex parte Hincks*,[18] Wien J. held that the 1977 Act did *not* give rise to a right for damages for a breach. This part of his judgment was, however, *obiter.*

These issues arose more recently in preliminary litigation on behalf of persons who had allegedly contracted the HIV virus from contaminated blood products. In the late 1980s British haemophiliacs who had contracted the virus from blood transfusions threatened to sue the Department of Health.[19] Britain did not start heat-treating blood products

---

[17] *ibid.* at 415–6, emphasis added.
[18] Unreported, January 1979.
[19] See *Re HIV Hemophiliac Litigation*, (1990) *N.L.J.*, 140, 1349.

until 1985 even though it was first suspected in 1982 that HIV could be transmitted by contaminated blood substances.[20]

The plaintiffs alleged that the Department of Health had been negligent in using blood from America. They claimed that this increased their risk of contracting HIV and hepatitis since the blood came from a pool of paid donors. Their argument that the Department was in breach of its statutory duty was based on section 1(1) of the 1977 Act, which states:

"It is the Secretary of State's duty to continue the promotion in England and Wales of a comprehensive Health Service designed to secure improvement (a) in the physical and mental health of the people of those countries and (b) in the prevention, diagnosis and treatment of illness, and for that purpose to provide or secure the effective provision of services in accordance with this Act."

In its defence the Department of Health argued:

"Firstly, ... that no cause of action lies against the Department for breach of statutory duty in respect of any of the provisions of the National Health Services Acts or of the Medicines Act 1968;
Secondly, that any duties that are owed by the Department are owed to the public at large and to the Crown and not to individual plaintiffs;
Thirdly, that there is not sufficient proximity between the Department of Health in exercising its functions under the National Health Service Acts, in particular when deciding on matters of policy or upon the implementation of policies, so as to give rise to a duty of care to individual plaintiffs;
Fourthly, that it would not be just and reasonable to impose a duty of care towards individual plaintiffs and that it would be contrary to public policy so to do; because policy decisions are such that ministers and officials already have a sufficiently difficult balancing exercise without having to consider the possibility of civil litigation;
Fifthly, those considerations apply with particular force where ministers have to allocate scarce resources between different demands and where they are balancing competing public interests because such decisions are not suitable for investigation in civil proceedings and should be regarded as 'non-justiciable'."[21]

At first instance Rougier J. held that the plaintiffs did not have a cause of

---

[20] Sherman, "Partial victory for campaigners" *The Times*, December 12, 1990. See also *The Independent*, September 20, 1990.
[21] *The Independent, ibid.*

action in respect of the alleged statutory breach, nor for any failure of the DoH to perform its statutory duties, but that they did have a cause of action in respect of the allegation that the Department had been negligent in the performance of its statutory duties.

In the Court of Appeal, Gibson L.J. concluded:

"... I share the judge's view of the apparent nature of the duties imposed by the 1977 Act. They do not clearly demonstrate the intention of Parliament to impose a duty which is to be enforced by individual civil action."[22]

However, he distinguished the case of *Murphy v. Brentwood District Council* and stated:

"In Murphy's case the claim was for economic loss. These [haemophiliac] plaintiffs have suffered personal injury. It is possible, in my judgment, that the court, after full consideration, may in this case be driven to hold that in the circumstances of these claims, and notwithstanding the difficulties of proof of negligence ... a duty of care is imposed by the law upon the Central Defendants in the discharge of their functions under the 1977 Act."[23]

This preliminary litigation concerned the issue of disclosure of certain documents, hence the dictum relating to the potential liability of government bodies was *obiter*. The suits themselves were later settled out of court.[24]

The liability of government regulatory bodies was also considered in interlocutory proceedings in one of the vaccine suits. In *DHSS v Kinnear*[25] the plaintiff alleged that the DHSS had been negligent in its *promotion* of the whooping cough vaccine. It was argued that the Department had been negligent in formulating its inoculation policy without first undertaking studies to ensure that the risks from vaccination were far less than those from the illness which the immunisation was designed to prevent. The court held that no cause of action lay against the Department in respect of its decision to promote immunisation, since it had acted within its

---

[22] *ibid.*

[23] *ibid.*

[24] The British Government was initially unwilling to offer a settlement, see "Clarke still refuses Aids virus payment for haemophiliacs", *The Independent*, October 1, 1990.

[25] *The Times*, July 7, 1984. See also (1984) 134, *N.L.J.*, 886.

discretionary powers.[26] So long as the Minister acted in good faith, no action would lie against his Department. A further allegation that the DHSS had been negligent in the advice and information it had given to health authorities *was* held to form a valid cause of action. This was a different ground of liability since it was being alleged, not that the Minister had been negligent in deciding to adopt a policy of immunisation, but rather that the policy had been *implemented* in a negligent fashion. However, this was based on a distinction made in the *Anns* case and, in the light of subsequent judicial dicta, some commentators have doubted whether *Kinnear* would now be followed.[27]

In the Scottish case of *Ross v. Secretary of State for Scotland*[28] the pursuer had been vaccinated against smallpox and claimed that this had caused her to sustain brain damage. The Secretary of State for Scotland represents the Scottish Home and Health Department and the pursuer averred, *inter alia*, that the Department had recommended to the general public that children should be immunised against smallpox but had failed to advise the public of the risks associated with vaccination. It was specifically contended that:

"... it was the department's duty in the exercise of reasonable care not to conduct an advertising campaign aimed at the general public in which a warning of the adverse consequences of contracting smallpox were emphasised, but the facts (a) that the prospects of contracting the disease were extremely remote, and (b) that there was a substantial risk of adverse reaction to the vaccine, were omitted."[29]

It was further contended that in the light of the above the department should have instituted a system whereby doctors were enjoined to inform parents of the advantages and disadvantages of vaccination. The Court of Session held that these arguments were concerned with matters of policy or the exercise of discretion by the Department of Health, and that it followed from this that the duties suggested by the pursuer were irrelevant in the absence of any averment of bad faith. According to Lord Milligan:

"... an important distinction fell to be made between matters which were

---

[26] This discretion was by virtue of s.26 of the National Health Service Act 1946.
[27] See Jones, *Medical Negligence* (London, Sweet & Maxwell, 1991) pp. 297–298, para. 8.5.
[28] 1990 S.L.T. 13; [1990] 1 Med L.R. 235.
[29] *ibid.*

matters of policy on the one hand and matters which concerned implementation of such policy and which have been, and suitably may be, described as operational matters, on the other hand . . . so far as matters falling within the latter or operational category are concerned ordinary principles of duty of reasonable care are applicable."[30]

A number of commentators have argued that it is unlikely that an action for breach of statutory duty would be available against the drug regulatory authorities.[31] There appear to be no reported cases in which a body such as the CSM or licensing authority has actually been held liable for the injuries caused by a pharmaceutical product. Even if such a claim is held to be competent a plaintiff would require to show that the body was negligent in licensing a drug or device, or in not withdrawing the product from the market once it became aware that the risks posed by the product outweighed its benefits. This may be a particularly difficult task, in view of the secrecy which surrounds the granting and withdrawal of licences for pharmaceutical products.

4. Conclusions

It is far from certain that it is competent to raise a personal injuries action against the regulatory bodies, either at Common Law or for the breach of statutory duty. It may be argued that it is in fact inadvisable for such bodies to be vulnerable to suit. Mann has warned that:

". . . unless inappropriate legal actions involving the Committee on Safety of Medicines lessen, the staffing of this Committee and the other [regulatory] Committees, is likely to become more and more difficult in a way that threatens the effective continuation of drug regulation in this country."[32]

One consequence of holding licensing authorities liable to compensate

---

[30] *ibid.* at 15.
[31] See, for example, Lawson, "Liability for Defective Drugs in the U.K." (1991) *P.L.I.*, 13:7, at 98; and Barton, "The Basis of Liability of the Licensing Authority and its Advisers under the Medicines Act 1968 to an Individual" Chap. 7 of Goldberg and Dodds-Smith, *Pharmaceutical Medicine and the Law* (Royal College of Physicians of London, 1991).
[32] See Mann and Havard, eds., *No Fault Compensation in Medicine* (London, Royal Society of Medicine Services, 1989) p. 9.

injured persons is likely to be that these bodies would become more conservative in their decisions to introduce new drugs. This may result in the public being denied the benefit of potentially beneficial pharmaceutical products.

Chapters 3 to 6 have illustrated the difficulties which plaintiffs face in establishing negligence on the part of pharmaceutical manufacturers, doctors and pharmacists, and the problems in establishing that government licensing bodies owe a duty of care to individual patients. One might imagine that the provisions of Part I of the Consumer Protection Act 1987, which imposes a system of strict liability on the producers of products, would greatly increase the prospects of obtaining a decision, favourable to the injured plaintiff. This is considered in the following chapter.

Chapter 7

Strict Liability

1. Introduction

In an attempt to harmonise the laws of the European Member States, and to overcome some of the difficulties plaintiffs face in establishing negligence for product liability injuries, the European Union introduced a directive which was designed to make producers strictly liable for their "defective" products.[1] Part I of the Consumer Protection Act 1987 implemented that directive for British law.[2] It does not replace the existing law, but provides additional remedies.[3]

Section 2(1) of the 1987 Act is a key section. It states:

> "where any damage is caused wholly or partly by a defect in a product, every person to whom subsection (2) applies shall be liable for the damage."

Section 2(2) makes it clear that this liability is imposed primarily on the producer, any persons putting their names or marks on products, or importing them. A producer includes the manufacturer of finished products, raw materials, or components.[4] In relation to pharmaceutical products it has been suggested that:

---

[1] Directive on the Approximation of the Laws, Regulations and Administrative Provisions of the Member States Concerning Liability for Defective Products, [1985] O.J. L210/29.

[2] The Act was given the Royal Assent on May 15, 1987. It came into force on the appointed day (March 1, 1988) by s.50(2). See the Consumer Protection Act 1987 (Commencement No. 1) Order 1987 (S.I. 1987 No. 1680).

[3] s.2(6). Its provisions do not have retrospective effect. s.50(7).

[4] s.1(2).

"The supplier of an active ingredient is in the position of the manufacturer of a component part and the act of formulating or tableting will constitute manufacture of the 'entire product'."[5]

A plaintiff must now prove that the product contained a defect and that this defect caused damage or injury.[6] The plaintiff need not be the owner or even the user of the product, nor need it be proved that the producer was negligent or at fault.[7]

2. Definitions

(A) "DAMAGE"

Section 5(1) of the Act defines "damage" as death or personal injury, or any loss of, or damage to property.[8] "Personal injury" includes any disease and any other impairment of a person's physical or mental condition.[9] In keeping with Article 9 of the Product Liability Directive, claims cannot be made for pain and suffering.[10] The costs of medical treatment and loss of earnings (actual and prospective) will be recoverable, as well as compensation for loss of earning capacity in the future.

---

[5] Cook, Doyle and Jabbari, *Pharmaceuticals, Biotechnology and the Law* (Hants, Macmillan Publishers Ltd, 1991) p. 357.

[6] Proving causation may be a particularly difficult task for persons alleging that they were injured by a pharmaceutical product. See Chap. 9, below.

[7] It should be noted that a producer will only be liable if it is established within the European Community, or in an EFTA country. Where a non-E.C. producer is responsible for manufacturing defective goods, the consumer's redress will be against the person who imported those goods into the Community.

[8] See Article 9 of the Product Liability Directive. Damage to property is outwith the scope of the present work.

[9] s.45(1).

[10] The Directive excludes compensation for "non-material" damage, such as pain and suffering, loss of consortium and loss of expectation of life. Any compensation to be awarded under these heads will be a matter for each State's existing law.

(B) "Product"

This term is defined in section 1(2) to include "any goods" and section 45(1) defines goods to include "any natural or artificial substance whether in solid, liquid or gaseous form or in the form of vapour and includes substances that are comprised in or mixed with other goods". It is clear that drugs fall within this definition but it is not so obvious that plasma, human tissue and other blood products do. Geddes is of the view that human blood and tissues are within the ambit of the new regime,[11] while Brazier argues the contrary. Her argument is based on the fact that blood and human tissues were expressly excluded from earlier drafts of the Directive. Furthermore, she doubts whether human tissues would be considered to be "goods".[12]

If blood plasmas *are* held to be "products" within the scope of the 1987 Act, a patient infected with the human immunodeficiency virus through contaminated blood may, in future, have grounds for an action under the 1987 Act against a health authority. With the advent of the HIV infection and AIDS, liability for contaminated blood products has become an increasing problem.[13] By 1985, 194 cases of AIDS contracted from blood transfusions had been reported in the United States of America and suits were taken against blood banks, laboratories and hospitals. In the late 1980s 400 British haemophiliacs attempted to obtain redress, having alleged that they were exposed to contamination with this virus as a result of blood transfusions. The transfusions took place prior to the passing of the 1987 Act, and these cases were settled by *ex gratia* payments from the government.[14]

---

[11] Geddes, *Product and Service Liability in the EEC: The New Strict Liability Regime* (London, Sweet & Maxwell, 1992) p. 12. The Pearson Commission recommended that blood be considered to be a "product" (*Royal Commission on Civil Liability and Compensation for Personal Injury*, Cmnd. 7054, 1978) para. 1276. See also Clark, "The Consumer Protection Act 1987" (1987) *M.L.R.*, 50, pp. 614–622; and Howells, *Comparative Product Liability* (Aldershot, Dartmouth, 1993) p. 32.

[12] Brazier, *Street on Torts* (London, Butterworths, 9th ed., 1993) p. 338.

[13] See "Negligence, Extra Blood Transfusions, and Risk of AIDS" (1991) *Medico-Legal Journal*, 59:2, p. 123.

[14] See "Major pledges another £42 million for haemophiliacs" *The Times*, December 12, 1990, p. 1.

(C) "Defective Products"

Section 3(1) of the 1987 Act states that "there is a defect in a product . . . if the *safety of the product is not such* as *persons generally* are entitled to expect".[15] It is clear that the law is applying an objective standard; it is not concerned with the expectations of the particular plaintiff. Much controversy surrounds the meaning of "defective". This is an important term, and is considered in more detail in chapter 8.

Section 3(2)(c) states that a product is not to be inferred to be defective merely because the safety of products supplied at a later date is greater than that of the product in question. This conforms to the position at Common Law.[16]

3. Potential Defendants

Consideration must be given to the position of the various categories of person who may be in danger of being sued under the 1987 Act. It should be borne in mind that the liability of the persons discussed below is joint and several. An injured plaintiff may be advised, therefore, to raise an action against a number of parties, leaving them to sort out their liability amongst themselves.

(A) The Producer

The producer is defined by the 1987 Act as the person who manufactured the product or where the substance has not been manufactured, it is the person who "won" or abstracted it.[17] Where a product has not been manufactured, won or abstracted and its essential characteristics are attributable to an industrial or other process having been carried out, then the producer is defined as the person who carried out that process.[18] A

---

[15] Emphases added.

[16] *Roe v. Ministry of Health* [1954] 2 W.L.R. 915; [1954] 2 Q.B. 66; [1954] 2 All E.R. 131.

[17] s.1(2)(a) and (b).

[18] s.1(2)(c).

processor is only liable as a producer if it has altered the product's characteristics. Hence a party does not generally become a producer merely by packaging products.

(B) The Own-brander

This is not a term used by the Act but it is a convenient title for a person described in the Act as one who "held himself out" to be the producer by putting his name, trade-mark or other distinguishing mark on the product.[19] The own-brander is treated as being a "producer" for the purposes of the Act. A Consultation Paper produced by the Medicines Division of the Department of Health suggested that a pharmacist who supplied "own-brand" medicines could be considered to be a producer under the Consumer Protection Act 1987.[20] The section could apply to a pharmacist who fills a prescription by supplying a drug to which a label, bearing the pharmacy details, has been affixed. It is now more common for drugs to come pre-packaged from the manufacturer, and comparatively rare for a pharmacist to have to bottle pills or decant liquid medicines from their original containers.

(C) The Importer

The importer is also treated by the 1987 Act as a "producer", but is defined as someone who has imported the product into a Member State from a place *outside* the European Community, in order to supply it to another in the course of a business.[21] Under the traditional tort system the importer of a product may be able to show that it exercised reasonable care simply by demonstrating that it acquired the product from a reputable source. This will not suffice under the 1987 Act since the importer's liability is strict. Despite this, an importer may limit its liability by ensuring that its contracts with the original producer include an indemnity clause, entitling the importer to recover any compensation paid out in respect of these goods.

---

[19] s.2(2)(b). This was recommended by the Pearson Commission, *op. cit.* at para. 1247.
[20] See *Product Liability: Special Features of the Medical Sector* (Consultation Paper).
[21] s.2(2)(c). See the Pearson Report, *op. cit.* at para. 1250.

(D) The Supplier

Section 2(3) imposes liability on the supplier of a product in certain circumstances. This will occur where an injured party requests the supplier to identify the producer, own-brander or importer of the product and the supplier fails to provide this information. This subsection imposes liability on the supplier even if he or she is not at fault in being unable to name the source of that particular product. The section is designed to protect the consumer from anonymous or counterfeit products.[22]

Section 46 of the Act gives a wide definition to the word "supply"; it includes not only the selling of goods, but also the performance of any contract for work and materials to furnish the goods; providing the goods for any consideration other than money; and providing the goods in or in connection with the performance of any statutory function. This is important in the field of pharmaceutical products, since it may cover pharmacists, and doctors who supply drugs directly to their patients.

i. The Pharmacist. As previously explained, a pharmacist who fills a NHS prescription is not "selling" the products to the patient, nor is there any contract of service between these two parties, but the pharmacist does provide the goods *in connection with the performance of a statutory function* and hence "supplies" them, within the meaning of section 46. To avoid liability pharmacists must keep a note of the make and manufacturer of drugs which are dispensed. They were required to keep such records even before the passing of the Consumer Protection Act; the Medicines Act 1968 obliges pharmacists to record the date on which a particular drug was supplied, its name, quantity, form and strength, the date of the prescription, and the names and addresses of both the practitioner who wrote it and the patient to whom the medication was dispensed.[23] However, the 1968 Act required that a register containing such information be kept for only two years. The provisions of the Consumer Protection Act as to time limits would suggest that such records should now be preserved for at least 10 years.[24]

ii. The Doctor. Where a hospital doctor administers a drug, it has been

---

[22] For a description of counterfeit drugs on the international market see Masland and Marshall, "The Pill Pirates", *Newsweek*, November 5, 1990, pp. 18–23.

[23] See Dale and Appelbe, *op. cit.* Chap. 7.

[24] See p. [102], below.

suggested that the hospital authority will be the supplier.[25] As already noted, General Practitioners do, occasionally, dispense drugs themselves, particularly in emergency situations. In such circumstances, the doctor becomes a supplier of the drug for the purposes of the Act since the goods are being provided in performance of a statutory function. It follows from this that a doctor must be able to identify the producer if called upon to do so. Accurate records must be kept of the name of the drug, the manufacturer, the date of purchase, batch number and expiry date. This should be cross-referenced with the records of the patient who was given the drugs.

In the Dalkon Shield litigation the women's IUDs had been removed in many cases before the injuries became manifest, and plaintiffs found it difficult to prove that their particular IUD had been manufactured by Robins. Most of their doctors had recorded that a device had been fitted, but had not specified its brand. It is now essential that these details be noted in future, if liability is to be avoided.

A supplier's duty under section 2(3) is only to provide the source of the product; a supplier who identifies the product's manufacturer within a reasonable time will not be liable, and this is so even if that manufacturer has ceased trading due to death or bankruptcy, or cannot be traced. This situation may lead to duplication of insurance, as all parties in the distribution chain will require to have adequate coverage.

4. Limitations to Compensation

Among the most important factors which may restrict a plaintiff's suit are the provisions as to time limits and financial limits.

(A) TIME LIMITS

The Act requires all actions relating to allegedly defective products to be commenced within three years from the date on which the injured party became aware of certain factors.[26] These are:

---

[25] See Dyer, "Strict Product Liability Arrives: Implications for Doctors", (1988) *B.M.J.*, 296, p. 635; and *Implementation of E.C. Directive on Product Liability*, DTI Consultative Note.
[26] By Sched. 1 Pt. IIA. The Pearson Commission had favoured a three year time limit. See para. 1270 of its Report.

1. that there was a defect in the product;
2. that the damage was caused or partly caused by the defect;
3. that the damage was sufficiently serious to justify the court action;
4. that the defendant was the person liable for the damage.

The 1987 Act also provides for a long-stop time limit of 10 years from the date on which the product was first put into circulation.[27]

Time limits pose a particular problem in "creeping disasters" since the injuries may not become apparent, or may not be associated with exposure to a particular substance, within a short period. One example of a drug with a long latency period between consumption and injury is Diethylstilbestrol; the rare forms of cancer which it caused took between 10 and 15 years to materialise. Another example is clioquinol, which was marketed in the 1930s but was only discovered to cause subacute myelo-optic neuropathy (SMON) in the 1970s.[28] The impact of lengthy latency periods has been recognised in relation to radiation injuries; the Nuclear Installations Act 1965 provides for a limitation period of 30 years.[29] In contrast to this, the 10 year limitation period imposed by the Consumer Protection Act means that plaintiffs in certain drug cases may lose their right of action before they are aware that they have been injured.

(B) FINANCIAL LIMITS

Article 16 of the Directive proposed a financial limit to the amount for which a producer could be liable in respect of any one defect in a product type.[30] The Pearson Commission was not in favour of a financial ceiling for compensation claims, fearing that this would encourage producers to procure insurance to cover themselves up to that limit, even when such cover was not necessary.[31]

The Commission was also concerned with the difficulty in allocating compensation to the limit where the effects of a particular product did not all become apparent at once, but emerged at intervals. It might be felt that a

---

[27] s.11A of the Limitation Act 1980, as inserted by Sched. 1 of the 1987 Act. In Scotland, this was achieved by the insertion of ss.22A–22D into the Prescription and Limitation (Scotland) Act 1973, by Sched. 1, Pt. II, para. 10 of the 1987 Act.
[28] See Strom, *Pharmacoepidemiology* (Chichester, John Wiley & Sons Ltd, 2nd ed., 1994) p. 6.
[29] By s.15(1).
[30] The current limit is 70 million ECUs.
[31] See the *Pearson Report, op. cit.* at paras. 1264 and 1265.

producer would require to delay payments to any injured party until the 10 year time limit had expired, in order to avoid those who were injured at a later date being unable to claim compensation. This would result in a lengthy delay for those persons injured at an earlier stage, and Pearson considered that this would be unacceptable. The Commission did, however, recognise that without a limit on liability a product catastrophe could result in a gap between the insurance acquired by a company and that company's legal liability. It did not envisage that an injured party would remain uncompensated in such an event, arguing that the government would be pressurised into providing financial assistance in the event of an under-insured tragedy. Interestingly, it gave as an example a catastrophe caused by a defective drug.[32] It has been suggested that this attitude might actually encourage producers to under-insure, in the knowledge that public money would provide compensation in the event of a major disaster.[33]

The Association of the British Pharmaceutical Industry was in favour of financial limits. It argued that:

> "The level of insurance cover available to the pharmaceutical industry is now such that sufficient even for the minimum financial limit permitted by Article 16 cannot usually be obtained. Not only is adequate cover simply not available, but also the cost of what cover is available has increased dramatically . . ."[34]

The 1987 Act has not imposed any financial ceiling on the amount of compensation which a producer may be required to pay, but this is not the case in other Member States. The operation of this limit is not made clear by the Directive and many of the concerns raised by the Pearson Commission remain to be addressed. The Directive was recently reviewed by the European Council, after it had been in operation for 10 years,[35] but the Council decided to make no changes to this. The Directive will be reviewed again after a further five years. In the meantime, as Geddes has argued:

---

[32] *op. cit.* at para. 1265.
[33] See Jolowicz, "Compensation for Personal Injury and Fault" Chap. 2 of Allen, Bourn and Holyoak, eds., *Accident Compensation After Pearson* (London, Sweet & Maxwell, 1979) p. 54.
[34] *Implementation of E.C. Directive on Product Liability: An Explanatory Note*: views of the Association of the British Pharmaceutical Industry (1985) p. 3.
[35] See Art. 15(3) of the Directive.

"... where there is a major disaster arising from a defective product such as the thalidomide tragedy, Plaintiffs would be well advised to bring their action in a member state that has not adopted a ceiling or where this is not possible to ensure that proceedings are commenced as soon as possible."[36]

5. Defences

Although liability is strict the 1987 Act does provide a number of defences. Along with contributory negligence, other defences contained in the Act include: that the injury was due to the manufacturer's compliance with mandatory regulations; that the product was not "supplied"; that the supply was not in the course of a business; that the product was not defective at the time of supply; and the "development risk" defence. A number of these may be particularly relevant in defending actions which involve pharmaceutical products.

(A) COMPLIANCE WITH REGULATIONS

The 1987 Act provides that it is a defence for a producer to show that the defect "... is attributable to compliance with any requirement imposed by or under any enactment."[37] This compliance must be with a statutory requirement or Community obligation, and must be mandatory, hence observance of British Standards or a Trade Practice Code will not be a defence. The fact that a producer has complied with these regulations is not of itself a defence; the defence is only available where the defect is *attributable* to compliance with the regulations. Hence the defendant must show that the product's defective condition is due to the fact that it required to conform to a particular regulation.

Numerous regulations relating to pharmaceutical products have been made under the Medicines Act 1968.[38] The ABPI stated in its evidence to the Pearson Commission that it did not regard approval of a new product by the Committee on Safety of Medicines as diminishing the responsibility

---

[36] Geddes, "Product Liability for Drugs in the U.K. and Europe" (Conference Paper: *Pharmaceuticals and the Law: European, U.S. & Canadian Developments*, London, November 3, 1992) p. 9.
[37] s.4(1)(a).
[38] See Chap. 2, above.

of its members for any defects in their products.[39] Pearson approved of this and recommended that there should be no defence of "official certification", as such. This defence might, however, be used where a manufacturer has asked the licensing authority to allow a particular side effect to be mentioned in a patient information leaflet, but the authority has refused to agree to this. A manufacturer may also introduce evidence of industry regulations as an indication of the standard of knowledge and practice in that industry at the relevant time, and this may assist it in establishing the "development risk defence".[40] Moreover, the existence of a government body which assesses the risks and benefits of drugs on behalf of the public means that it will be difficult for a plaintiff to establish that a drug is "defective". This is an important aspect of the 1987 Act and is explored in more detail in chapter 8.

(B) NON-SUPPLY

Liability can be avoided if the defendant proves that it did not at any time supply the product to another, or that the product was supplied without a view to profit or otherwise than in the course of a business.[41] This defence will therefore negate liability for items which are stolen, or for prototypes. It may also protect a pharmaceutical manufacturer while it is engaged in clinical trials as part of the initial research into the safety of its products.[42]

(C) NO DEFECT AT THE TIME OF SUPPLY

A manufacturer which is sued under traditional tort principles may have a defence if it is able to show that the defect was not present when the product was supplied by it. Product-tampering cases in America have illustrated this issue. Seven people died in Chicago in 1982 following their consumption of Extra-Strength Tylenol (acetaminophen) capsules which had been contaminated with cyanide by a third party. Another person was killed in this way in 1986 prompting Johnson and Johnson, the drug's

---

[39] *op. cit.* para. 1260.
[40] See p. [106], below.
[41] See Art. 7(a) and (c) of Dir. 85/374 and ss.4(1)(b) and (c) of the 1987 Act.
[42] This view is supported by the Department of Trade and Industry: *Implementation of E.C. Directive on Product Liability*, DTI Consultation Document, para. 56.

producers, to stop manufacturing this medication in capsule form.[43] In March 1991 two people died as a result of ingesting Sudafed capsules which had been laced with cyanide.[44] Suits against these manufacturers have failed, since the products were not defective when supplied by them.[45]

The 1987 Act embodies a similar defence to that available at Common Law, on the basis that it would not be appropriate to impose liability for a product which had been rendered defective by improper use or variation by a third party.[46] Despite this, were such a product to injure a consumer, the latter may argue that it *was* defective when circulated by the manufacturer, due to the lack of a "tamper-proof", or more accurately, tamper-evident, container. To date, this argument has failed to satisfy the courts, even in the United States.[47]

(D) THE DEVELOPMENT RISK DEFENCE

This is arguably the most controversial of the defences provided by the 1987 Act.[48] According to section 4(1)(e), it is a defence for a producer to show:

"that the state of scientific and technical knowledge at the relevant time was not such that a producer of products of the same description as the product in question might be expected to have discovered the defect if it had existed in his products while they were under his control."

---

[43] See Abbot, "The Story Behind the Tylenol Story" (1991) *P.L.I.*, 13:1, at p. 4.

[44] 1991 *P.L.I.*, 13:3, at p. 38. Sudafed Cold Capsules, manufactured by Burroughs Wellcome, account for over $15 million worth of sales each year.

[45] See *Elsroth v. Johnson & Johnson* S.D. N.Y. 1988, 700 F.Supp. 151.

[46] s.4(1)(d). This is based on Art. 7(b) of the Directive.

[47] See Patterson, *Drugs in Litigation: Damage Awards involving Prescription and Nonprescription Drugs* (Virginia, Michie, 1992), p. 1.

[48] See Griffiths, "Defectiveness in EEC Product Liability" (1987) *Journal of Business Law*, 222; Miller, *Product Liability and Safety Encyclopaedia* (London, Butterworths, 1979) Division III, 11, para. 22; Newdick, "The Development Risk Defence of the Consumer Protection Act 1987" (1988) *Camb. L.J.*, 47, 455; Stoppa, "The Concept of Defectiveness in the Consumer Protection Act 1987: A Critical Analysis" (1992) *Legal Studies*, 12:2, 210; Clark, "Product Liability—The New Rules" (1987) *S.L.T.* 257; Goldberg, "The Development Risk Defence and Medicinal Products" (1991) *J.L.S.S.* 376, Young, "Product Liability: Are Industrialists Protesting Too Much?" *The Times* March 6, 1980; "Doubts on New Consumer Bill" *The Independent* November 13, 1986.

The defence was not available in the original draft of the Directive, which stated that a producer was to be held liable for damage caused by a defect in a product "whether or not he knew or *could have known* of the defect".[49] According to this version, a producer was to be held liable "even if the article could not have been regarded as defective in the light of the scientific and technological development at the time when he put the article into circulation." Several Member States, including Britain in particular, were unwilling to impose strict liability without a "development risk" defence and this accounts, at least in part, for the delay in the implementation of the Directive.

The defence was subject to a derogation procedure, with Member States being free to accept or reject it.[50] It has been implemented by all countries except Luxembourg.[51] The British government was warned that innovation would be discouraged if the defence was not available and was fearful that this country's competitive position would be jeopardised. The fate of the pharmaceutical industry, in particular, was invoked to support this contention. The ABPI pointed out that Britain is a significant exporter of pharmaceutical products, and that its major competitors are countries such as Japan, Switzerland, Sweden and the United States of America, all of which are outside the European Community.[52] The Association argued that without a development risk defence "innovation would inevitably be inhibited in this and other high risk and high technology industries . . ." and that "it would be wrong in principle for manufacturers to be held liable for defects which they could not reasonably have discovered."[53]

Pharmaceutical manufacturers were also concerned about the insurance implications. According to David Willingham of the Wellcome Foundation:

"The Pharmaceutical Industry in the U.K. received a clear message from the insurance industry that, if the defence were not incorporated into U.K.

---

[49] Emphasis added.
[50] Art. 15(1)(b). See also Art. 15(3).
[51] No development risk defence operates in Germany, nor for medical and food products in Spain. In the recent review of the Directive, the European Commission concluded that the option for Member States to include a development risk defence should be left unchanged.
[52] *Implementation of E.C. Directive on Product Liability: An Explanatory and Consultative Note, op. cit.* p. 2.
[53] *ibid.* p. 2.

national law, pharmaceutical product liability insurance would become not just even more expensive than it already was, but virtually unavailable at any price."[54]

Similar fears had been expressed by Allan Sanders of Smith Kline and French; a strict liability regime without a development risk defence:

"... could herald a flow of frivolous, punitive or blackmailing claims such as are common in the United States, where strict liability has led to rocketing insurance premiums and fantastic levels of damages. Increased costs to cover such liability would necessarily have a damaging effect on competitiveness and employment and would inevitably be passed on to the patient through insurance premiums and higher costs."[55]

The wording of the development risk defence in the Consumer Protection Act may, however, have given manufacturers greater protection than that envisaged by the Directive. According to Miller:

"there is a real danger that the defence will be equated with simply carrying out such tests as are customary in technically advanced sectors of the relevant industry. Since this is broadly equivalent to the requirements of a negligence-based liability the directive and the Act will have little effect—beyond reversing the burden of proof—where the problem is one of unknown side effects or health hazards."[56]

One of the purported advantages of a system of strict liability is that suits will be simplified and cheaper than claims based on negligence. The development risk defence is likely to increase greatly the complexity, and hence the expense, of any court case. Indeed, the existence of a strict

---

[54] "How Pharmaceutical Firms are Coping with the Difficulties of Obtaining Insurance Cover" (Fulbright Colloquium on *Product Liability, Insurance and the Pharmaceutical Industry: an Anglo-American Comparison*, University of Keele, September 18–19, 1989) p. 17.
[55] "Drug safety and the concept of Product Liability: The Industry Viewpoint", (1983) *P.L.I.*, 55:5, p. 76 at p. 77.
[56] Miller, *Product Liability and Safety Encyclopaedia* (London, Butterworths 1979) at Division III, para. 131.

liability regime may *itself* result in cases becoming more complex, because plaintiffs are likely to pursue their claims on the basis of both strict liability and fault.[57] This does seem to have occurred in the United States.[58]

Despite the criticisms which have been directed at the defence, David McIntosh, a solicitor who often acts for the pharmaceutical industry, has suggested that:

> "... a defendant who can only resist a claim on the basis that the injuries sued upon were 'unforeseen' and thus not warned against will find itself in a very weak position ..."[59]

He has argued that a company which attempts to rely solely on the development risk defence will find that the media will portray it as putting forward a "technical defence", only.

The development risk defence does at least reverse the burden of proof. Under the pre-existing law the plaintiff had the onus of establishing that a manufacturer which was exercising reasonable care would have foreseen that its product was likely to cause injury or damage. The 1987 Act seems to allow consideration of similar issues, but the onus is now on the manufacturer to establish that it was not, and could not reasonably have been expected to have been, aware of the defect in its product.

6. European Harmonisation?

We have already noted the different approaches adopted by various Member States in relation to financial limits.[60] One of the arguments in favour of the Directive was that the differing regimes of liability distorted competition and thereby impeded the free movement of goods. That some states have acted differently to the rights of derogation contained within the Directive, coupled with the fact that the pre-existing liability regime in

---

[57] See Dodds-Smith, "The Impact of Product Liability on Pharmaceutical Companies" Chap. 12 of Howells, ed., *Product Liability, Insurance and the Pharmaceutical Industry: an Anglo-American Comparison* (Manchester University Press, 1991) p. 156 at p. 158.

[58] See DeSimone, "The State of the Art Defense in Product Liability: 'Unreasonably Dangerous' to the Injured Consumer" (1980) *Duquesne Law Review*, 18, 915 at 932.

[59] McIntosh, "Defending a Pharmaceutical Company in Multi-Plaintiff Litigation" Chap. 4 of Howells, *op. cit.* p. 40.

[60] See p. [103], above.

each country continues in force, means that the laws of Member States will continue to be different from one another, and that harmonisation has not been achieved.[61]

The new liability regime can be attacked at a more fundamental level. Stapleton has contended that:

> ". . . the acceptance and implementation by the U.K. of the EC Directive not only defused what little domestic political impetus there was for *comprehensive* personal-injuries reform along the lines of the Woodhouse scheme operating in New Zealand since 1972, but introduced significant new barriers to such change."[62]

She argues that Britain could not now introduce a more comprehensive compensation system, which would repeal the 1987 Act, since this would place us in breach of our Community obligations. Even if the product liability regime was retained by any new scheme, she suggests that this would alter the "level playing field" of liability which the Directive was attempting to establish within the Community. Stapleton concludes that the Directive has in fact "severely put back the cause of personal injuries reform".[63] Of course, it is arguable that the Directive was not in fact capable of achieving equality of liability. As we have seen, the derogation procedures, which cover such important aspects of liability as financial limits and the development risk defence, coupled with the fact that the pre-existing laws of Member States continue in force, mean that the new regime is incapable of achieving much in the way of harmonisation.

7. Conclusions

A plaintiff now requires to prove that he or she has sustained injury and that a product which was manufactured, imported or supplied by the defendant was responsible for that injury. There is no need to prove that the

---

[61] Art. 13 of the Product Liability Directive states that the implementation of the strict liability regime "shall not affect any rights which an injured person may have according to the rules of the law of contractual or non-contractual liability . . .".

[62] Stapleton, "Three Problems with the New Product Liability" Chap. 11 in Cane and Stapleton, eds., *Essays for Patrick Atiyah* (Oxford, Clarendon Press, 1991), p. 257 at p. 278, emphasis in original.

[63] *ibid.* p. 287.

defendant was negligent in designing, manufacturing or marketing the product. This is the case even where there is no contractual relationship between the parties. Despite this, a manufacturer's potential liability is still less than that of a seller, since the latter may not invoke a "development risk" defence. It is clear, therefore, that the impact of the strict liability regime has been weakened by the inclusion of that defence.

As has already been noted, the new regime does not prevent a defendant from alleging that a plaintiff has been contributorily negligent. In addition, plaintiffs may pursue their claims on the basis of *both* strict liability and fault. That resources may still require to be spent in investigating such claims of negligence goes against one of the goals of a strict liability system, namely that the court process should become simpler and less expensive. Furthermore, there is no guarantee that a plaintiff will ultimately be able to recover any compensation which has been awarded under the 1987 Act; the defendant may not have adequate insurance to meet any award, or indeed, may not be insured at all.

It must also be emphasised that the new strict liability regime does not alter that fact that a plaintiff has to prove that his or her injuries were *caused by the product.* This may be especially difficult in cases involving pharmaceutical products.[64] In short, although the Consumer Protection Act has removed the burden of establishing negligence on the part of the defendant, other important hurdles remain for the injured plaintiff. The preamble to the Product Liability Directive states that:

> "... liability without fault on the part of the producer is the sole means of adequately solving the problem, peculiar to our age of increasing technicality, of *a fair apportionment of the risks* inherent in modern technological production."[65]

The existence of the development risk defence, and the failure of the 1987 Act to tackle the problem of establishing causation, mean that the risks which are inherent in pharmaceutical drugs and devices will generally continue to lie with the injured plaintiff.

---

[64] See Chap. 9, below.
[65] Emphasis added.

Chapter 8

Determining "Defectiveness"

1. Introduction

As we have seen, the strict liability regime which is imposed by the Consumer Protection Act requires a determination that the product was "defective" in some way.[1] Similarly, strict liability for product injuries in the majority of American states is based on section 402A of the Restatement (Second) of Torts 1965.[2] This provides that:

> "One who sells any product in a *defective condition* unreasonably dangerous to the user or consumer ... is subject to liability for physical harm thereby caused ..."[3]

As already noted, pharmaceutical products can be regarded as being "defective" in one of three ways: by having a manufacturing defect, by being defectively designed, or by reason of a marketing defect. The last of these commonly involves an allegation that there has been inadequate information supplied with the product, particularly that there has been a

---

[1] See Chap. 7, above.
[2] Restatements are treatise-like publications which are drafted by committees of eminent judges, legal academics and practising lawyers, all of whom work under the auspices of the American Law Institute. Restatements are not usually adopted by state legislatures in a formal sense, hence are not primary authorities, but a number of them, such as that on the law of torts, have become so respected and have been applied so frequently by the courts that they seem to have achieved the status of primary authority. A Third Restatement of Torts, in relation to its product liability aspects, is currently in preparation, see Ross and Bowbeer, "American Product Liability Law Undergoing Revision" [1994] *Consum. L.J.*, and Twerski, "From A Reporter: A Prospective Agenda" (1993) *Touro Law Review*, 10:1.
[3] Emphasis in original.

failure to provide appropriate warning of its risks.[4] Despite the fact that many American states have operated strict liability for products for over thirty years, the most appropriate definition of "defective" remains a highly controversial issue in that country.[5] Three main tests have been utilised by different states in America: these are the "Reasonably Prudent Manufacturer", the "Consumer Expectations" and the "Risks/Benefits" tests. Examination of these may shed some light on how a British court may interpret the definition which is provided by the Consumer Protection Act. As we shall see, the determination of defectiveness is a far from simple matter, and this may be particularly problematic in respect of certain products, such as pharmaceutical drugs and devices.

2. Definitions of "Defective"

(A) THE REASONABLY PRUDENT MANUFACTURER

In a number of American states the test of defectiveness has become based on "the reasonably prudent manufacturer", such that a product is to be considered as defective if such a manufacturer, being fully aware of the risk, would not have put its product on the market.[6] Hence Keeton has proposed that:

> "a product ought to be regarded as 'unreasonably dangerous' . . . if a reasonable man with knowledge of the product's condition, and an appreciation of all the risks found to exist by the jury at the time of the trial would not now market the product, or, if he did market it, would at least market it pursuant to a different set of warnings and instruction as to its use."[7]

This differs from the traditional negligence standard of reasonable care in that the manufacturer is *presumed* to be aware of the flaw or danger in its

---

[4] See page [16], *supra*.

[5] See, for example, Clark, "Product Liability: Oklahoma's Defective Test for Defect—The Consumer Expectation Test and Its Limitations" (1986) *Okla. L. Rev.*, 39, 318; and Wade, "On Product 'Design Defects' and Their Actionability" (1980) *Vand. L. Rev.*, 33, 551.

[6] Hulsen, "Design Liability and State of the Art: The United States and Europe at a Crossroads" (1981) *St Johns Law Review*, 55, 450 at 464.

[7] Keeton, "Manufacturer's Liability: The Meaning of 'Defect' in the Manufacture and Design of Products" (1969) *Syracuse Law Review*, 20, 559 at 568.

product. In relation to a drug such as thalidomide this test would ask: "would the manufacturer have marketed thalidomide for use by pregnant women had it been aware of the drug's tendency to cause congenital deformities?" It is clear that this standard will operate against the manufacturer of a pharmaceutical drug in most cases; a defendant will only be able to avoid liability if it satisfies the court that any alterations in the design of the product which would make it safer were not feasible at the time, either because they would make the product non-viable, commercially, or because the very nature of the product would be altered in the process.

(B) THE CONSUMER EXPECTATION TEST

It has been suggested that the definition of defectiveness should focus more on the expectations of the *consumer*, rather than on those of the person who marketed the product. Hence McClellan argued that a product ought to be regarded as defective if ordinary consumers would not now use it, or would only do so subject to a different set of procedures and precautions.[8] Comment i to section 402A of the Second Restatement of Torts lends some support to this. It states that the product in question:

" . . . must be dangerous to an extent beyond that which would be contemplated *by the ordinary consumer* who purchases it with the ordinary knowledge common to the community as to its characteristics."[9]

A "consumer expectation" test is easily understandable in the context of manufacturing defects; it can readily be determined that consumers expect each product to be as safe as its counterparts on the production line. Hence the test can be applied with ease to cases such as *Donoghue v. Stevenson*; the ordinary consumer does *not* expect to find a decomposing snail in a bottle of ginger beer. Such a product has failed to meet even its manufacturer's own expectations. It is, however, arguable that traditional tort liability is in fact "strict" in relation to manufacturing defects, in that the courts are quick to infer negligence where such a defect has occurred.[10]

---

[8] McClellan, "Strict Liability for Drug Induced Injuries: An Excursion through the Maze of Products Liability, Negligence and Absolute Liability" (1978) *Wayne Law Review*, 25, 4.
[9] Emphasis added.
[10] See, for example, *Grant v. Australian Knitting Mills Ltd* [1936] A.C. 85.

As one might imagine, cases of alleged design defect are harder to determine under a consumer expectation test. In *Dart v. Wiebe Manufacturing Incorporated*[11] it was stated that this test:

"... provides no resolution for those cases in which the consumer would not know what to expect, because he would have no idea how safe the product could be made."[12]

The risk in asking a jury in a design defect case to determine whether the product at issue was "more dangerous than the ordinary consumer would expect" has been pointed out by Hermann. As he puts it:

"Since *any* latent danger and, in particular, any danger of which the jury was not previously aware, will likely make the product seem more dangerous than the typical juror would expect, a consumer expectation type of instruction in design or toxic tort cases will arguably increase the likelihood that a jury will deem the product defective, even when the product was properly designed and consistent with the medical or scientific state of the art at the time."[13]

The notion of a consumer expectation test does not fit easily to the position regarding pharmaceutical products. While one can accept that consumers may develop certain expectations as to the safety of most consumer goods, pharmaceutical drugs and devices are in a different position since they have to pass strict requirements, laid down by government bodies, before they can be marketed. It is arguable that a consumer should not expect a product which has satisfied the standards imposed by such bodies to be any safer than in fact it is. If this approach is not taken, then it would be all too easy for a jury to hold that ordinary consumers expect their drugs to be 100 per cent safe, hence that *any* side effect which was not warned about in advance of the treatment rendered the product less safe than consumers expect.

The consumer expectation test was ultimately rejected in the United States by the drafters of the Model Uniform Product Liability Act, on the basis that:

---

[11] 147 Ariz. 242; 709 P. 2d 876.

[12] *ibid.*

[13] Hermann, "The Consumer Expectation Test—Application of a Difficult Standard for Determining Product Defects" (1991) *Federation of Insurance and Corporate Counsel Quarterly*, 41, 251 at 255 (emphasis in original).

"... it takes subjectivity to its most extreme end. Each trier of fact is likely to have a different understanding of abstract consumer expectations. Moreover, most consumers are not familiar with the details of the manufacturing process and cannot abstractly evaluate conscious design alternatives."[14]

(C) THE RISKS/BENEFITS TEST

An alternative method of determining whether a product is defective was proposed in the case of *Barker v. Lull Engineering Co.*[15] Known as the "risks/benefits" test,[16] this allows defectiveness to be determined by an assessment of the advantages and disadvantages offered by the product. It permits the manufacturer to lead evidence to demonstrate that its product could not really have been made any safer. In some cases, it may be possible for a court to hold that a pharmaceutical product offered nothing in the way of benefits which could be balanced against its risks. One example of this is Diethylstilbestrol which was designed to prevent miscarriages but was not even effective at doing this.

The cases which will prove to be most controversial will be those in which the drug has caused an adverse reaction which was not expected by its manufacturer, let alone by consumers. The test is concerned with the risks and benefits to persons generally, rather than simply to the injured plaintiff. As Stapleton has pointed out, under this test:

"... the enterprise would be liable only where the overall social benefits were outweighed by the overall social costs and would not be liable in cases where the social benefits outweighed the high cost to the few victims."[17]

The test would allow a drug company to show that its product did offer an appropriate level of safety, notwithstanding that it produced an unavoidable side effect in the particular consumer.

---

[14] Model Uniform Product Liability Act (UPLA), Analysis 104(B), reprinted in 44 Fed. Reg. 62, 714 (1979) 62, 724. See Stoppa, "The Concept of Defectiveness in the Consumer Protection Act 1987: A Critical Analysis" (1992) *Legal Studies*, 12:2, 210 at 215.

[15] 20 Cal. 3d 413, 573 P. 2d 443, 143 Cal. Rptr. 225 (1978).

[16] It has also been called the "risks–utility analysis"; see Leacock, "A General Conspectus of American Law on Product Liability" (1989) *Journal of Business Law*, 273 at 275.

[17] Stapleton, "Products Liability Reform—Real or Illusory?" (1986) *Oxf. J.L.S.*, 6:3, 392 at 405.

Some American courts have held that a drug can be considered to be defective if other drugs are available which confer the same benefits as the drug in question, but which do not have similar risks. This was the position in the case of *Stromsodt v. Parke-Davis & Co.*[18] in which the defendants were the manufacturers of Quadrigen, a combination of vaccines designed to provide immunisation against diphtheria, tetanus, pertussis (whooping-cough) and poliomyelitis. The court held that the inclusion of the pertussis vaccine in this concoction made the other vaccines more likely to cause an anaphylactic type of reaction. Accordingly, the drug was "defective".[19]

Similarly, in *Brochu v. Ortho Pharmaceutical Corporation*[20] an oral contraceptive manufactured by the defendant company was held to be defective since there were other low-oestrogen pills on the market which were safer than that produced by Ortho. It is possible that a British court could adopt a similar stance in relation to the recent concerns over the safety of certain types of "mini Pill".[21] It seems that the risks of thrombosis which these Pills offer is twice as high as for other oral contraceptives.[22] This may lead a court to conclude that the higher risk Pills are defective.

In the *Brochu* case the court stated:

"[L]iability may attach if the manufacturer did not take available and reasonable steps to lessen or eliminate the danger of even a significantly useful and desirable product . . . [W]hen an unreasonable danger could have been eliminated without excessive cost or loss of product efficiency, liability may attach even though the danger was obvious or there was adequate warning."[23]

One key point here is that the danger has to be capable of being eliminated without "loss of product efficiency". In practice, if you modify the chemical composition of a drug even slightly, you often end up with a totally different drug, and one which may have a whole range of side effects of its own.[24]

Another important factor according to the court in *Brochu* is that the danger has to be capable of elimination "without excessive cost". The

---

[18] 257 F. Supp. 991 (1966).
[19] The plaintiff was awarded $500,000 in compensation.
[20] 642 F. 2d 652 (1st Cir. 1981).
[21] See p. [15], above.
[22] The risk of thrombosis posed by these Pills is estimated to be 30 injuries in 100,000 users.
[23] *op. cit.* at 654–55.
[24] See Bauer and Stith, "Duty to Warn" Chap. 4 of Vinson and Slaughter, eds., *Products Liability: Pharmaceutical Drug Cases* (Colorado, Shepard's/McGraw-Hill Inc, 1988) p. 134.

potential profitability of some drugs is, of course, greater than for others; a drug which is designed for the treatment of a commonly occurring condition, such as hypertension or arthritis, is more likely to make a profit than one which is intended for a much rarer condition.

It has been recognised in the United States that there is little incentive for a pharmaceutical company to devote resources to find a treatment which will alleviate a rare condition, such as muscular dystrophy, Huntington's disease, or Tourette syndrome. A pharmaceutical company will aim to recover the costs it has devoted in the development of a new drug from sales of that drug before its patent expires. If the market for a new drug is limited then the company may find it difficult to do this. The FDA has estimated that a drug must be used to treat 100,000 people or more before it may be said to be profitable to its manufacturer.

Drugs which are designed to benefit less common medical conditions are referred to as "Orphan Drugs" in the United States and that country has passed legislation, specifically designed to provide financial incentives for their manufacture.[25] A drug is entitled to the benefits of the Orphan Drug legislation if it has an estimated patient market of less than 200,000 people. In terms of product liability one might imagine that since many Orphan Drugs offer the *only* known treatment for certain medical conditions, the courts are likely to acknowledge that the benefits to be derived from such drugs generally outweigh the risks. In practice, however, while the legislation led to the development of 42 Orphan products in six years, it did not make any concessions over product liability, and one in five of these products has been the subject of suit.[26]

(D) THE CONSUMER PROTECTION ACT

As already noted, section 3(1) of the 1987 Act states that:

"there is a defect in a product . . . if the safety of the product is not such as *persons generally* are entitled to expect".[27]

---

[25] See the Oprhan Drug Act, Pub. L. No. 97–414, 96 Stat. 2049 (1983) and 21 USC at 360ee and 360cc (1988).

[26] See Asbury, "The Orphan Drug Act: The First 7 Years" (1991) *J.A.M.A.*, 265, 893; and Jackson, "Pharmaceutical Product Liability may be Hazardous to your Health: A No-fault Alternative to Concurrent Regulation" (1992) *American University Law Review*, 42, 199 at 207–208.

[27] Emphasis added.

This sounds very much like a "consumer expectation" test. Newdick has argued that:

> "We are probably *entitled* to rather less [safety] than we actually *expect*. Many appear to be largely unaware of the inevitable risks connected with pharmaceuticals. Perhaps it is fair to say that we are entitled to expect as much safety as is reasonable, taking all the circumstances into account."[28]

This smacks of the negligence test of reasonable care.

In applying the "consumer expectation" test to cases involving pharmaceutical drugs or devices, some American courts have held that the "consumer" is not always the patient. In *Rosburg v. Minnesota Mining & Manufacturing Co.*[29] for example, a woman whose breast implants deflated six years after their insertion claimed that this rendered them "defective". She relied on the consumer expectation test, claiming that this was certainly not something she had contemplated. However, the court founded on the testimony given by the plaintiff's doctor, who stated that *he* was aware of the risks of deflation of the implants. The court held that the test to be applied here was to assess the reasonable expectations of her *doctor*, since he was the consumer in these circumstances. The use of the term "persons generally" in the British legislation should prevent a similar interpretation applying in this country.

Where any danger posed by a product is recognised and well-known, a court may consider that the product is not defective, since such an obvious danger ought to have been apparent to "persons generally". Similarly, if a consumer misuses the product no claim will generally lie against the manufacturer.[30]

Section 3(2) of the 1987 Act requires a court to take "all relevant circumstances" into account in assessing the safety of a product, thus incorporating a risks/benefits element into the test of defectiveness. When the Consumer Protection Bill was before the House of Lords, Lord Denning quoted a report in *The Times* newspaper that the Wellcome Pharmaceutical Company was developing a drug against the AIDS virus, at a cost of $80 million. He questioned whether such a manufacturer "which

---

[28] Newdick, "Special Problems of Compensating Those Damaged by Medicinal Products" Chap. 1 in McLean, ed., *Compensation for Damage* (Aldershot, Dartmouth, 1993) p. 7 at p. 8, emphases in original.

[29] 721 P. 2d 611 (Alaska 1986).

[30] See *Heil v. Hedges* [1951] 1 T.L.R. 512.

is doing such valuable research" ought "to be strictly liable to a person who suffers side-effects in the course of it?"[31] It is respectfully submitted that Lord Denning's fears have little foundation; section 3(2) will allow consideration of the amount of research which might have been required to eliminate the defect, as well as the cost of this additional research, not only in financial terms, but also the human costs. A court would consider how urgently the product was needed and its general utility.

In determining the level of safety which may be expected from a pharmaceutical product, therefore, a court will compare the seriousness of the illness and potential benefits of the drug with its adverse effects. Consideration may also be given to any alternative treatments which may be available; where an illness is particularly serious or life-threatening it may be that the courts will be justified in concluding that the patient was not entitled to expect a high level of safety from the product.

As already noted, several diabetics had considered raising personal injury actions against the manufacturers of human insulins.[32] The insulin producers eventually agreed to include a warning with their products, drawing patients' attention to the fact that less warning symptoms might occur prior to a hypoglycaemic attack with human insulin than with animal insulin. The shelf-life of human insulin is up to two years, hence there may have been patients who did not receive this warning. Would such patients be able to claim that the insulin was thereby "defective"? Section 3(2)(c) of the 1987 Act makes it clear that the defectiveness of a product is to be judged at "the time when the product was supplied by its producer to another". It is therefore unlikely that insulin which was delivered to a distributor or wholesaler before the warning information was considered to be necessary would be considered to be defective, within the provisions of that Act.

3. Conclusions

There has been a great deal of difficulty in defining "defectiveness" for the purpose of products liability. Clark has argued that:

---

[31] See "The Consumer Protection Bill: Lord Denning Moves the Lords on New Drugs" (1987) *The Lancet*, 284.

[32] See p. [12], above.

"The major difficulty with the definition of defect in the 1987 Act is that it fails to provide a readily ascertainable objective standard against which a manufacturer, or indeed a court, can measure the safety of a product."[33]

As one author has put it, under the British strict liability regime "fault" must still be proved by the plaintiff "but the relevant fault becomes that a 'defect' in the product resulted in injury, rather than want of care".[34] Writing of the American experience, Dutton has noted that, in practice, "proof that a product was in fact 'defective' can involve many of the same arguments and evidence that would be necessary for proof of negligence".[35] It does seem that the need to establish that a product was defective may be as much of a hurdle for the plaintiff under the strict liability regime as the requirement to prove negligence under tort law.

This problem is exacerbated when the product at issue is a pharmaceutical drug or device. We have noted that a distinction can be made between adverse reactions which are recognised as a risk prior to marketing, and those which are unforeseen (and commonly unforeseeable) until the drug has been consumed by a large number of people.[36] Information about recognised risks must be provided in the label or leaflet which accompanies a drug,[37] and the 1987 Act requires a court to take account of "any instructions for, or warnings with respect to" a product.[38] Furthermore, since the CSM is charged with the regulation of pharmaceutical products, a court may hold that it is the Committee's job to assess the risks and benefits of a drug. Where the side effect which has materialised was a recognised one, the court may feel that the drug's benefits must be said to outweigh the risks for the majority of users. Many drugs, such as vaccines and oral contraceptives, for example, pose risks to a small proportion of users, but these risk are outweighed by the benefits conferred on the great majority.[39]

Clozaril is used in the treatment of schizophrenia and represents a

---

[33] Clark, *Product Liability* (London, Sweet & Maxwell, 1989) p. 29.

[34] Brazier, *Street on Torts* (London, Butterworths, 9th ed., 1993) p. 338.

[35] Dutton, *Worse than the Disease: Pitfalls of Medical Progress* (Cambridge University Press, 1988) p. 257, n. 10.

[36] See Chap. 2, above.

[37] See p. [27], above.

[38] By s.3(2)(a).

[39] The risk of thrombosis associated with taking the Pill is between 15 and 30 in 100,000 women, depending on the type of Pill. The risk of thrombosis associated with pregnancy is 60 in 100,000.

significant advance in the treatment of that illness, but its side effects can be fatal in two per cent of patients.[40] Thalidomide has been referred to as "the classic example" of a design defect,[41] and at first sight would seem to be the epitome of a defective product, yet it offers great benefits to many patients. Recent studies have shown that it is effective in the treament of leprosy, and is currently being tested in clinical trials for the symptoms of AIDS and cancer.[42] Live vaccines cause more side effects than killed ones, but the former also confer better immunity and can even protect people who have not been immunised, but who come into contact with persons who have been. Where does the balance of risk and benefits lie between those vaccines? It may be argued that, by deciding to license such products, the government regulatory authority has assessed the risks and benefits for the community as a whole and has determined that the balance lies in favour of marketing the drug.

The above examples relate to foreseeable risks. Where an unknown and unforeseeable risk materialises, as was the case with drugs such as Opren and Halcion, it may be decided that the extent or severity of the injuries is such that the risks *do* outweigh the benefits; this is presumably the conclusion which the CSM itself ultimately reached since it decided to withdraw the licences from both of these drugs.[43] Yet even in these cases, a plaintiff may not be successful in claiming compensation under the 1987 Act; even if such products may be regarded as being "defective", the very fact that these side effects were unforeseeable means that a drug company may be able to invoke the development risk defence,[44] and establish that "the producer of similar products" would not have discovered the defect, due to the state of scientific and technical knowledge which was available at the time of marketing.

Hulsen has argued that, if we really feel that the provision of compensation to consumers who sustain product injuries is of such importance, then we ought not to insist that the product be shown to be

---

[40] See p. [173], below.

[41] Cook, Doyle and Jabbari, *Pharmaceuticals, Biotechnology and the Law* (Hants, Macmillan Publishers Ltd, 1991) p. 364.

[42] See Garfield, "The return of thalidomide" *The Independent*, September 23, 1995.

[43] It should be noted, however, that the American FDA decided not to withdraw its licence for Halcion, illustrating that a determination of the risks and benefits posed by a particular drug may be decided differently by different agencies.

[44] See p. [106], above.

defective in some way, but rather should compensate all persons who are injured by products.[45] This approach is considered in chapter 12, below.

Finally, it must be borne in mind that even where a product is judged to be defective, a plaintiff must still prove that it was the defective product which *caused* his or her injury. This considerable hurdle is explored in the following chapter.

---

[45] *op. cit.* at 482.

Chapter 9

Establishing Causation

"Although causation is often seen as an ancillary issue, in practice it is the greatest hurdle for a plaintiff in a drug injury case to overcome and it provides the best and most effective defence; that the drug did not cause the damage."[1]

1. Introduction

In a negligence-based action a plaintiff is required to prove a causal connection between the fault of the defendant and the former's loss or injury. The plaintiff must show that this damage would not have occurred had it not been for the defendant's fault.[2] Notwithstanding the reforms enacted by the Consumer Protection Act 1987 a plaintiff is still required to establish the causal link between the defendant's act or omission and the former's loss. This is emphasised by Article 4 of the Product Liability Directive which states that the injured person shall be required to prove the damage, the defect and the *causal relationship* between the defect and damage. Hence as Cook *et al* have put it:

> "... the same thorny issues of proving causation which have stood in the way of successful pharmaceutical negligence claims, still exist under strict liability."[3]

---

[1] Cook, Doyle and Jabbari, *Pharmaceuticals, Biotechnology and the Law* (Hants, Macmillan Publishers Ltd, 1991) p. 359.
[2] See Stapleton, "The Gist of Negligence: Part I: Minimum Actionable Damage" (1988) *L.Q.R.*, 104, 213, and "Part II: The Relationship Between 'Damage' and Causation" (1988) *L.Q.R.*, 104, 389.
[3] *op. cit.* at 355.

2. Causation and Pharmaceutical Products

A detailed discussion of the general issues posed by the requirement to establish causation is outwith the scope of this book.[4] In respect of pharmaceutical products, it is their very nature which leads to causation difficulties. Drugs are intended to be consumed and to have a biological effect. The action of any drug in the body of a particular individual can never be predicted with complete accuracy. Many symptoms which may be ascribed to an adverse effect of a medication may actually be due to the natural progression of an underlying disease or illness. Drugs are absorbed at varying rates by different persons, they may be metabolised and excreted differently. A drug may interact with others which are being taken concurrently by a patient, or with foodstuffs. Studies have shown that many people who are neither ill nor taking any medication perceive that they are suffering from "symptoms".[5] Had such people been receiving drug therapy, they might have attributed their symptoms to the treatment.

A person who is injured by a car which has faulty brakes or by an exploding kettle is at least aware of the fact that the car or the kettle was "involved" in causing the injury. While this does not mean that the injured person will find it easy to establish that the manufacturer of the car or kettle was negligent, or that these items were "defective" within the meaning of the 1987 Act, the very fact that the injury has occurred suggests that this might be the case, and that the matter should be further investigated. The injured party does at least have a starting point from which to explore the issue of liability, and the remnants of the product might be available for examination. At the very least, the injured party is likely to be able to identify the product as a potential source of the harm.

This is in contrast to the position with pharmaceutical drugs, which leave little or no trace once consumed.[6] Suits involving food or drink may face similar problems, but since any "adverse reactions" to such substances usually occur very soon after consumption, a causal link will generally be

---

[4] See Hart and Honore, *Causation and the Law* (Oxford, Clarendon Press, 2nd ed., 1985).

[5] Stephens, "Has the patient suffered an ADR?—assessment of drug causality" in Glaxo Group Research, *Drug Safety: A Shared Responsibility* (New York, Churchill Livingstone, 1991) p. 47.

[6] Similar causation problems do occur in other areas, such as in environmental law. See, for example, the case of *Graham and Graham v. ReChem*, discussed in *ENDS Report*, 245, June 1995, p. 18 on.

suspected at an early stage. As we have seen, while some people do suffer from immediate allergic reactions to drugs, in the majority of cases, such as those involving Diethylstilbestrol, Opren, and problems associated with certain tranquillisers, the injuries which are alleged to have been caused by these drugs took several months, or in some cases, years, to become manifest. That consumption of a particular drug by a pregnant woman may have resulted in pre-natal injury may only be suspected once the child is born; thalidomide is an example of this.

Several suits involving pharmaceutical products have failed, at least in part, due to the difficulty of establishing that the drugs in question caused the plaintiffs' injuries. A brief description of these cases serves to illustrate the extent of the problem.

(A) THALIDOMIDE

Several hurdles confronted the thalidomide victims. For example, it was unclear whether the manufacturer of a pharmaceutical drug owed a duty of care to a person *in utero*.[7] Furthermore, it would have been difficult for the plaintiffs to establish that Distillers had been negligent in not testing the drug more fully, since it was not common practice at that time for drug companies to test their products on pregnant animals. Since the case was settled out of court it is impossible to know which, if any, of these would have proved fatal to the plaintiffs' case had it proceeded to trial. Nevertheless, one might have thought that the causation issue was one obstacle which it would have been relatively easy for the victims of thalidomide to surmount, since the types of handicap sustained by many of its victims occurred very rarely under normal circumstances. In fact, a court in Germany spent several years considering the causation issue. One expert even testified that, in his opinion, the injuries sustained by these children could not have been caused by thalidomide.[8]

---

[7] The situation is now governed by the Congenital Disabilities (Civil Liability) Act 1976. See p. [43], above.
[8] See Chap. 3 of Allen, Bourne and Holyoak, eds., *Accident Compensation after Pearson* (London, Sweet & Maxwell, 1979) p. 161.

(B) The Benzodiazepine Litigation

Several factors contributed to the eventual collapse of these suits. There were at one point 17,000 potential plaintiffs and the sheer numbers involved meant that there were inevitable problems associated with legal aid funding and multi-party actions.[9] The defendant manufacturers were, however, convinced that the plaintiffs' case was doomed to fail over the causation issue. A report on the benzodiazepine litigation was prepared by McKenna & Co., the firm of solicitors which represented Ativan's manufacturers, Wyeth & Brother Ltd. This stressed the difficulties which the plaintiffs would have faced in establishing that their symptoms were caused by Ativan:

> "The injuries alleged by the plaintiffs as side-effects during ingestion of the drug were similar to the injuries alleged as withdrawal effects following cessation of the drug and these injuries were similar to the pre-existing symptoms/conditions of which the plaintiffs complained, and for which benzodiazepines were indicated and prescribed."[10]

The report also emphasised the problems which can occur where the illness being treated is a long-term one, such as depression:

> "The difficulties of establishing causation are accentuated where, as is common, a person has taken many different products for separate conditions or a series of similar products from different manufacturers for one condition."[11]

(C) The Kay Case

The Scottish case of *Kay's Tutor v. Ayrshire and Arran Health Board*[12] was a medical negligence suit, rather than a product liability action against a

---

[9] See Chap. 10, below.
[10] See McKinney, "A Bitter Pill", *Legal Business*, November 1994, 66, at p. 69.
[11] *ibid.*
[12] [1987] 2 All E.R. 417 H.L.; 1987 S.L.T. 577.

manufacturer. It does, however, illustrate the difficulties a plaintiff may face in establishing causation where pharmaceutical drugs are involved. In *Kay* it was alleged that the infant pursuer had become deaf due to a large overdose of penicillin. This had been administered to him while he was suffering from meningitis. The case illustrates that a patient's claim may fail even where negligence has been accepted; the dose given to the child was 30 times the recommended amount and the issue at trial was solely one of causation. At first instance the court accepted the medical evidence led by the defenders to the effect that deafness was a common consequence of meningitis, and rejected the evidence of the pursuer's expert that the injury was due in part to the penicillin overdose. Nevertheless, the court found in favour of the pursuer, holding that the overdose had weakened the child's defences, thus making it more likely that he would be susceptible to the effects of meningitis.

This was, however, reversed by the Inner House of the Court of Session, which ruled that there was no medical evidence for the theory that there was a causal connection between the overdose and the deafness. The pursuer then appealed from this ruling to the House of Lords, basing his case on the decision in *McGhee v. National Coal Board*.[13] At one time it was thought that the House of Lords had held in the *McGhee* case that where the defender's fault materially increased the risk of a certain kind of injury, such as dermatitis, and an injury of that nature subsequently occurred, the defender was deemed to have caused it, unless it proved otherwise.[14] However, in the *McGhee* case both risks were of the same kind (that is, the risk of dermatitis from dust) hence operated cumulatively to cause the injury.

The later case of *Wilsher v. Essex Area Health Authority*[15] reaffirmed that where there are alternative causes of injury the onus of proving that it was the defendant's act or omission which was a material cause of that injury remains with the plaintiff.[16] In short, the principle in *McGhee* is only of assistance to a plaintiff who can demonstrate that the defendant's negligence was *a* cause of injury, even if it was one of a number of causes. It

---

[13] 1973 S.C., H.L., 37; [1973] 1 W.L.R. 1.
[14] See also *Clark v. MacLennan* [1983] 1 All E.R. 416; and *Bonnington Castings v. Wardlaw* [1956] A.C. 613; [1956] 1 All E.R. 615.
[15] [1988] A.C. 1074.
[16] See also the opinion of Musthill J. in *Thompson v. Smiths Ship-Repairers (North Shields) Ltd* [1984] 1 All E.R. 881, at 909.

is not sufficient for the plaintiff to establish that the defendant's negligence was one of a number of *possible* causes. In *Kay* their Lordships held that the *McGhee* case would only have been in point if there had been medical evidence that an overdose of penicillin was known to increase the risk that the meningitis would cause deafness.

(D) VACCINE INJURIES

The recent controversy surrounding vaccines, such as the whooping cough (pertussis) vaccine also illustrates the causation difficulty. In the American case of *Stromsodt v. Parke-Davis & Co.*[17] it was held that, in the absence of other known causes for the infant plaintiff's seizures, this could be ascribed to the inoculation process:

> "there is no competent evidence in the entire record, medical or otherwise, to show that [the baby's] condition arose out of or from any susceptibility or predisposition, nor that the child had any congenital disease or disorder or defect of any kind, nor that he had any allergy or idiosyncrasy, nor that heredity was a factor that might account for his present condition."[18]

Things are seldom so straight forward. Where seizures or convulsions occur in a child who has recently been immunised, it is understandable that the child's parents will presume that it is the vaccine which was responsible. However, infantile spasms can occur at this time in a child's life, unconnected to the vaccination. In the Canadian case of *Rothwell v. Raes*[19] Mr Justice Osler stated:

> "... it has been easy and natural for laypersons, and probably the great majority of physicians, to conclude that, because there was sometimes a temporal association between vaccine administration and the development of devastating brain damage, the one was caused by the other. The logical fallacy encompassed in the term 'post hoc ergo proper hoc' is an error into which it is easy to fall."[20]

It is interesting to note that he concluded in this case that a no-fault compensation fund ought to be established to assist such plaintiffs.[21]

---

[17] 275 F.Supp. 991 (D.N.D. 1966).
[18] *ibid.* at 997.
[19] (1986) 66 O.R. (2nd) 449.
[20] *ibid.* at 464.
[21] See p. [193], below.

One author has argued that:

"Because the human body and its functions are only imperfectly understood by medical science, proof of causation in fact must usually take the form of a two-step analysis. First, it must be established that the drug or device in question can and does inflict the type of injury involved. This is a question of *general* causation. Second, it must be established that the drug or device inflicted injury on this particular plaintiff. This may be termed *specific* causation."[22]

A similar approach was taken by the trial judge in the English case of *Loveday v. Renton*.[23] Stuart-Smith L.J. decided to hear the trial in two parts; the first part would determine whether the whooping cough vaccine was ever capable of causing brain damage (general causation), while the subsequent trial would consider whether it had caused injury to the plaintiff (specific causation), and whether the defendant had been negligent. In the event, at the end of the first trial, which lasted four months and had included evidence from 19 medical experts, Stuart-Smith L.J. held that he was not satisfied that the vaccine could cause permanent brain damage. He said:

"... when I embarked on the consideration of the preliminary issue, I was impressed by the case reports and what was evidently a widely held belief that the vaccine could, albeit rarely, cause permanent brain damage. I was ready to accept that this belief was well founded. But over the weeks that I have listened to and examined the evidence and arguments I have become more and more doubtful that this is so. I have now come to the clear conclusion that the Plaintiff fails to satisfy me on the balance of probability that pertussis vaccine can cause permanent brain damage in young children. It is possible that it does; the contrary cannot be proved. But in the result the Plaintiff's claim must fail."[24]

It seemed likely that any cases alleging pertussis vaccine damage would suffer a similar fate in the future. However, in 1991 an Irish court held the pertussis vaccine *was* capable of causing brain damage[25] and this was upheld

---

[22] Woodside in Vinson and Slaughter, eds., *Product Liability: Pharmaceutical Drug Cases* (Colorado, Shephard's McGraw/Hill Inc., 1988) p. 225, emphases in original.
[23] [1990] 1 Med.L.R. 117. See also *The Times*, March 31, 1988.
[24] See Lee, "Vaccine Damage: Adjudicating Scientific Disputes" Chap. 5 in Howells, ed., *Product Liability, Insurance and the Pharmaceutical Industry: an Anglo-American Comparison* (Manchester University Press, 1991) p. 52 at pp. 55–56.
[25] See "U.K. solicitors focus on Irish vaccine case" (1989) L.S.G., 86:25, at 9.

in the Irish Supreme Court.[26] The court heard evidence which had not been presented during the *Loveday* case. Following *Loveday*, Legal Aid Boards had been refusing aid for plaintiffs in vaccine damage cases.[27] It should, however, be noted that the Irish case concerned a particularly potent batch of pertussis vaccine, hence the issue as to whether vaccine which is of normal strength is capable of causing brain damage has yet to be decided in that country.[28]

Reference has already been made to the Canadian case of *Rothwell v. Raes*,[29] in which the plaintiff failed to establish that the pertussis vaccine had caused his injury. Mr Justice Osler preferred the evidence of the defence witnesses, stating:

"On the whole, they have a higher level of expertise, their clinical experience or their academic eminence, as the case may be, tends to be somewhat greater and the fact that in almost every instance the witness originally accepted the post pertussis theory that was popular wisdom some years ago but as experience, study and technology developed he came to prefer another explanation, lends added credence to the views expressed."[30]

Similarly in *Loveday* the judge opined that he was more impressed with the cogency and quality of the experts cited on behalf of the defendants. It may be argued that courts do not have the expertise which is necessary to assess scientific evidence of this nature. The issue of causation then becomes "merely an analysis of the credibility and demeanour of competing expert witnesses, and may often yield outcomes in conflict with generally accepted scientific understandings".[31] A comparison of the decision in the *Loveday* case with the earlier American case of *Graham v. Wyeth Laboratories*[32] illustrates that courts in different jurisdictions may reach

---

[26] *Best v. Wellcome Foundation* [1992] I.L.R.M. 609.

[27] McKeone, "Legal Aid for Vaccine Cases" (1991) *L.S.G.*, 88:4, at 4. See also "Whooping cough" (1990) *L.S.G.*, 87:9, at 9, and s.15(2) of the Legal Aid Act 1988, which states: "A person shall not be granted representation for the purposes of any proceedings unless he satisfies the Board that he has reasonable grounds for taking, defending, or being a party to the proceedings." See also *R. v. Legal Aid Area No. 8, ex parte Parkinson, The Times*, March 13, 1990.

[28] See p. [146], above.

[29] (1986) 66 O.R. (2nd) 449. See p. [130], above.

[30] *ibid.* at 507.

[31] "A Question of Competence: The Judicial Role in the Regulation of Pharmaceuticals" (1990) *Harvard Law Review*, 103:3, 773 at 780.

[32] U.S. Dist. Ct., (Kansas) 666 F.Supp. 1483; 1987 U.S. Dist.

differing assessments as to the credibility of particular witnesses; some of the defence experts whose testimonies were rejected in the case of *Graham* were accepted in the *Loveday* case. As a result, Ms Loveday's claim failed, while Mr Graham's succeeded, and he was awarded $15 million in compensation.[33]

While there is a certain amount of logic in separating general and specific causation, and requiring the plaintiff to establish the former before the latter, in practice the courts have tended to consider the two simultaneously. Even where general causation is established, or where the courts have been prepared to assume that a particular drug is capable of causing the type of injury complained of, a plaintiff may still face great difficulty in establishing *specific* causation, that is, that his or her injuries were due to the pharmaceutical drug. A recent illustration of this is the litigation being contemplated by a number of women who have taken the oral contraceptive. It seems that several women are considering suing the manufacturers of these contraceptives for injuries which they allegedly sustained from taking the Pill.[34] The injury of which these women complain, pulmonary embolism, *is* a recognised side effect but each woman will have a difficult task in establishing that her particular stroke was caused by the Pill, since a small number of women suffer from strokes who have not used oral contraceptives.

3. Alternative Methods of Proving Causation

Although the civil law standard of proof on the "balance of probability" is obviously lower than a standard which requires causation to be established beyond all scientific doubt, it is nevertheless clear that the task of showing that a drug caused a patient's injury can be a daunting one. One technique which can help to demonstrate causation is known as "drug rechallenge". This has been defined as the giving of a further dose or doses of a drug to a person who had previously taken that drug, and who had experienced an

---

[33] See Campbell, "Pertussis Vaccine Litigation in Three Countries" (1990) *Law, Medicine and Health Care*, 18, 59 at 62–63.
[34] See Aitkenhead, "A hard pill to swallow" *The Independent*, May 1, 1995 and Ferguson, "An Ill for every Pill" (1995) *N.L.J.*, 836.

adverse reaction which might be due to the drug.[35] While the result of a drug rechallenge may be the most reliable method of establishing causality between a drug and a suspected adverse reaction, it is, in practice, a procedure which is rarely attempted, due to ethical considerations surrounding the re-administration of such a therapy to a patient.[36]

The adoption of a less stringent approach to causation in British law would improve an injured party's chances of establishing that his or her injury was caused by a drug. A precedent for reducing the burden of causation already exists in Britain. Certain industrial injuries are covered by a state-funded compensation scheme which provides compensation for death or long-term disability; there is a rebuttable presumption that the injury was caused by the exposure to the industrial hazard.[37]

Sweden has operated a no-fault compensation scheme for pharmaceutical injuries since 1978. Under this system injured parties must establish that there is a "preponderant probability" that it was a pharmaceutical product which caused their injury.[38] Without a similar relaxation of the rules for pharmaceutical drugs in Britain, establishing causation will only be straightforward in cases where the drug caused an injury which is particularly unusual. A rare example of this occurred in the diethylstilbestrol litigation.[39] The causal link between their mothers' consumption of DES and the plaintiffs' injuries was relatively easy to establish due to the fact that the injury which it induced was an extremely uncommon form of vaginal cancer. The "DES daughters" faced another problem, however; that of identifying the appropriate defendant.

---

[35] See Mann and Havard, eds., *No Fault Compensation in Medicine* (London, Royal Society of Medicine Services, 1989) p. 6.
[36] See Wolf and Wolf, "Drug Rechallenge and Patients' Rights" (1992) 11 *Medicine and Law*, 33–36. Ciba-Geigy report that under 5 per cent of all adverse reactions which are reported to them have had the benefit of a rechallenge. See Stephens, *Detection of New Adverse Drug Reactions* (Basingstoke, The Macmillan Press Ltd, 3rd ed., 1992) p. 126.
[37] See the Social Security (Industrial Injuries) (Prescribed Diseases) Regulations 1985 (S.I. 1985 No. 967) and s.50(3) of the Social Security Act 1975.
[38] See Chap. 12, below.
[39] See Chap. 1, above.

4. Identifying the Defendant

To succeed in a product liability action an injured party must establish a link between the defendant and the product which is alleged to have caused the injury.[40] Hence in the case of *Gray v. United States*[41] it was stated that:

> "It is a fundamental principle of products liability law that a plaintiff must prove, as an essential element of his case, that a defendant manufacturer actually made the particular product which caused the injury."[42]

Where a patient has consumed more than one medication, it may be difficult to ascertain which one was responsible for the injury. Even where a patient was only taking one drug, it may nonetheless be hard to determine who the appropriate defendant is; by the time the side effects become manifest, a patient may be unable to recall many details about a drug which was taken some years earlier.

This problem is exacerbated once the patent for a pharmaceutical product expires, since a large number of different companies may then produce the same drug. In the case of *Mann and Close v. Wellcome Foundation Ltd*,[43] for example, the plaintiffs alleged that a neomycin spray had caused deafness. The case against the Wellcome pharmaceutical company foundered when it became apparent that the injured parties were unable to prove that their sprays had been manufactured by one of Wellcome's subsidiaries. Reference has already been made to the case of *Loveday v. Renton*, involving the pertussis vaccine.[44] In *Loveday* the Wellcome Foundation successfully applied to be conjoined as defendants. The company was at that time the only manufacturer which continued to produce that vaccine for the British market. Ms Loveday had not, however, attempted to sue the manufacturer of the vaccine since she did not know which particular company had produced the one which had been administered to her.

By virtue of the Consumer Protection Act 1987, if a plaintiff knows the

---

[40] See *Oresman v. GD Searle & Co.*, 321 F.Supp. 449 (D.R.I. 1971) and *McCreery v. Eli Lilly & Co.* 87 Cal.App. 3d 77, 150 Cal.Rptr. 730 (1978).

[41] 445 F.Supp. 337 (S.D. Tex. 1978).

[42] *ibid.* at 338.

[43] January 20, 1989, Q.B.D. (unreported).

[44] See p. [131], above.

identity of the person who *supplied* the drug (that is, the identity of the doctor or pharmacist), then the fact that he or she does not know the identity of its manufacturer is no longer a bar to recovering compensation. As explained in Chapter 7, although liability is imposed primarily on the producer, section 2(3) of that Act imposes liability on the "supplier" of a product in certain circumstances, and this may cover the activities of pharmacists, as well as doctors who supply drugs directly to their patients.

As already noted, problems of identifying the appropriate defendant have arisen in America in cases involving Diethylstilbestrol. More than 300 companies manufactured this drug at some time, although about one-third of these have ceased to operate. It has been suggested that "pharmacists commonly filled prescriptions for a designated brand of DES with whatever brand they happen to have on hand".[45] Several American states have refused to apply traditional rules of tort law to these cases, and have argued that product liability law should adapt to accommodate victims who are faced with such difficult problems of proof.[46] The question raised by the DES cases has been described as follows:

> "may a plaintiff, injured as a result of a drug administered to her mother during pregnancy, who knows the type of drug involved but cannot identify the manufacturer of the precise product, hold liable for her injuries *a maker of a drug produced from an identical formula*?"[47]

Some American courts have answered this question in the affirmative, and have devised several novel theories of liability in an attempt to overcome these difficulties.[48]

---

[45] Schreiber and Hirssh, "Theories of Liability Applied to Overcome the Unique 'Identification Problem' in DES Cases" (1985) *Medicine and Law*, 4, 337 at 338.

[46] See, for example, *Bichler v. Eli Lilly & Co.*, 450 N.Y.S. 2d 776 (1982), at 779, quoting from *Capara v. Chrysler Corporation*, 436 N.Y.S. 2d 251 (1981). See also Meagher, "Market Share Liability: A New Method of Recovery for DES Litigants" (1981) *Catholic University Law Review*, 30:1, 551.

[47] *Sindell v. Abbott Laboratories*, 607 P.2d 924 (1980), *per* Justice Mosk, emphasis added.

[48] See Fern and Sichel, "Evolving Tort Liability Theories: Are They Taking the Pharmaceutical Industry into an Era of Absolute Liability?" (1985) *St Louis University Law Journal*, 29, 763; and Maedgen and McCall, "A Survey of Law Regarding the Liability of Manufacturers and Sellers of Drug Products and Medical Devices" (1986) *St Mary's Law Journal*, 18:2, 395 at 418–431.

(A) ENTERPRISE LIABILITY

In *Hall v. E.I. Du Pont De Nemours & Co.*[49] the 13 plaintiffs were children who had been injured in incidents involving blasting caps. The children were from 10 different states and the injuries occurred during 12 unrelated incidents. However, the court allowed the plaintiffs to sue all six cap manufacturers under a theory of joint liability, since the particular cap manufacturer could not be identified and the defendants had all followed national safety standards. The case illustrates the doctrine of Enterprise Liability. This theory may be applied if it can be shown that the defendants acted essentially in concert, and that their safety requirements were determined by a trade association of the industry. It is a prerequisite that the industry consists of only a few members, virtually all of whom are cited as defendants.

In relation to pharmaceutical products, the Enterprise Liability theory was proposed in the case of *Collins v. Eli Lilly & Co.*[50] The plaintiff's mother was given DES during her pregnancy and the plaintiff had developed adenocarcinoma. This had required removal of her uterus and part of her vagina. She was attempting to sue 17 parties, alleging that they had each produced or marketed DES at the relevant time.[51] The Enterprise Liability approach was, however, rejected by the court in this case. As already noted, hundreds of different drug companies had been responsible for manufacturing DES and it was felt to be unreasonable to assume that the 17 defendants had jointly controlled the risk of injury.

(B) ALTERNATIVE LIABILITY

This was a second theory proposed in *Collins*. The leading authority here is *Summers v. Tice*[52] in which the plaintiff was shot in the eye by one of two negligent hunters.[53] Both hunters had fired in the direction of the plaintiff but the latter was unable to ascertain which of the two had fired the actual

---

[49] 345 F.Supp. 353 (E.D.N.Y. 1972).

[50] 342 N.W. 2d 37 (1984).

[51] That is, in 1957, when Ms Collins was *in utero*.

[52] 33 Cal.2d 80, 199 P.2d 1 (1948).

[53] See also the Canadian case of *Cook v. Lewis* [1952] 1 D.L.R. 1.

shot which caused his injury. The Alternative Liability theory placed the onus on each defendant to show that he was not responsible. This principle is now contained in the Second Restatement of Torts, which states:

> "Where the conduct of two or more actors is tortious, and it is proved that harm has been caused to the plaintiff by only one of them, but there is uncertainty as to which one has caused it, the burden is upon each actor to prove that he has not caused the harm."[54]

It has been argued that the principle in *Summers v. Tice* is a sound one:

> "... it is fairer that the burden of identification be borne by the wrongdoers rather than their victim when it is their multiplicity alone which precludes the latter from identifying the responsible culprit."[55]

The Alternative Liability theory has been used successfully in some DES actions[56] but has been rejected in the majority of cases. One principle behind the theory is that the defendants are in a better position than the plaintiff to identify the negligent party or the source of the injury. In many DES cases even the defendants have encountered problems in recovering vital information. Furthermore, in *Summers v. Tice* both hunters were cited as co-defendants by the plaintiff. In many DES suits the plaintiff is attempting to sue a large number of manufacturers or suppliers, but all potential defendants are not before the court. This has proved fatal in a number of cases,[57] since the Restatement of Torts provides that all potential tortfeasors must be before the court before the burden of proof can shift from plaintiff to defendants.[58] In general, the DES cases in which the Alternative Liability theory has been successful are those where the plaintiff has attempted to sue all the companies which manufactured DES at the relevant time.[59]

---

[54] s.433B(3).

[55] Hart and Honore, *Causation in the Law* (Oxford, OUP, 2nd ed., 1985) p. 424, n. omitted.

[56] For example, *Ferringo v. Eli Lilly & Co.*, 420 A.2d 1305, N.J. Super.Ct. Law Div. 1980.

[57] See *Sindell v. Abbott Laboratories*, 26 Cal.3d 588; 163 Cal.Rpu. 132, 607 P.2d 924 (1980).

[58] Comment h to s.433B.

[59] This was the position in the case of *Abel v. Eli Lilly & Co.*, 343 N.W. 2d 164 (1979).

(C) CONCERTED ACTION

Similar to the idea of Enterprise Liability is the theory of "Concerted Action". This was also proposed in the *Collins* case. According to this theory:

"All those who, in pursuance of a common plan or design to commit a tortious act, actively take part in it, or further it by cooperation or request, or who lend aid or encouragement to the wrongdoer, or ratify and adopt the wrongdoer's acts done for their benefit, are equally liable."[60]

The plaintiff must demonstrate that there was some agreement, express or implicit, among the defendants. By virtue of section 876 of the Second Restatement of Torts:

"For harm resulting to a third person from the tortious conduct of another, one is subject to liability if he:
   (a) does a tortious act in concert with the other pursuant to a common design with him, or
   (b) knows that the other's conduct constitutes a breach of duty and gives substantial encouragement to the other ... or
   (c) gives substantial assistance to the other in accomplishing a tortious result and his own conduct, separately considered, constitutes a breach of duty to the third person."

Liability based on this theory has been imposed by some states in DES litigation. In *Bichler v. Eli Lilly & Co.*[61] the "concerted action" was based on:

"... the original cooperation by the twelve manufacturers (which included Lilly) and pooling of information, the agreement on the same basic chemical formula, and the adoption of Lilly's literature as a model for package insets for joint submission to the FDA ..."[62]

It was argued in *Collins* that the defendant manufacturers had acted in concert since each had relied upon the tests of its fellow producers and had

---

[60] Prosser and Keaton, *On Torts* (St Paul, Minn, West Publishing Co., 5th ed., 1984) p. 323.
[61] 79 App.Div. 2d 317, 436 N.Y.S. 2d 625 (App.Div. 1981); 55 N.Y. 2d 571, 450 N.Y.S. 2d 776, 436 N.E. 2d 182 (1982).
[62] *ibid.* 436 N.Y.S. 2d 625, at 633.

139

derived advantage from the promotional activities and advertising of the others. This argument was rejected by the court on the basis that the defendants' activities were more in the nature of parallel conduct than concerted action.[63]

Similarly, in the case of *Sindell v. Abbott Laboratories*[64] the court stated:

"What the [plaintiff's] complaint appears to charge is defendants' parallel or imitative conduct in that they relied upon each others' testing and promotion methods. But such conduct describes a common practice in industry: a producer avails himself of the experience and methods of others making the same or similar products. Application of the concept of concert of action to this situation would expand the doctrine far beyond its intended scope and would render virtually any manufacturer liable for the defective products of an entire industry, even if it could be demonstrated that the product which caused the injury was not made by the defendant."[65]

(D) MARKET SHARE LIABILITY

The three theories which have been looked at so far were already recognised by the law at the time of the DES litigation. A fourth theory which has gained some acceptance in DES litigation is that of "Market Share" liability.[66] This was a novel theory of liability, invented by some American courts specifically to assist DES plaintiffs. The theory was successfully applied in the case of *Sindell v. Abbott Laboratories*, mentioned above. The plaintiff attempted to sue 11 named and 100 unnamed pharmaceutical companies. Ultimately, the Supreme Court of California held that she had a valid cause of action against five of the companies, the Upjohn Company; ER Squibb & Co.; Eli Lilly; the Rexall Drug Company and Abbott Laboratories.

The Market Share theory requires a plaintiff to demonstrate that the defendants were responsible for a substantial share of the drug market. Each defendant must then show that it did not produce the particular drug which

---

[63] This theory was also rejected in *Morton v. Abbott Laboratories*, 538 F.Supp. 593 (M.D. Fla. 1982); *Payton v. Abbott Laboratories*, 512 F.Supp. 1031, (D.Mass. 1981) and *Conley v. Boyle Drug Co.*, 420 A.2d 185 (N.J. Super.Ct.App.Div. 1979).

[64] 26 Cal. 3d 588, 607 P.2d 924, 163 Cal.Rptr. 132 (1980).

[65] *ibid*. 26 Cal. 3d at 605.

[66] See "Market Share Liability: An Answer to the DES Causation Problem" (1981) *Harvard Law Review*, 94, 668.

was responsible for the plaintiff's injury.[67] Each manufacturer which fails to demonstrate this is liable to pay a percentage of the compensation awarded to the plaintiff, and this percentage is dependant on the share of the market for which the company was responsible at the relevant time (that is, at the time when the plaintiff's injury or loss occurred). A defendant may bring other producers of the drug into the action as co-defendants.[68]

The reasoning in *Sindell* was rejected in the later cases of *Mizell v. Eli Lilly & Co.*[69] *Ryan v. Eli Lilly & Co.*[70] and in the *Collins* case itself. One major reason for this was the recognition that in any particular case none of the companies being sued might have actually been responsible for producing the drug which caused the plaintiff's injuries.

Where a Market Share liability approach is accepted, this may allow a plaintiff to claim punitive damages from the defendants. In the case of *Morris v. Parke-Davis & Co.*[71] the plaintiff could not identify the manufacturer of the DTP vaccine which had caused his brain damage.[72] In allowing the plaintiff to seek punitive damages from all five defendants the court stated:

> "If manufacturers act with conscious disregard for human safety, they should not be allowed to escape punitive damages simply because the nature of their activity makes it impossible to identify which of them is responsible for the resulting harm."[73]

(E) RISK CONTRIBUTION

A further theory which has been developed by some American courts can be described as one of "Risk Contribution". This does not require the

---

[67] It has been held that a manufacturer who had 10 per cent of the DES market did not have a sufficiently large "market share" to be subject to this form of liability—see *Murphy v. E R Squibb & Sons* (1985) 40 Cal. 3d 672, 221 Cal.Rptr. 447, 710 P.2d 247.

[68] Market Share liability has also been applied against the makers of blood concentrates where persons have contracted the AIDS virus as a result, see *Smith v. Cutter Biologicals Incorporated*, 823 P.2d 717 (Haw. 1991).

[69] 526 F.Supp. 589 (D.S.C. 1981).

[70] 514 F.Supp. 1004 (D.S.C. 1981). See also *Smith v. Eli Lilly & Co.*, 560 N.E. 2d 324 (Ill. 1990), and *Gorman v. Abbott Labs*, 599 A.2d 1364 (R.I. 1991).

[71] 573 F.Supp. 1324 (C.D. Cal. 1983).

[72] The DTP vaccine is designed to immunise against diphtheria, tetanus and pertussis.

[73] Quoted in Vinson and Slaughter, eds., *Product Liability: Pharmaceutical Drug Cases* (Colorado, Shepard's/McGraw-Hill Inc., 1988) p. 286.

plaintiff to raise suit against all possible defendants, but rather to act against some of the potential tortfeasors, only. The injured party requires to show that the defendants manufactured the type of drug involved. It is still open to each of the defendants to prove that it did not produce the particular DES in question. The theory is an amalgam of the "Market Share" and "Alternative Liability" theories, and was applied in the case of *Martin v. Abbott Laboratories.*[74] The criteria which the plaintiff requires to meet are similar to those specified in the *Collins* case. However, the defendants in *Collins* may have been found jointly liable for the total amount of the plaintiff's loss, despite the fact that all potential tortfeasors might not have been before the court. In *Martin's* case the court determined that the defendants could only be found liable for a percentage of the plaintiff's compensation, equivalent to their percentage share of the market at the time. Hence a plaintiff who sues manufacturers who were responsible for 60 per cent of the market will recover only 60 per cent of the compensation that would otherwise be due.

(F) THE *HYMOWITZ* Approach

A yet more radical development was made by the New York Court of Appeals[75] in the case of *Hymowitz v. Eli Lilly & Co.*[76] All previous theories had been justified on the basis that the courts were attempting to make it easier for plaintiffs to establish causation. The effect of many of these theories was to reverse the onus of proof such that each defendant was deemed to have produced the drug which harmed the plaintiff *unless* it established, on a balance of probabilities, that it did not do so. Manufacturers have therefore escaped liability by establishing that they did not market DES in the state in which the plaintiff resides, or during the time when the plaintiff's mother was taking the drug, or have managed to demonstrate that their pills differed in shape, size or colour from those described by the plaintiff. The law of passing off has been used by pharmaceutical manufacturers to prevent other companies from copying distinctive product colours and shapes. One example of this is *Hoffman la*

---

[74] 689 P.2d 368 (Wash. 1984).
[75] This is the highest court in New York.
[76] 73 N.Y. 2d 487, 539 N.E. 2d 1069, 541 N.Y.S. 2d 941 (1989).

Roche v. DDSA Pharmaceuticals[77] in which the plaintiff was successful in preventing other pharmaceutical companies from copying its distinctive green and black capsules. In the future, companies would be advised to consider developing unique colour and size combinations for their products in order that they may more easily defend themselves against unwarranted claims arising from generic drugs. In the case of *Krist v. Eli Lilly & Co.*[78] for example, the plaintiff's mother testified that the DES which she had taken consisted of red pills, and the defendant was entitled to summary judgment when it established that it had never manufactured pills matching that description. Such a defendant is exonerated since it has proved that it could not have caused the injury, since it had not even manufactured the drug to which the plaintiff had been exposed.

In contrast to this, in a development of the Risk Contribution theory, the *Hymowitz* case focused on the fact that each manufacturer who marketed DES was responsible for increasing the risk of injury to the general public, and should therefore compensate any person who is injured by DES. The amount to be contributed by each defendant would reflect that company's share of the DES market. A defendant is unable to escape liability even if it shows that it did *not* make the drug in question and therefore could not have caused the injuries sustained by that particular plaintiff.

5. A Critique

Newdick has pointed out some of the difficulties associated with the more radical American theories. In relation to Market Share liability he asks:

> "Should the claim fail entirely if a less than 50 per cent share of the market can be identified, on the basis that it is more likely that a member of the unidentified share was responsible? On what basis is the share to be calculated—net or gross profits of the company generally, or from the drug alone? From which market is

---

[77] [1969] F.S.R. 410. See also *Roche Products v. Berk Pharmaceutical* [1973] F.S.R. 345; [1973] R.P.C. 473.
[78] (CA-7 Wis. 1990) 897 F.2d 293.

the share to be taken; regional, national or international? And should account be taken of the 'culpable' companies which have ceased trading?"[79]

He concludes that these difficulties are likely to persuade British courts not to adopt such theories.

The difference in approach to causation in Britain and America may be partly due to the differing constitutional position of the judiciary in the two countries—under the American Constitution the courts are a branch of government which is "of equal and independent status to that of the executive and legislature".[80] As Atiyah and Summers have pointed out:

". . . an English judge is expected to give reasons for his findings of fact where the facts have been seriously controverted, and this itself is a salutary discipline which restrains any tendency to sloppy fact finding, or *any temptation to do substantive justice or equity between the parties by fudging the fact-finding process.*"[81]

In the case of *Wilsher v. Essex Area Health Authority*[82] Lord Bridge referred to "the shortcomings of a system in which the victim of some grievous misfortune will recover substantial compensation or none at all according to the unpredictable hazards of the forensic process".[83] However, he continued:

"But, whether we like it or not, the law, which only Parliament can change, requires proof of fault *causing damage* as the basis of liability in tort. We should do society nothing but disservice if we made the forensic process still more unpredictable and hazardous by *distorting the law* to accommodate the exigencies of what may seem hard cases."[84]

This makes it clear that, despite their sympathy for injured plaintiffs, British judges have little intention of following their American brethren in devising novel methods of liability.

Although the concept of "fault" has been diluted by the prevalence of

---

[79] Newdick, "Special Problems of Compensating Those Damaged by Medicinal Products" Chap. 1 of McLean, ed., *Compensation for Damage* (Dartmouth, Aldershot, 1993) p. 24.

[80] See Fleming, *The American Tort Process* (Oxford, Clarendon Press, 1988) p. 68.

[81] Atiyah and Summers, *Form and Substance in Anglo-American Law: A Comparative Study of Legal Reasoning, Legal Theory and Legal Institutions* (Oxford, Clarendon Press, 1987) p. 165, emphasis added.

[82] [1988] 2 W.L.R. 557; [1988] 1 All E.R. 871.

[83] *ibid.* [1988] 1 All E.R. 871 at 883.

[84] *ibid.* emphases added.

insurance and the existence of vicarious liability, one can at least justify the negligence action on the basis that those defendants who are found liable have in some sense been "responsible" for causing injury.[85] Strict liability regimes such as the Consumer Protection Act remove the requirement to establish any kind of fault, but defendants have nonetheless caused injury, albeit that they may not have been blameworthy in any moral sense. Causation therefore provides a minimum link between plaintiff and defendant. In cases such as *Hymowitz*, however, the connection between defendant and plaintiff is highly tenuous; we can say only that the former was responsible for producing a drug which is of a similar type to that which injured the latter. Alternatively, we could describe the relationship as being that the former has produced a product which is likely to have injured several members of a class of people, and that while the plaintiff was not one of those injured by the defendant's product, she was a member of a class of injured people, and is thus deserving of compensation.

Once this minimal link of a causative relationship between the parties is breached, then one must question why it is that the defendant manufacturer is to be held responsible for compensating the plaintiff, rather than some other person or body. It may be said to be a form of "rough justice", in that the defendant has caused injury, hence ought to pay for its actions, while the plaintiff has been injured and ought to be compensated. It is submitted, however, that in cases such as *Hymowitz* the link between the defendant and the plaintiff has become so tenuous that a preferable option might be to acknowledge that tort law is not necessarily the best method of reallocating funds in such circumstances.

A number of compensation systems do not require injured parties to exercise their private law remedies. These are commonly referred to as "no-fault" schemes, since what they have in common is that there is no need for claimants to establish fault or negligence on the part of any party. Such schemes are usually funded by an insurance consortium, or by the state itself. If pharmaceutical manufacturers are to be required to provide financial compensation to persons who are injured by a drug, even where there is no direct link between a particular plaintiff and a particular

---

[85] For a criticism of the present Tort system see Cane, *Atiyah's Accidents, Compensation and the Law* (London, Butterworths, 5th ed., 1993) and Harris, "Evaluating the Goals of Personal Injury Law: Some Empirical Evidence" Chap. 12 in Cane and Stapleton, eds., *Essays for Patrick Atiyah* (Oxford, Clarendon Press, 1991) p. 290.

company then a no-fault compensation scheme, funded by the pharmaceutical industry as a whole would at least have the merit of being honest about the looseness of the link between any particular company and any particular injured party.

6. Conclusions

The requirement that British plaintiffs establish, on the balance of probability, that their injuries were *caused* by a pharmaceutical drug or device has proved to be difficult to fulfil. As one author has noted, the causation problem:

> "is compounded by the nature of drug associated adverse events. They vary in their frequency, their manifestations, their timing relative to exposure, and their mechanisms, and mimic almost the entire range of human pathology . . .".[86]

Although intended to improve the position of the plaintiff, the Consumer Protection Act has failed to address the problem of causation, and this therefore remains an important hurdle. It is equally clear that some American judges are prepared to mould the law to provide compensation for injured plaintiffs in ways which would not be countenanced by their British counterparts. While one cannot help but sympathise with the victim of a harmful pharmaceutical product who is unable to identify the manufacturer of that drug or device, it is nonetheless difficult to find a legal rationale for the imposition of liability on a manufacturer in cases such as that of *Sindell* or *Hymowitz*. It is clear that a particular defendant may have acted in a wholly proper fashion, yet may still be found liable under these theories. In such cases, each manufacturer of the drug has become an insurer of similar products, produced by fellow manufacturers.

Such decisions have fundamental implications for tort law since they abandon the traditional requirement that a plaintiff prove that there was a causal connection between the defendant's act or omission and the former's injury. Referring to the *Sindell* case[87] one author has pointed out that:

---

[86] Jones, "Determining Causation from Case Reports" Chap. 26 of Strom, ed., *Pharmacoepidemiology* (John Wiley & Sons, 2nd ed., 1994) p. 365 at p. 370.
[87] See p. [140], above.

"The drug companies ... see this as an awful decision. The costs will be enormous, they argue; drug prices will rise steeply; competition and innovation will be reduced; companies will go bankrupt ..."[88]

Chapter 11 attempts to determine whether the development of new pharmaceutical drugs and devices has in fact been stifled by the strictness of the products liability laws and the novel theories of causation adopted by some American states, and chapter 12 explores alternative compensation systems. It must be noted, however, that many of the issues which have been examined so far have not as yet been tackled by a British court, since no personal injuries claim against a pharmaceutical company has managed to reach the trial stage. The following chapter therefore considers some of the procedural hurdles which may confront plaintiffs in their quest for compensation.

---

[88] Smith, "Product liability all dressed up American style" (1981) *B.M.J.*, 282, 1536.

Chapter 10

Procedural Problems and Multi-Party Actions

1. Introduction

Chapters 3 to 9 have illustrated the considerable problems of substantive law which face the victims of drug disasters. Certain aspects of pre-trial procedure can present equally great obstacles. This chapter considers certain procedural problems which may be of particular relevance in litigation involving pharmaceutical products.

2. Aspects of Civil Court Procedure

(A) LEGAL AID

In America the use of a contingency fee system and the rule that parties to litigation pay their own costs, win or lose, mean that a potential plaintiff has little at stake, financially, in commencing an action.[1] In theory, civil legal aid could put British plaintiffs in a similar position. In practice, however, the acquiring and retaining of legal aid has proved to be yet

---

[1] Contingency fees are discussed at p. [153], below.

another hurdle for plaintiffs in drug-disasters.[2] It has been estimated that the number of households eligible for legal aid has dropped from 80 per cent in 1979 to 48 per cent in 1994.[3] While reductions in the availability of legal aid can affect all types of litigation, it may present a particularly acute problem in certain drug cases. Opren is a good example of a drug which affected mainly older patients. Such persons may have a greater disposable income, and therefore may not qualify for legal aid.[4]

The financial position of the plaintiffs in cases involving pharmaceutical products can be contrasted to that of the defendant drug companies. It has, for example, been suggested that the "biggest hurdle of all" which faced the Association of Parents of Vaccine Damaged Children[5] in their quest for compensation was the fact that the Wellcome Foundation was "willing and able to incur legal costs later estimated to exceed £1 million . . . to defend the vaccine's safety record".[6]

In other mass disasters the number of persons who are likely to raise an action can usually be determined at an early stage. This is in contrast to the position with respect to "creeping disasters" such as drugs, where the number of claimants is difficult to determine at the outset. The funding of any form of group action is complex, since the current structuring of legal aid "presupposes that the problems of applicants are best tackled on an individual basis".[7] This can be particularly problematic in pharmaceutical product cases where the number of potential litigants is often far greater than in other mass disasters. In the Benzodiazepine litigation, for example, there were 17,000 applications for legal aid[8] and in the Myodil litigation there were approximately 700 claimants, 75 per cent of whom were legally aided.[9]

---

[2] See Chittenden and Rufford, "Legal Aid Cuts Curb Fight by Drug Victims", *Sunday Times*, January 2, 1994. The difficulty the legal aid system caused in the Opren ligitation is discussed at p. [164], below.

[3] See Wells, *Negotiating Tragedy: Law and Disasters* (London, Sweet & Maxwell, 1995) p. 99.

[4] See *Legal Aid for Multi-Party Actions in Scotland* (Working Party's Report, 1992) p. 6. There is also increased pressure on elderly persons to settle their claims—many Opren sufferers died before they were able to seek compensation.

[5] See p. [9], above.

[6] Harlow and Rawlings, *Pressure Through Law* (London, Routledge, 1992) pp. 121–122.

[7] Paterson and Bates, *The Legal System of Scotland: Cases and Materials* (Edinburgh, W. Green & Son Ltd, 2nd ed., 1986) p. 255.

[8] See the Report of the Legal Aid Board: *Issues Arising from the Legal Aid Board and The Lord Chancellor's Department from Multi-Party Actions*, May 1994, p. 1.

[9] Harlow and Rawlings, *op. cit.* p. 135.

The Opren litigation clearly highlights the expense of such suits. Had the case proceeded all the way to judgment after trial it has been estimated that the damages may have exceeded £10 million, with both sides incurring costs of £6 million. The litigation was halted after the Court of Appeal held that all potential plaintiffs had to share the costs of the action; they could not simply select a few legally aided plaintiffs to act as a test case.[10]

The Lord Chancellor tabled various Parliamentary amendments to the Legal Aid Bill, now the Legal Aid Act 1988.[11] These amendments were designed to facilitate the granting of legal aid for group actions, and allow the Legal Aid Board to enter into contracts with solicitors' firms for the provision of co-ordinated work in multiple claims actions.[12]

While these changes may make it easier for Legal Aid boards to handle group actions, the criteria for the granting of legal aid remain the same. Section 15(2) of the Legal Aid Act 1988 states:

> "A person shall not be granted representation for the purposes of any proceedings unless he satisfies the board that he has reasonable grounds for taking, defending or being a party to the proceedings."[13]

Section 15(3) provides a second test, namely that a person may be refused legal aid if it appears to the board "unreasonable that he should be granted representation . . . ". The Legal Aid Handbook provides guidance on the Act, including the statement that legal aid is likely to be refused if the action is "not likely to be cost effective, *i.e.*, the benefit to be achieved does not justify the costs". This may occur where:

> "(i) the amount of the claim is small;
> (ii) the estimated costs of the proceedings are likely to exceed the benefit to the client . . ."[14]

This is known as the "paying client" test—would these costs be incurred by a person who had the means to pay?

---

[10] See "Opren and the Ailing Legal System" (1987) *Solicitors Journal 31:25*, 815 and (1987) *Commonwealth Law Bulletin*, 13:3, 900.

[11] See ss.4(5) and 15(5).

[12] See Curle, "Enabling Multi-party Actions" (1992) *L.S.G.*, 89:44, at 17.

[13] See also the Legal Aid (Scotland) Act 1986, s.14(1)(b).

[14] At para. 6.07(b).

In *R. v. Legal Aid Committee No 10, ex parte McKenna*[15] a refusal to grant legal aid to an alleged Opren victim was successfully challenged. Mrs McKenna had been denied legal aid to continue proceedings against Eli Lilly, but on appeal it was held that the committee had based its decision on a mistaken view of the facts. Roch J. also held that the cost of the litigation should not be the only criterion, or even the major criterion, in deciding whether or not to grant legal aid, since this would "place multinational corporations in a position of advantage *vis-à-vis* individual claimants".[16]

In the Benzodiazepine litigation, the defendants inundated the Legal Aid Board with written submissions, opposing the continuation of legal aid for the plaintiffs.[17] The Legal Aid Regulations allow for aid to be withdrawn as a result of such information.[18] As the Legal Aid Board itself accepts:

> "Opponents in multi-party actions will almost always be large or multinational companies who are able to devote almost unlimited resources to opposing legal aid at the outset."[19]

The benzodiazepine litigation collapsed when the Legal Aid Board decided that the plaintiffs no longer satisfied the "paying client" test, and withdrew funding. It has been estimated that £30–35m of legal aid expenditure was incurred in these suits.[20] Hickinbottom has argued that:

> "The Legal Aid Board should impose the same criteria in respect of claims forming part of a group action, as an individual claim. They should not fund such a claim unless a solicitor would advise the applicant to take proceedings privately, if he had adequate means. They should not grant funding to a claim where the benefit to be achieved does not justify the costs."[21]

While this seems a sound argument in theory, in practice very few cases involving injuries allegedly sustained from pharmaceutical drugs will satisfy this test. Even where the injury has been serious and the damages sought are

---

[15] *The Times*, December 20, 1989. See also *R. v. Legal Aid Area No. 8, ex parte Parkinson*, *The Times*, March 13, 1990.

[16] *ibid.* cited in Pugh and Day, *Toxic Torts* (London, Cameron May, 1992) p. 20.

[17] Legal Aid Report, May 1994, *ibid.* at 20.

[18] See reg. 82(5) of the Civil Legal Aid (General) Regulations 1989.

[19] *ibid.* at 21.

[20] *ibid.*

[21] Hickinbottom, "Multi-Claimant Group Litigation: A Defendant's Perspective" (1994) *Personal Injury Law and Medical Review*, 72 at 77.

relatively large, as in the whooping cough vaccine cases, for example, the costs of attempting to establish causation are likely to be considerably greater.

(B) CONTINGENCY FEES

It is frequently suggested that American society is more litigious than the British and one factor which may account for this, at least in part, is the existence of a contingency fee system in the United States. A contingency fee arrangement may be defined as:

> "a contract for the provision of legal services in which the amount of the lawyer's fee is contingent in whole or in part upon the successful outcome of the case, either through settlement or litigation. Usually such agreements involve rewarding lawyers with higher fees than they would normally receive if they win, in return for running the risk of going without a fee if the case is lost."[22]

In the United States a successful claimant may require to give his solicitor up to 50 per cent of any award while an unsuccessful litigant requires to pay nothing.

Contingency fee arrangements are unlawful in England, being regarded as contrary to public policy.[23] As regards Scots law, a contract by which a solicitor's fee is to be a proportion of the court award would be considered void.[24] When an Aberdeen company by the name of Quantum Claims Compensation Specialists Ltd purported to operate a contingency fee system the Law Society of Scotland obtained a declarator in the Court of Session against the company, to the effect that the latter's fee charging method was contrary to law and unenforceable.[25] It has, however, always been permissible for a Scottish lawyer to act on a speculative basis—*i.e.* on a "no win, no fee" contract.[26]

Rodger Pannone, co-founder of the major "disaster law" firm, Pannone

---

[22] Paterson, "Contingent Fees and their Rivals" (1989) *S.L.T.* 81.
[23] See *Wallersteiner v. Moir (No. 2)* [1975] 1 All E.R. 849.
[24] See Walker, *Principles of Scottish Private Law* (Oxford, Clarendon Press, 4th edition, 1988) 2, pp. 27–28.
[25] See (1991) *J.L.S.S.* 462. Quantum's method of fee charging was described as a *pactum de quota litis*, and the company gave a written undertaking to observe the terms of the declarator.
[26] See Paterson and Bates, *op. cit.* pp. 262–263.

Napier, claims that a contingency fee system would have public support in this country:

> "If you ask the consumers whether they prefer to pay a lawyer only if they win and nothing if they lose, overwhelmingly the answer will be: 'we want a contingency fee system'."[27]

Others who favour the introduction of such a system in Britain argue that it allows greater access to the courts than would otherwise be the case. It is also said to encourage law firms to specialise, hence improving the services offered to potential plaintiffs.

It is clear that under a contingency fee system a lawyer has a personal interest in the outcome of the litigation. It may therefore be feared that lawyers might prefer to settle their clients' cases for smaller sums than might have been awarded after trial, since this will involve less work for the lawyer. Studies which have attempted to compare the amount of work undertaken by lawyers under different fee-charging systems have however failed to demonstrate this.[28]

Its detractors also contend that contingency fees encourage juries to give inflated awards of compensation, in order to ensure that an injured party receives an appropriate amount of money *after* the lawyer's percentage has been deducted.[29] This is said to have been responsible for the increasing number of damage awards in the United States which exceed $1 million. It has also been claimed that contingency fee systems lead to groundless suits and the soliciting of clients. The latter practice, known colloquially as "ambulance chasing", has however been upheld by the American Supreme Court. While allowing a state to impose restrictons on such activities, the Supreme Court held that the practice could not be proscribed as it was covered by the Constitutional right to free speech.[30]

The nature of fee-charging in both Scotland and England has changed in recent years. The Law Reform (Miscellaneous Provisions) (Scotland) Act

---

[27] Berlins and Dyer, "Pannone Napier: Developing a Disaster Practice" (1986) *N.L.J.*, 136, 783 at 786.

[28] See, for example, Kritzer *et al*, "The Impact of Fee Arrangements on Lawyer Effort" (1985) *Law and Society Review*, 19, 251.

[29] See Atiyah and Summers, *Form and Substance in Anglo-American Law: A Comparative Study of Legal Reasoning, Legal Theory and Legal Institutions* (Oxford, Clarendon Press, 1987) p. 198.

[30] See "Contingency fees: Can British clients win with a U.S.-style system?" (1989) *L.S.G.*, 86:12, at 6.

1990 allows an uplift in the fee in speculative actions, but not contingency fees.[31] In England, the Courts and Legal Services Act 1990 allows solicitors to charge an additional fee if they win their case.[32]

It is difficult to determine the impact which these reforms will have on personal injury suits involving pharmaceutical products. It has been suggested that the impact of the contingency fee provisions in the United States has been exaggerated, since American lawyers who offer such a service refuse to take on about 85 per cent of potential suits on the basis that these actions do not have a reasonable chance of success.[33] McIntosh has argued against the introduction of such a system in Britain for that reason. He cites the recent litigation involving Opren and the whooping cough vaccine:

> "Contingency fees are not the answer in these cases. This is because the damages in prospect, when weighed against the expense of prosecuting the claims, would not be enough to provide a contingency fee incentive which would be bearable."[34]

It must be borne in mind that the unsuccessful party in the USA is not liable for the legal costs of the other side. The British requirement that the loser pays may act as a great disincentive to the bringing of an action by an injured party, particularly in actions such as drug liability suits in which there may require to be a wealth of documentary and expert evidence, often at considerable expense. This may be of greater importance than the availability of contingency fees.

(c) Jury Trials

In Scotland the Court of Session Act 1988 provides that actions for damages for personal injuries should normally be tried by a jury.[35] In

---

[31] See s.36, which inserted s.61A into the Solicitors (Scotland) Act 1980. The relevant rules are contained in the Solicitors (Scotland) (Written Fee Charging Agreements) Practice Rules 1993.

[32] See s.58; the Green Paper on Contingency Fees, Cm. 571, 1989, and S.I. 1993 No. 2132.

[33] Quam, Fenn and Dingwall, "Medical Malpractice in Perspective: II—The Implications for Britain" (1987) *B.M.J.*, 294, p. 1597 at p. 1598.

[34] McIntosh, "Against Contingency Fees: Why the English Legal System should not apply them" (1989) *P.L.I.*, 11:4, 65 at 66.

[35] See s.11(a).

practice, however, such trials are rare. They are also seldom found in English personal injury suits, and the English Court of Appeal has ruled that juries should only be used in exceptional cases.[36] In contrast to this, personal injury claims based on product liability are commonly tried by juries in the United States; injured parties have a right to this which is enshrined in the American Constitution.

The amount of compensation to be awarded in personal injury cases is usually decided by an American jury hence those awards tend to be much higher than in Britain. The American Civil jury has been subject to a great deal of criticism, and it has been suggested that juries in product liability cases may be influenced by "extra-legal" characteristics, such as the fact that the defendant is a company, rather than an individual.[37] It is generally accepted that juries in personal injuries suits tend to be pro-plaintiff, and this is especially so when the defendant is a wealthy multinational company such as a pharmaceutical manufacturer. In America this is referred to as the "deep pocket" rule. In relation to pharmaceutical products, in particular, it has been suggested that:

> "The often complex nature of causation in these cases raises doubts regarding the ability of jurors to comprehend the technical evidence establishing or refuting the relationship between the product and the injury."[38]

Jury verdicts have been overturned in a number of cases involving pharmaceutical drugs, where it was found that the evidence did not support the jury's decision.[39]

An increased use of jury trials in Britain might well result in a greater number of cases being decided in favour of plaintiffs, and to higher damage awards being granted. It must, however, be borne in mind that any compensation recoverable in the United States includes a large amount for medical care, since medical costs in the U.S. are high. The lack of a

---

[36] See *Ward v. James* [1965] 2 W.L.R. 455; [1966] 1 Q.B. 273; [1965] 1 All E.R. 563.

[37] See Bornstein and Rajki, "Extra-Legal Factors and Product Liability: The Influence of Mock Jurors' Demographic Characteristics and Intuitions about the Cause of an Injury" (1994) *Behavioural Sciences and the Law*, 12, 127 at 138.

[38] Cecil, Hans and Wiggins, "Citizen Comprehension of Difficult Issues: Lessons from Civil Jury Trials" (1991) *The American University Law Review*, 40, 727 at 740.

[39] See *Brock v. Merrell Dow Pharmaceuticals, Incorporated* 874 F. 2d 307 (5th Cir.); 884 F. 2d 166 (5th Cir. 1989); 110 S.Ct. 1511 (1990); and *Richardson v. Richardson-Merrell Incorporated* 649 F.Supp. 799 (1986), discussed at p. [175], below.

developed social security system in that country has been highlighted by Dutton:

"More than 38 million Americans, 19 percent of the population, do not even have basic health insurance. No other industrialized country gives people who have been injured so little assistance. Every industrial nation but the United States provides its citizens with some form of national health insurance covering medical expenses, and most also have much more generous social and disability benefits. For many Americans who are injured, the courts may offer the only hope of redress."[40]

American jury awards are generally higher than in Britain even where a plaintiff has been covered by adequate medical insurance. This is due to the fact that a person who has sustained a permanent disability will require to pay increased premiums in order to acquire insurance in the future, and this is often taken into account by juries.

It seems, therefore, that although greater use of juries in Britian may increase the plaintiff's chances of success in pharmaceutical product liability actions, the belief that injured parties would receive compensation awards of a similar size to their American counterparts is unfounded. Furthermore, where the defendant is a wealthy pharmaceutical company American juries often appear to be biased in favour of the injured plaintiff, and this may have contributed towards a product liability crisis and a lack of new drugs in the United States.[41]

3. Multi-Party Actions

A number of the drugs described in chapter 1 were several responsible for injuring large numbers of people. Were such people able to sue in one action, this would save time and expense, both for plaintiffs and defendants. Group actions may also attract more publicity for the plight of the plaintiffs.[42] One might have thought that adverse reactions to pharmaceut-

---

[40] Dutton, *Worse than the Disease: Pitfalls of Medical Progress* (Cambridge University Press, 1988) p. 256.
[41] This is explored in greater detail in Chap. 11, below.
[42] For a criticism of the role of the media and advertising by solicitors in group actions, see Hickinbottom, *op. cit.*

ical products would be the very type of cases for which some sort of group action would be suited; the evidence as to *general* causation (that is, that the particular drug was capable of causing the injuries or symptoms complained of) would be the same in all cases, and plaintiffs' solicitors could save time and money by pooling their information and resources. In fact, even in America there has been less use of this type of action than one might have expected.

A "class action" may be defined as "a procedure by which, in a situation where numerous persons have a similar interest in the resolution of a particular question, one [court] action can take the place of many".[43] In other words, all plaintiffs join together in one action. Alternatively, a "representative action" allows a single claim to be taken on behalf of the group.

In the United States, representative actions are available in both federal and state courts. The bringing of such actions in the federal courts is governed by Rule 23 of the Federal Rules of Civil Procedure. Four pre-requisites are specified:

1. The group must be so numerous that it is impracticable to have all the members joined in the action.
2. There must be questions of law or of fact which are common to all members of the group.
3. The claims or defences of the parties must be typical of those of the group.
4. The representative parties must fairly and adequately protect the interests of the other members.

The court must also determine that the questions of fact or law which are common to the group predominate over any questions which affect only individual members, and that this action is better that any other available method for determining the issues.

Once a representative action has been commenced it may not be dismissed or settled without the approval of the courts, and notice of the proposed settlement must be given to all members of the group. In the case of *Eisen v. Carlisle and Jacquelin*[44] the Supreme Court held that where it is reasonably possible to identify group members, individual notice is

---

[43] *Class Actions in the Scottish Courts: A New Way for Consumers to Obtain Redress?* Scottish Consumer Council Report, 1982, p. 2, para. 1.6.
[44] 417 U.S. 156 (1974).

required, regardless of cost. This was justified on the basis that it was only after such notice that the courts could be satisfied that a plaintiff was competent to represent the group. Once notification has been given to a party, that party may decide to opt out of the action.

Generally speaking, English law requires actions to be taken personally; the procedural rules which have evolved over the years were not designed for actions involving a multiplicity of claimants or defendants and hence are not entirely suited to the disposal of such actions. Order 15, Rule 12(i) of the English Rules of the Supreme Court does, however, provide as follows:

> "Where numerous persons have the same interest in any proceedings ... the proceedings may be begun, and, unless the Court otherwise orders, continued, by or against any one or more of them as representing all or as representing all except one or more of them."

Any decree obtained by a representative party is binding upon all members of the group, including those who are not named in the action and who may not even be aware that such an action had been raised.

The leading case here is *The Duke of Bedford v. Ellis*[45] in which a group of Covent Garden stall-holders sued on behalf of other stall-holders to enforce certain privileges conferred on them. The House of Lords emphasised that, in determining whether a case is suitable for a representative action, a court requires to consider which aspects of the case are common to the group and what their differences are. A representative action would be appropriate where the plaintiffs had common interest and grievance, and where the relief sought was "in its nature beneficial to all whom the plaintiff proposed to represent".[46]

This restriction has, however, been taken to mean that the relief sought must be of equal benefit to all plaintiffs. Such an interpretation restricts the representative action to cases where damages are recovered for a collective fund rather than for individuals, since no individual would have an interest in the damages recoverable by another individual. This is illustrated by *Markt & Co. v. Knight Steamship Co. Ltd.*[47] The case involved the loss of cargo from a ship. There were several contracts, each of which included an

---

[45] [1901] A.C. 1.
[46] *ibid.* at 8, *per* Lord Macnaghten.
[47] [1910] 2 K.B. 1021.

identical clause, between the defendant company and a number of shippers. Despite the fact that the essentials of each contract were the same it was judged that they were distinct contracts which gave rise to differing claims for damages, hence the plaintiffs did not have a sufficiently shared interest for the purposes of a representative action. Fletcher Moulton L.J. stated:

> "Damages are personal only. To my mind no repesentative action can lie where the sole relief sought is damages, because they have to be proved separately in the case of each plaintiff, and therefore the possibility of representation ceases."[48]

This was because the relief sought was seen as being a personal relief, applicable to the particular plaintiff alone, and did not benefit those for whom the representative purported to be bringing the action.

More recent cases indicate that the courts are now willing to interpret the requirement that plaintiffs have the same interest in a more liberal fashion. In *Prudential Assurance Co. Ltd v. Newman Industries Ltd*[49] several shareholders were held to have sufficiently similar interest in a misleading circular issued by the defendants. The court decided that a representative action could be used, even where each of the persons represented did not have an equal interest in the claim of the other members of the group.

Vinelott J. specified two conditions to this. First, an Order could not be made in favour of a representative plaintiff if that Order could confer a right to a member which that member would not have had in a separate action. Equally, the Order could not prevent a defendant from exercising a right which might have been available had separate actions been taken. For example, a defendant who would have had a defence under the Limitation Acts cannot be deprived of that defence merely because that particular plaintiff did not bring an action himself but allowed someone else to represent his interest. Secondly, an Order would only be made in favour of a representative plaintiff if there was a common element in the claim of all members of the class which the plaintiff purports to represent. Thirdly, the court must be satisfied that it is for the benefit of the group that the plaintiff

---

[48] *ibid.* at 1040–1041.
[49] [1980] 2 W.L.R. 339; [1979] 3 All E.R. 507.

be permitted to sue in a representative capacity.[50] Such actions allow for representative defendants as well as plaintiffs.[51]

In Scotland there is no provision in the law for representative or class actions. If two or more pursuers have the same interest in a particular issue, then their actions may be conjoined[52] but if their claims arose from separate contracts, then each pursuer requires to raise a separate action.[53] A report by the Scottish Consumer Council recommended over a decade ago that a class action procedure be adopted in Scotland.[54] These recommendations have not been implemented. Test cases or "lead actions" have no legal significance since defenders, even if they lose a test case, are under no legal requirement to apply that decision to other, similar cases which may be pending.[55] In England, Order 4, Rule 9(1) of the Rules of the Supreme Court allows for a "lead action" to be taken, by providing that a number of actions may be stayed until one with "common questions of law or fact" has been determined. This procedure was used in some of the vaccine cases.[56]

Recent cases involving pharmaceutical drugs and devices have illustrated the short-comings of available British procedures.

(A) The Tranquilliser Cases

In November 1990 Mr Justice Ian Kennedy, who had been appointed by the Lord Chief Justice to determine preliminary matters in the benzodiazepine litigation, decided that the thousands of claims against the maunfacturers of these tranquillisers could be dealt with as a group action. In January 1991 he approved a list of benzodiazepines which might be included in the litigation,[57] and in July of that year he established various deadlines for these actions; all applications for legal aid required to be made

---

[50] *ibid.* at 520. The case has been followed in *EMI Records Ltd v. Riley* [1981] 1 W.L.R. 923; [1981] 2 All E.R. 838.

[51] See *Michaels (Furriers) Ltd v. Askew* [1983] 127 S.J. 597. This case was distinguished in *U.K. Nirex v. Barton, The Times,* October 14, 1986.

[52] See *Duke of Buccleuch v. Cowan and Others,* 1876 4R, H.L., 14.

[53] *Fishof v. Cheapside Bonding Co.,* 1972 S.L.T. (Notes) 7.

[54] *Class Actions in the Scottish Courts: A New Way for Consumers to Obtain Redress?* (1982). See also the Editorial in 1988 *SCOLAG* No. 139, at 50.

[55] This is illustrated by the case of *Electrolux Ltd v. Hutchison,* 1977 I.C.R. 252, an employment law case. A case may, however, be treated as determining the issue for the future, see *McColl v. Strathclyde Regional Council,* 1983 S.L.T. 616.

[56] See p. [131], above.

by September 1991, and the deadline for the issuing of writs was April 1992. The effect of these cut-off dates was not to prevent an additional claimant from suing the company, but it did mean that such a person would be unable to take advantage of the scheme.[58]

A Solicitors' Steering Committee was formed by the Law Society, comprising six lead firms. The Committee represented 2,000 other firms of solicitors and its role was limited to the co-ordination of the generic aspects of the suits. It had hoped that the generic issues could be resolved by a small number of cases, but on November 9, 1990 Mr Justice Kennedy ruled that each plaintiff required to provide the defendant manufacturers with their medical records and individual medical reports. This decision was upheld by the Court of Appeal. Woolf L.J. stated that it was "essential for the defendants to know the detailed nature of the case which has been put forward by each plaintiff."[59] This ruling has been referred to as "the real nail in the plaintiffs' solicitors' coffin".[60] In June 1992 solicitors acting for the drug companies served a 700 page defence document on the plaintiffs. The Legal Aid Board concluded that the potential damages which plaintiffs would be likely to receive if successful did not justify the continuing, and escalating, legal aid costs, and legal aid was withdrawn from the majority of plaintiffs. The group action has now been abandoned.[61]

(B) The Opren Litigation

The Opren Action Group was formed in 1982 and a large number of actions for personal injuries were commenced against Eli Lilly, the manufacturers, as well as against the DHSS and the CSM. Given the wide range of injuries alleged to have been caused by Opren and the varying degrees of knowledge among the plaintiffs as to the risks associated with this drug, a class action was unlikely to be a realistic possibility. The case of

---

[57] This included not only Valium, Ativan, Librium and Halcion, but also Mogadon (nitrazepam), Serenid (oxazepam), Nobrium (medazepam), Tranxene (clorazepate), Dalmane (flurazepam), Euhypnos (temazepam), Frisium (clobazam), Anxon (ketazolam), Noctamid (lormetazepam), Rohypnol (flunitrazepam), Lexotan (bromazepam), Centrax (prazepam) and Xanax (alprazolam).
[58] See *B. and Others v. John Wyeth & Brother Ltd and Others* [1992] 1 W.L.R. 168, C.A. [1992] 1 All E.R. 443; [1992] 3 Med.L.R. 190, C.A.
[59] McKinney, "A Bitter Pill", *Legal Business*, November 1994, 66 at 69.
[60] *ibid.*
[61] See Barton, "A Case for Treatment", *Financial Times*, July 26, 1994.

Davies v. Eli Lilly & Co.[62] was, however, commenced as a test case, and Hirst J. approved certain measures, designed to reduce the expenditure involved in the case. These have been referred to as "the co-ordinated arrangements" and included a master set of pleadings which applied to all cases, and the selection of a number of lead plaintiffs as representative of the several types of Opren victims. This grouping was based on the various categories of disability, among other things. All other actions against the defendants for alleged Opren related injuries were stayed pending the outcome of this action.[63]

Hirst J. recognised that this was an unusual procedure but emphasised that it had been devised to fit the special needs of the litigation. He explained that his intention was "to be fair to all interested parties, including the present plaintiffs, serious claimants, and all the defendants, and to strike a fair balance between their interests".[64] According to one commentator, this case was:

"... the first time an English court has agreed that common issues of liability should be litigated in proceedings which are effectively, if not formally, representative—that findings of fact in an action for damages should bind others who were not parties to the action. However, this is not a change in the law or procedure—Opren plaintiffs and defendants can, at some stage, fight to the end any action which has not been tried whatever the result of the lead cases. In the case of the plaintiffs, at least, such an option is, however, wholly theoretical. Those on legal aid would not be allowed to carry on and the rest could not afford to do so anyway ..."[65]

This arrangement was made with the agreement of all parties. However, the defendants asked the court to determine the responsibilities amongst the claimants for their own costs and for any costs which they might be required to pay, should their case fail. The court's attempt at clarifying this has been described as resulting in "a mess which reflected badly both on the

---

[62] [1987] 1 W.L.R. 1136. See also [1987] 3 All E.R. 94 and [1987] 2 F.T.L.R. 154.

[63] A similar procedure had been adopted in relation to the pertussis vaccine litigation in the case of *DHSS v. Kinnear* (unreported, but see (1984) 134, *N.L.J.*, 886). Legal aid was, however, withdrawn in that case when it became clear that the evidence given by the plaintiff's mother did not match the medical reports.

[64] See Harvey and Parry, *The Law of Consumer Protection and Fair Trading* (London, Butterworths, 4th ed., 1992) at 212; see also Hansen, "Opren—Court Bars Plaintiff's Expert from Discovery" (1986) *N.L.J.*, 136, 883.

[65] Hansen, *ibid.* at 883–884.

legal system and the legal aid scheme".[66] The 20 lead plaintiffs had been chosen from persons who were entitled to qualify for full legal aid, despite the fact that about a third of the plaintiffs were not in receipt of legal aid. Mr Justice Hirst ruled, however, that the issue of legal aid should not be taken into account in the selection of cases, and that all plaintiffs, including those who were not entitled to legal aid, were required to bear an equal share of the costs of the action should the case be determined in favour of the defendants.[67]

His decision was upheld on appeal. Lord Donaldson, the Master of the Rolls stated:

> "Very naturally no individual plaintiff wanted to undertake the burden, including the costs, of a lead action. So unfair would this burden be, that consideration was given to how, within the powers and procedures of the court, the costs of the lead actions could be taken off the shoulders of the plaintiffs in whose names they were being brought. In this way, it was thought, the whole cost of the lead actions, which might well be a very significant part of the cost of the whole proceedings, could be transferred to the broad shoulders of the state in the shape of the legal aid fund ... [This] betrays a woeful misunderstanding of how the legal aid scheme works ... legal aid helps those who lose cases, not those who win them. Legal aid makes 'out and out' grants to those who lose cases. It makes loans to those who win them."[68]

The case would have had to be abandoned as a result of this ruling had it not been for the fact that a wealthy philanthropist offered to underwrite the claim.[69] In February 1988 the vast majority of the plaintiffs agreed to an out of court settlement of their claims. About £2.25 million was shared among 2,000 claimants, giving each about £1,000.

4. Future Reforms

Might a procedure such as that which was commenced in the Opren case be used in the future? Following the Opren litigation, Hirst J. stated:

---

[66] NCC Report, January 1989, at 25.

[67] See s.7(6)(b) of the Legal Aid Act 1974 and s.31 of the Legal Aid Act 1988.

[68] *Davies v. Eli Lilly & Co.* [1987] 3 All E.R. 94, at 97.

[69] The philanthropist was Geoffrey Bradman, co-founder of the Citizen Action Compensation Campaign.

"What would be suitable for an Opren type case might well not work well in other types of relevant actions . . . What is needed is an enabling rule, subject to very broadly drawn criteria, empowering the Court to set up a scheme to fit an individual case which falls under one or other of the relevant categories, and to do so by binding order if necessary if the parties cannot themselves agree."[70]

A similar procedure was adopted in respect of the Myodil litigation. In the case of *Chrzanowska v. Glaxo Laboratories Ltd*[71] the plaintiffs sought an order that one judge should hear all actions concerning Myodil, and that all their costs should be borne equally by all of them. The court decided that all applications involving Myodil would be reserved for hearing by Mr Justice Rose and Mr Justice Stern, and granted the plaintiffs' order in respect of costs. As already noted, this case was ultimately settled by *ex gratia* payments from the defendants.[72]

A number of changes have been proposed to facilitate the bringing of such actions. A Report by the National Consumer Council suggested that courts should be able to certify litigation as being suitable for group action if certain criteria are fulfilled.[73] One area of controversy was the requirement that the action must have a "reasonable possibility of success". Although recognising that this was a contentious issue, the Council stressed that this test was similar to that applied in determining legal aid applications.[74]

In a recent Discussion Paper, the Scottish Law Commission argued that a new representative action procedure be adopted by the Scottish courts.[75] The four criteria suggested by the Commission for certification of such an action by the courts are as follows:

1. that there are so many potential pursuers that it would be impracticable for all to sue in a single conventional action;
2. that the potential pursuers are an identifiable class whose claims give rise to similar or common issues of fact or law;
3. that a class action is preferable or superior to any other available procedure for the fair and efficient determination of the issues; and

---

[70] See Newdick, "Special Problems of Compensating Those Damaged by Medicinal Products" Chap. 1 in McLean, ed., *Compensation for Damage* (Dartmouth, Aldershot, 1993) p. 29 and n. 69.
[71] *Times Law Reports*, March 16, 1990, 212.
[72] See Chap. 1, above.
[73] *Group Actions: Learning from Opren*, NCC January 1989.
[74] See p. [151], above.
[75] *Multi-Party Actions: Court Proceedings and Funding* (Scot. Law Com. D.P. No. 98).

4. that the representative pursuer will fairly and adequately protect the interests of the class.[76]

These criteria are very similar to the American Federal Rules of Civil Procedure.[77]

One criticism that is made of group action procedures in the United States is that the mere threat of suit can lead to defendants settling claims of little merit. It must be noted, however, that the financial risk taken by British plaintiffs in pursuing such actions is far greater than that undertaken by their American counterparts, since each party to a suit in the United States pays only its own costs.

Furthermore, it may be argued that group actions are particularly unsuitable for cases involving pharmaceutical products since an alleged iatrogenic injury or symptom may in fact be attributable to some other cause, such as personal idiosyncrasy or hereditary factors. An additional complicating factor is that the state of the manufacturer's knowledge of adverse reactions is often at issue, and this will obviously vary with time.

Such actions have met with limited success in the United States.[78] In *Rose v. Medtronics Incorporated*,[79] for example, the defendant manufacturer had recalled its pacemaker due to a suspected defect. The plaintiff was required to undergo a further operation to replace his pacemaker and sought to sue Medtronics on behalf of himself and 4,000 others, all of whom were affected by the recall of this product. The court concluded, however, that this type of claim was particularly ill-suited for a representative action since the liability of the defendant would vary from case to case. The claims themselves would be very different in respect of the extent of compensation being claimed, in that for some plaintiffs, such as Mr Rose, a second operation had become necessary, while for others this was only a possibility for the future.

Similarly in *Ryan v. Eli Lilly & Co.*[80] several women were not permitted to sue in a group action for alleged DES injuries. According to Vinson and Slaughter:

---

[76] See also Barker, Willock and McManus, *Multi-Party Actions in Scotland* (Research Report, Central Research Unit, Scottish Office, 1994).

[77] Federal Rules of Civil Procedure, Rule 23.

[78] See Dutton, *op. cit.* p. 264, regarding the failure of DES class actions; *McElhaney v. Eli Lilly & Co.* (D.S.D. 1992) 93 F.R.D. 875 and *Mertens v. Abbott Laboratories* (D.N.H. 1983) 99 F.R.D. 38.

[79] 166 Cal. Rptr. 16 (1980).

[80] 84 F.R.D. 230 (D.S.C. 1979).

" . . . the courts to date have been impressed, not by the common issues present in such litigation, but by the numerous peculiarities that affect the resolution of each individual case."[81]

They argue that group actions in cases involving pharmaceutical products appear to have been successful only where the individual claims are quite small, or, at the other end of the spectrum, where the claims are so large that there may not be sufficient funds for later plaintiffs unless all cases are dealt with in one action.

One might have expected the American Tetracycline litigation to be an example of a class action suit based on the first of these two types of claim. Tetracycline causes a discolouration of the teeth and a class action was sought by many people who had been affected in this way. They argued that since their claims were small and their injuries less serious than in most mass disaster cases the cost of each individual action could out-weigh the amount of compensation ultimately awarded.[82] Although the court was sympathetic to these arguments it held that class action would not be appropriate. The Tetracycline suits were based on the failure of the manufacturer to provide adequate information to the medical profession, warning of the likelihood of teeth discolouration. In order to succeed in such an action a plaintiff would require to establish that his or her doctor had not been made aware of these dangers, *and* that the doctor would have decided not to prescribe Tetracycline had further information been available. These factors would vary from case to case, hence group action was considered to be inappropriate.

It seems likely that some form of group action will be introduced into Britain in the future. In the course of the Opren litigation Sir John Donaldson M.R. said that class action procedure:

". . . is something which should be looked at by the appropriate authorities with a view to seeing whether it has anything to offer and, if so, introducing the necessary procedural rules."[83]

---

[81] Vinson and Slaughter, eds., *Products Liability: Pharmaceutical Drug Cases* (Colorado, Shepard's/McGraw-Hill Inc, 1988) p. 44.
[82] See *In re Tetracycline Cases*, 107 F.R.D. 719 (W.D. Mo. 1985).
[83] See *Davies v. Eli Lilly & Co.* [1987] 3 All E.R. 94, at 96.

167

5. Conclusions

It is apparent that the procedures of British courts are unsuited to dealing with multiple plaintiffs. The limitations of the legal aid system have been highlighted by suits involving pharmaceutical drugs and there is clearly a need for the development of better multi-party procedures in this country. It must, however, be borne in mind that better group action procedures would not overcome all the difficulties faced by plaintiffs. As already noted, a pharmaceutical product tragedy differs from other mass disasters since it does not involve one incident in which all plaintiffs are injured at the same time and in the same location. Nor are all the injuries sustained likely to be of a similar nature; drugs affect different people in different ways depending on each individual's metabolism. In relation to Opren, for example, it has been pointed out that:

> "... even if the drug was *capable* of causing the harmful effects complained of, the question whether it *actually caused* them in each individual case would depend on numerous individual factors varying with each patient."[84]

It would seem, therefore, that the development of better group action procedures in Britain would go some way towards improving the position of plaintiffs in mass pharmaceutical product litigation, but that important hurdles, such as that of establishing causation, would still require to be dealt with on an individual basis.

---

[84] Hacking, "Class Action", paper given at the 7th Annual Canadian Law Conference: *Pharmaceuticals and the Law: European, U.S. & Canadian Developments* (London, November 3, 1992) p. 15, emphases in original.

Chapter 11

Stricter Liability? Lessons from America

1. Introduction

One solution to the difficulties faced by plaintiffs in pharmaceutical product suits might be to impose a tougher system of legal liability on the manufacturers of harmful drugs and devices. The legal systems operating in the United States of America each have their own substantive law and procedures. These differ from that of the British legal systems, and the greater use of jury trials, the more developed class action procedures, and the availability of contingency fees all contribute to making the United States a more litigious society than our own, and one where the odds are less favourable to the defendant than in Britain.[1] For more than 30 years many states have had a system of strict liability for product injuries, which is not dissimilar to our own, but which does not provide for a development risk defence.[2] Recent legal developments in that country, such as the application of novel identification theories,[3] seem to favour the plaintiff at the expense of the defendant.

It is clear that there is a great fear on the part of some commentators that Britain may become too like the United States in its product liability laws. John Banham, former Director General of the Confederation of British Industry, has argued that developments in America during the past two decades "supply a horrible example, to put it bluntly, of what can happen if

---

[1] See Chap. 10, above, for a description of some of these procedural aspects.
[2] This is based on the Second Restatement of Torts 1965. See p. [113], above.
[3] These theories are discussed in Chap. 9, above.

we get it wrong".[4] Banham cites the example of a British manufacturer of anaesthetic equipment which has decided not to export its product to America, despite the success of the product in other markets, due to the perceived risk of product liability claims in the States. Are these fears justified? To answer this, one must consider the effect which American product liability law has had on the availability of pharmaceutical products in that country.

2. The American Product Liability Crisis

It has been claimed that there is a lack of new pharmaceutical products being developed in the United States, and that new drugs and devices are introduced into that country's market much later than in other Western countries. This is commonly referred to as the "drug lag". The belief that there are fewer new pharmaceutical products being introduced in America is one which is held by many commentators:

> ". . . the USA's share of world spending on pharmaceutical research has allegedly dropped in the past 20 years, its share in world trade has fallen, and the number of new chemical entities (NCEs) discovered by American companies has declined."[5]

In 1961 American pharmaceutical companies were responsible for the introduction of one third of all new chemical entities, world-wide. By 1963 this had fallen to a quarter, and by 1976 less than a sixth of new drugs were manufactured by U.S. companies.[6] According to Isaacs and Holt: "Virtually all researchers investigating the drug lag conclude that it does, in

---

[4] In Abbott: *Safer By Design: the Management of Product Design Risks under Strict Liability*, (London, Design Council, 1987) Foreword.

[5] Hancher, *Regulating for Competition: Government, Law and the Pharmaceutical Industry in the United Kingdom and France* (Oxford, Clarendon Press, 1990) p. 46, citing the National Academy of Engineering/National Research Council, *The Competitive Status of the U.S. Pharmaceutical Industry* (Washington, National Academy Press, 1983). See also Hancher, *ibid.* p. 111.

[6] Brozen in Grabowski, *Drug Regulation and Innovation* (Washington, American Enterprise Institute for Public Policy Research, 1976) Foreword, p. 2.

fact, exist and that the United States falls behind other Western countries."[7] They too cite a number of studies in support of this claim.

One reason for this lack of new drugs may be the fact that the American Food and Drug Administration operates a very exacting licensing system. This does seem to have had an adverse impact on its pharmaceutical industry. Between 1965 and 1969 new drugs were introduced to the American market a year later than in France, more than 18 months later than West Germany and in excess of two years later than in Britain. A study by Wardell of drugs marketed between 1972 and 1976 found that 2.4 times as many drugs became available in Britain before the United States.[8] The controversy has continued since then, and in the 1980s it was again argued that important new drugs were being licensed more quickly in other countries.[9]

The lack of new drug products can also be partly attributed to the occasional, perverse jury verdict against a pharmaceutical manufacturer,[10] or to the general explosion of product liability suits in the United States, where the number of claims in the federal courts alone increased from 1974 to 1984 by 580 per cent. Nevertheless many commentators, including Isaacs and Holt, have argued that the main reason for the dearth of new drugs in the USA is due to the strictness of that country's product liability laws, which has led to an increasing number of judgments against pharmaceutical manufacturers. It has been claimed that certain drugs, freely available in Europe, are being priced beyond the reach of patients in the United States, due to the rising costs of product liability insurance in the pharmaceutical industry. Hence Inman notes:

> "Because most suits are against manufacturers... the cost of insurance is becoming prohibitive. Many products available in other countries are not sold in the USA, and the American public, sooner or later, will have to decide if the loss of a wide range of treatments may not be too high a price to pay."[11]

---

[7] Isaacs and Holt, "Drug Regulation, Product Liability, and the Contraceptive Crunch: Choices are Dwindling" (1987) *Journal of Legal Medicine*, 8:4, 533 at 537–538.

[8] Wardell, "The Drug Lag Revisited: Comparison by Therapeutic Area of Patterns of Drugs Marketed in the United States and Great Britain from 1972 through 1976" (1978) *Clinical Pharmacology and Therapeutics*, 24:5, 499.

[9] Hutt, "Investigations and reports respecting FDA regulation of new drugs (Part II)" (1983) *Clinical Pharmacology and Therapeutics*, 674 at 679.

[10] See pp. 156, above and 175, below.

[11] Inman, *Monitoring for Drug Safety* (Lancaster, MTP Press, 1980) p. 480.

The existence of a product liability crisis has, however, been denied by some authors. Pretl and Osborne have argued that the perception of a drug lag is based on "misunderstanding and distortion of the facts".[12] They state:

> "Responsible independent analysis gives the lie to the widespread notion of a US pharmaceutical industry under siege by greedy patients and their unscrupulous lawyers. A minuscule percentage of the tens of thousands of drug products and medical devices marketed in the United States have been the subject of lawsuits."[13]

This does not take into account the number of products which have failed even to reach the market, due to manufacturers' fear of suit. According to one author a study in 1988:

> "... showed that uncertainty over potential liability had led almost 50% of the responding companies to discontinue product lines, nearly 40% to withhold new products, including beneficial drugs and 25% to discontinue products research."[14]

Some examples of this pharmaceutical product liability crisis are given, below.

(A) TREATMENTS FOR BLEPHAROSPASM AND SCHIZOPHRENIA

That fear of litigation is inhibiting the development of new drugs is illustrated by the problems which confronted the producers of Oculinium. This drug, which is made from botulism-A toxin, had been used on an experimental basis for the treatment of blepharospasm, sufferers of which experience continual spasms of the eye muscles. This can cause the eyes to clamp shut for minutes at a time. Oculinium had been used to treat 2,300 patients with this condition, but trials were temporarily halted in 1986 after six years of experimental testing since its manufacturer had been unable to

---

[12] Pretl and Osborne, "Trends in U.S. Drug Product Liability—the Plaintiff's Perspective" Chap. 9 of Howells, ed., *Product Liability, Insurance and the Pharmaceutical Industry: an Anglo-American Comparison* (Manchester University Press, 1991) p. 109.

[13] *ibid.* p. 110

[14] See Mahoney and Littlejohn, "Innovation on Trial: Punitive Damages Versus New Products" (1989) 246 *Science* 1395.

find affordable insurance cover.[15] It seems that the insurers were "afraid they will be hit with huge damage suits if any untoward side effects occur"[16].

In January 1991 *Product Liability International* noted that Clozaril, a drug used in the treatment of schizophrenia, cost $40 in most European countries for a week's treatment. The journal records:

"Fearing lawsuits, the manufacturer of Clozaril has established an elaborate testing system prior to administering the drug for use in the United States. The result: Clozaril costs $172 per week in the United States, which effectively places it out of reach of most of those who need it most."[17]

(B) VACCINES

Dutton has argued that:

"For vaccine manufacturers, the law seemed to be heading beyond strict liability toward absolute liability—that is, liability for any and all vaccine-related injuries, regardless of fault, warnings issued, or foreseeability of risks."[18]

It has been claimed that vaccine development has ceased in the United States because "prospective liability outweighs prospective profits".[19] In 1984 a hearing before the Subcommittee on Health and the Environment in the United States reported that Merck, Sharp and Dohme was the sole manufacturer of the MMR (measles, mumps and rubella) vaccine, and Lederle Labs and Connaught were the only remaining producers of the polio and pertussis vaccines.[20] It now seems that very few manufacturers are

---

[15] See "A Question of Competence: The Judicial Role in the Regulation of Pharmaceuticals" (1990) *Harvard Law Review*, 103, 773.
[16] *ibid*. See also "Eye Misery: Insurance Loss Halts Drug Test", *Time*, October 27, 1986, p. 71.
[17] (1991) *P.L.I.*, 13:1, p. 11.
[18] See Dutton, *Worse than the Disease: Pitfalls of Medical Progress* (Cambridge University Press, 1988) p. 266.
[19] Institute of Med. Vaccine Supply and Innovation, 85, 116–119 (1985), cited in Gilhooley, "Learned Intermediaries, Prescription Drugs, and Patient Information" (1986) *St Louis Uni L.J.*, 30, 633 at 689. See also McKenna, "The Impact of Product Liability Law on the Development of a Vaccine Against the AIDS Virus" (1988) *Uni Chicago L.Rev*, 55, 943 at 944 and 955.
[20] Vaccine Injury Compensation, 1984: Hearings on H.R. 556 before the Subcommittee on Health and the Environment, 98th Cong., 2d Sess. 140, at pp. 86–87.

willing to undertake the risk of marketing a new vaccine in that country. According to Mullady:

"The pertussis vaccine has been the target of so much litigation that there has been an exodus from the market by manufacturers of the vaccine and the cost of the product has risen exponentially."[21]

He noted that the price of the pertussis vaccine rose from 11 cents to 11 *dollars* in a five year period. Rosenfeld advises:

"... while only one out of every 312,500 doses of pertussis vaccine might cause brain damage and only one out of every 3.2 million doses of polio vaccine results in paralysis, products liability concerns have become so problematic that in 1984, the Centre for Disease Control (CDC) reported shortages of pertussis vaccine because a manufacturer [had] left the market."[22]

Banham claims that a composite vaccine for common childhood illnesses is now being produced by one manufacturer only, the rest having decided to withdraw from that particular market for fear of lawsuits.[23] This is hardly suprising; in the case of *Toner v. Lederle Laboratories*[24] the plaintiff was awarded $1.13 million in damages following a vaccine injury.

In relation to the development of an AIDS vaccine, one commentator has stated that concern over product liability suits has caused companies to be reluctant to market a vaccine unless the American government itself assumes the risk of suit.[25] Hence it has been argued that:

"... manufacturers must overcome the disincentives to making and marketing

---

[21] Mullady, "Considerations in the Management and Defence of Pharmaceutical Litigation in the United States" Chap. 10 of Howells, ed., *Product Liability, Insurance and the Pharmaceutical Industry: an Anglo-American Comparison, op. cit.* p. 125.

[22] Rosenfeld, "The Strict Products Liability Crisis and Beyond: Is there Hope for an AIDS Vaccine?" (1991) *Jurimetrics: Journal of Law, Science, and Technology,* 31:2, 187 at 195 (n. omitted).

[23] Abbott, *op. cit.* Foreword. These contentions are supported in "A Question of Competence: The Judicial Role in the Regulation of Pharmaceuticals", *op. cit.* at 775. See also Herzog, "Recent Developments in Products Liability in the United States" (1990) *American Journal of Comparative Law,* 38, 539 at p. 548.

[24] 779 F.2d 1429 (9th Cir. 1986); 831 F.2d 180 (9th Cir. 1987).

[25] See Games, "The Race for an AIDS Vaccine", *Fortune* 115, at p. 118 (December 21, 1987). See also Huber, "AIDS and Lawyers" *New Republic* 14 (May 5, 1986), in which the author states "under present legal conditions, even if a vaccine were available tomorrow, no one would produce it".

such a vaccine posed by products liability. To facilitate this process, it appears that the federal government will have to take a staunch stand against traditional state torts systems. Whether through express preemption of strict liability, federal recovery limitations imposed on state courts, a federal purchase plan or total government assumption of liability and distribution, something must be done to curb a system of liability that has already sent most manufacturers of lifesaving vaccines, as well as their insurers, fleeing."[26]

The American government's response to these concerns is considered in chapter 12, below.

(C) ANTI-NAUSEANTS AND CONTRACEPTIVES

Some very useful drugs have been forced from the American market, despite the fact that the allegations as to the harm caused by these drugs proved to be unfounded. One example of this is Merrell Dow Bendectin (Doxylamine Succinate, sold in Britain as Debendox). Bendectin was the only anti-nauseant ever approved for pregnant women in the United States. Since 1957 it had been used in more than 33 million pregnancies, worldwide.[27] It had, however, been alleged that the drug could cause birth defects. The British CSM had reviewed its safety on three separate occasions and had concluded each time that there was no evidence that this drug caused an increase in congenital abnormalities. The American FDA had also concluded that the drug was not responsible for an increased incidence of birth defects. Despite this, in the case of *Richardson v. Richardson-Merrell Incorporated*,[28] a jury awarded $1.16 million in compensation to the plaintiff. It was held on appeal, however, that "reasonable jurors could not reject [the] scientific consensus that Bendectin is not a teratogen without indulging in speculation and conjecture".[29]

Even though Merrell Dow was vindicated in this and other suits, the company submitted to a $120 million class action settlement and

---

[26] Rosenfield, *op. cit.* p. 187.

[27] Mullady, *op. cit.* p. 123.

[28] 649 F.Supp. 799 (1986).

[29] Quoted by Willig and Ruger, "Pharmacoepidemiology: A View from the U.S. Court Room" Chap. 9 of Strom, ed., *Pharmacoepidemiology* (Chichester, John Wiley & Sons Ltd, 2nd ed., 1994) at p. 102. See also *Turpin v. Merrell Dow Pharmaceuticals*, 959 F.2d 1349 (6th Cir. 1992) and *Lynch v. Merrell National Laboratory*, 646 F.Supp. 799 (D.D.C. 1986) which both found insufficient evidence that Bendectin could cause such defects.

voluntarily withdrew Bendectin from the American market in 1983. Many plaintiffs' attorneys now concede that this anti-nauseant was driven from the market by unjustified litigation.[30] According to Mullady:

"The Bendectin experience is an example of the deleterious effect litigation can have on a manufacturer's ability to market and sell a prescription drug, even when there is no scientific proof that a drug is problematic and the litigation is defended successfully."[31]

The United States of America has the highest teenage pregnancy rate in the world, yet only one American company is continuing to conduct extensive research into contraceptives. The many multi-million dollar awards given to plaintiffs in suits involving contraceptive injury has greatly increased liability insurance for such products. Isaacs and Holt contend that contraceptives "are being removed from the market faster than they can be replaced".[32] According to the American National Academy of Sciences:

"... contraceptive technology in the United States lags a decade behind Europe as a result of the impact of products liability litigation."[33]

In relation to oral conraceptives, it has been claimed that the chemical composition of contraceptive pills available in America has not changed since the 1960s. This is in contrast to the position in Europe, where the early 1980s saw the development of three new ingredients.[34]

Following the litigation over the Dalkon Shield intrauterine device, the Cu-7 and Tatum-T IUDs came under attack. Both these devices were manufactured by GD Searle. The company succeeded in defending itself against claims that its IUDs had caused injury in eight out of the first ten law suits which were started against them.[35] The cost to the company of just four of these suits was $1.5 million. Despite its success, 300 further suits were pending and in 1986 the company decided to cease selling IUDs in

---

[30] See Pretl and Osborne, *op. cit.* p. 114.

[31] *op. cit.* p. 124.

[32] *op. cit.* p. 533.

[33] See Roccamo, "Medical Implants and Other Health Care Products: Theories of Liability and Modern Trends" (1994) 16 *Advocates' Quarterly*, 421–451, at p. 442.

[34] *ibid.* p. 442.

[35] In *Marder v. GD Searle & Co.* 630 F.Supp. 1087, (D.Md. 1986) 17 women sued for alleged pelvic inflammatory disease, uterine perforation and ectopic pregnancy. Judgment was entered in favour of the company due to the plaintiffs' failure to establish causation.

the United States. Searle's experience tends to support the view that the American legal system:

"undermines the availability of pharmaceuticals. Even in the absence of liability judgments, the mere fear of astronomical liability may render a drug uninsurable."[36]

As a result of Searle's withdrawal, the Alza Progestasert remains the only IUD available to American women.

At one time, it was thought that there was a connection between the use of certain spermicidal contraceptives and birth defects. There has been serious criticism of the way the studies which had suggested such a link had been carried out, and several later studies have failed to confirm their findings. In 1986 the issue was considered by the FDA's Fertility and Maternal Health Drugs Advisory Committee, which was unanimous in concluding that there was insufficient evidence to link spermicides with birth defects. Despite this, in the case of *Wells vi. Ortho Pharmaceutical Corporation*,[37] decided several months after the FDA's determinations, the plaintiff succeeded in obtaining compensation from the manufacturer of Ortho-Gynol spermicidal jelly following the birth of a handicapped child. This illustrates the willingness of some American courts to find in favour of an injured plaintiff, sometimes on the flimsiest of evidence. This was a judicial decision, which suggests that the American jury system cannot be given the entire blame for that country's product liability crisis. The plaintiff's compensation was reduced to $4.7 million from $5.1 million on appeal, but the judgment itself was upheld.

3. Compensation Theories

(A) NEGLIGENCE

As well as providing compensation for persons who had suffered loss, the tort of negligence traditionally had several other objectives, namely to

---

[36] "A Question of Competence: The Judicial Role in the Regulation of Pharmaceuticals", *op. cit.* p. 773.
[37] 615 F.Supp. 262 (N.D. Ga. 1985); 788 F.2d 741 (1986).

punish a party who was in some sense responsible for that loss; to act as a deterrent by attempting to encourage the defendant, as well as persons in a similar position to the defendant, to act or refrain from acting in a particular way in the future, and to educate persons generally about accident avoidance. Its supporters argue that liability based on "fault" serves to discourage harmful conduct by giving adverse publicity to defendants who have failed to take reasonable care and by drawing attention to dangerous practices, thereby promoting accident prevention. It is also claimed that the negligence action allows for a detailed inquiry into the circumstances of a plaintiff's injury and that, compared to a system of strict liability, tort is a more just system, since only the "morally blameworthy" are held responsible.

Doubts have been expressed as to the ability of tort law to achieve any of these goals.[38] Its detractors claim that the link between the morality of a defendant's conduct and its liability is tenuous, since the amount of damages awarded is related to the severity of the plaintiff's injury rather than to the degree of the defendant's fault; that the deterrent aspect has been diluted by insurance; and that detailed investigation of the plaintiff's accident, which is so important to many who advocate retention of the tort process, is a rare event indeed since most cases are settled prior to trial.[39] They also point out that the tort system is protracted and expensive, with the legal costs frequently swallowing much of the damages.[40]

(B) STRICT LIABILITY

The imposition of "strict" or "no fault" liability for product injuries in the United States was originally devised by the courts, rather than by the legislature. The judges were motivated in this by certain considerations of

---

[38] See Cane, *Atiyah's Accidents, Compensation and the Law* (London, Butterworths, 5th ed., 1993) and Harris, "Evaluating the Goals of Personal Injury Law: Some Empirical Evidence" Chap. 12 in Cane and Stapleton, eds., *Essays for Patrick Atiyah* (Oxford, Clarendon Press, 1991) p. 290.

[39] See Ison, *The Forensic Lottery: A Critique on Tort Liability as a System of Personal Injury Compensation* (London, Staples Press, 1967) and Cane, "Justice and Justifications for Tort Liability" (1982) *Oxf. J.L.S.*, 2:1, at 30.

[40] The Pearson Commission estimated that the operating costs of the tort system amounted to about 85 per cent of the value of tort compensation payments. (*The Report of the Royal Commission on Civil Liabiity and Compensation for Personal Injury*, Cmnd. 7054, 1978, Volume 1, at para. 83.)

public policy. Three policies have been used by American courts to justify strict liability, namely "marketplace honesty","loss spreading" and "injury prevention".[41] All three are defined in the commentary to the Second Restatement of Torts:

"... the justification for ... strict liability has been said to be that the seller, by marketing his product for use and consumption, has undertaken and assumed a special responsibility towards any member of the consuming public who may be injured by it; that the public has the right to and does expect, in the case of products which it needs and for which it is forced to rely on the seller, that reputable sellers will stand behind their goods [*marketplace honesty*]; that public policy demands that the burden of accidental injuries caused by products intended for consumption be placed upon those who market them, and be treated as a cost of production against which liability insurance can be obtained [*loss spreading*]; and that the consumer of such products is entitled to the maximum of protection at the hands of someone, and the proper persons to afford it are those who market the products [*injury prevention*]."[42]

The threads of the last two of these policies, in particular, are discernible in many of the landmark American product liability cases. Hence in *Henningsen v. Bloomfield Motors Incorporated*[43] the court held that the burden of losses consequent upon the use of a defective product should be borne by those who are in a position to "make equitable distribution" of such losses, and who are able to control the danger.[44] This illustrates the court's concern to spread the risk of injury, but also emphasises the deterrent aspect of products liability.[45] Similarly, in the case of *Escola v. Coca Cola Bottling Co.*[46] Judge Traynor justified the move to strict liability as follows:

"... the risk of injury can be insured by the manufacturer and distributed among

---

[41] See Britain, "Product Honesty is the Best Policy: A Comparison of Doctors' and Manufacturers' Duty to Disclose Drug Risks and the Importance of Consumer Expectations in Determining Product Defect" (1984) *Northwester University Law Review*, 79:2, 342.

[42] Comment c to s.402A.

[43] 32 N.J. 358, 161 A.2d 69 (1960).

[44] *ibid.* at 379, and 81.

[45] See also *Greenman v. Yuba Power Products Incorporated* 59 Cal.2d 57, 377 P.2d 897, 27 Cal.Rptr. 697 (1962), in which it was stated that the purpose of strict liability "is to insure that the cost of injuries resulting from defective products are borne by the manufacturers that put such products on the market rather than by the injured persons who are powerless to protect themselves" (at 63, 901 and 701, respectively).

[46] 24 Cal.2d 453; 150 P.2d 436 (1944).

the public as a cost of doing business. [*Loss spreading*] . . . It is evident that the manufacturer can anticipate some hazards and guard against the recurrence of others, as the public cannot [*injury prevention*]."[47]

(c) PHARMACEUTICAL PRODUCTS: AN EXCEPTION?

When the idea of imposing strict liability for defective products was first mooted in Britain there were many who contended that the pharmaceutical industry should be exempted from the application of any such provisions.[48] It was argued that the imposition of strict liability for pharmaceutical product injuries would inhibit research into new drugs, and would ultimately deprive the public of the benefit of those drugs. This view was supported by the Royal College of Physicians which expressed concern that strict liability could lead to the practice of defensive medicine by members of the medical profession. Miller has argued that additional arguments against the application of strict liability to the pharmaceutical industry include the difficulty members of the industry may face in obtaining insurance cover,[49] and the fact that a government body exists to screen drugs, to ensure their safety before they are licensed.[50]

The Pearson Commission declined to make an exception for pharmaceutical products. Its reasoning was similar to that found in the American Restatement of Torts. It emphasised that since producers reap the benefits if their products are successful, they should also accept losses if their products fail and injure people. This is comparable to the "marketplace honesty" approach. Pearson also felt that strict liability would encourage higher safety standards (injury prevention) and that manufacturers were in the best position to arrange insurance cover, and could pass the extra cost to consumers through the price mechanism (loss spreading).[51]

---

[47] *ibid.* at 462 and 440–441, respectively.

[48] See the arguments presented to the Law Commissions, in *Liability for Defective Products*, Cmnd. 6831 (1977) No. 82, and No. 45, respectively, and also Pearson, *op. cit.* at para. 1260 and 1256.

[49] This argument was indeed utilised by a member of the pharmaceutical industry in explaining the lobbying undertaken by that industry to ensure that the development risk defence was included in the U.K. legislation. See p. [107], above.

[50] Miller, *Product Liability and Safety Encyclopaedia* (London, Butterworths, 1979) Div. III, p. 55.

[51] *op. cit.* paras. 1230–1236.

4. Conclusions

It is clear that the law of tort in the United States has increasingly placed less emphasis on notions of morality, fault and deterrence, and may now be regarded as having "the allocation of losses" as its primary purpose. Hence Fleming refers to the transformation of tort law "from its one-time admonitory to its new compensatory and loss-distributive purpose".[52] According to Waddams:

"In some cases, it appears that the courts attempt to make a genuine evaluation of fault, in others it appears that the most important question has become which party can more easily *bear the loss*."[53]

This is made explicit in many of the cases; in *Collins v. Eli Lilly & Co.*[54] the court held that:

"as between the injured plaintiff and the *possibly responsible* drug company, the drug company is in a better position to absorb the cost of the injury. The drug company can either insure itself against liability, absorb the damage award, or pass the cost along to the consuming public as a cost of doing business."[55]

Similarly, the finding in favour of the plaintiff in the *Sindell* case[56] has been justified as follows:

"several women have suffered awful injuries and they should be compensated; the drug companies make money out of successful drugs, and they should be prepared to compensate for damages; the question of fault is irrelevant—it is simply a case that the drug companies are *best able to pay*."[57]

In short, many American courts seem to have viewed the provision of compensation to injured plaintiffs as being the dominant goal of product liability. They have attempted to ensure that the burden of injuries caused

---

[52] Fleming, *The Law of Torts* (Sydney Law Book Company, 6th ed., 1983) p. 274.

[53] Waddams, *Products Liability* (Toronto, The Carswell Co. Ltd, 1974) Chap. 2, p. 13, emphasis added.

[54] 342 N.W. 2d 37 (1844). See p. [137], above.

[55] *ibid.* emphasis added, at 49.

[56] 607 p. 2d 924 (1980). See p. [193], above.

[57] (1981) *B.M.J.*, 282, at see p. [140], above. 1536, emphasis added.

by products is treated as part of the cost of manufacturing those products; the manufacturer can obtain insurance to cover its liability, and this is ultimately paid for by all consumers. Even in Britain it has been argued that:

> "In modern times, the deterrent and retributive effects of the law have been considerably blunted by the pervasiveness of insurance, and it seems reasonable to assume that compensation to injured people, or the allocation of losses, is a major objective of English tort law."[58]

This chapter has demonstrated, however, that if the policy of loss spreading is taken to extremes then fear of product liability suits may lead to a dearth of new products—particularly in a research dependent activity such as the pharmaceutical industry.

Rather than distort traditional tort theories to benefit plaintiffs, consideration should be given to alternative methods of ensuring that adequate compensation is provided for injured parties. This is addressed in the following chapter.

---

[58] Genn, *Hard Bargaining: Out of Court Settlement in Personal Injury Actions* (Oxford, Clarendon Press, 1987) p. 168.

Chapter 12

The Provision of Compensation

"[T]he expansion of manufacturers' liability cannot continue indefinitely. At some point, it makes sense to consider more fundamental kinds of legal reform."[1]

1. Introduction

The fear that America was experiencing a product liability crisis led to a backlash, and the development of reform programmes designed to protect the producers of certain pharmaceutical drugs and devices from unjustified suits. At the same time, there were calls for the provision of more secure prospects of compensation for injured persons. Despite the introduction of strict liability into British law, it seems clear that a personal injuries action may not be the best method of accomplishing even the limited goal of providing financial recompense.[2] As Rosenberg has argued:

"Current criticism of the tort system as a scheme too cumbersome, costly, and haphazard to accomplish its accident prevention and compensation objectives suggests that our reliance on private damage actions is misplaced."[3]

A number of compensation systems do not require injured parties to

---

[1] Dutton, *Worse than the Disease: Pitfalls of Medical Progress* (Cambridge University Press, 1988) p. 279.
[2] For an excellent critique of civil litigation in the realm of personal injuries, see Cane, *Atiyah's Accidents, Compensation and the Law* (London, Butterworths, 5th ed., 1993).
[3] Rosenberg, "The Causal Connection in Mass Exposure Cases: A 'Public Law' Vision of the Tort System" (1984) *Harvard Law Review*, 97, 849 at 854 (n. omitted).

exercise their private law remedies. These schemes are usually funded by an insurance consortium, or by the state itself and are commonly referred to as "no-fault" schemes, since they have in common that there is no need for claimants to establish "fault" or negligence on the part of any party.

The Pearson Commission considered the introduction of a state funded scheme for medical injuries in Britain, but decided against this. It did, however, add: "All of us appreciate that circumstances may change, and that our conclusions may have to be reviewed in the future."[4] It is 18 years since the publication of that Report, hence a reassessment of this conclusion may now be in order.

No-fault compensation systems pertinent to pharmaceutical products may be divided into three categories: those which provide compensation to the victims of certain types of pharmaceutical products only (commonly, vaccines); those which compensate the victims of *all* pharmaceutical product injuries, and those which provide more comprehensive cover, of which persons injured by pharmaceutical drugs or devices are merely one group of individuals who may be entitled to recompense.

2. No Fault Schemes for Vaccines

(A) FLU VACCINES

It has been estimated that more than 45 million Americans were vaccinated against Swine Flu, and that one in 100,000 of them developed Guillain-Barre Syndrome as a result.[5] Under the Swine Flu Immunisation Program of 1976 all parties who allege that they have been injured as a result of immunisation against Swine Flu are required to seek compensation through a national compensation scheme.[6] In its first eight years the scheme paid out $73 million in compensation.

---

[4] *Report of the Royal Commission on Civil Liability and Compensation for Personal Injury*, Cmnd. 7054, 1978, Vol. I, para. 1370.

[5] Guillain-Barre syndrome causes polyneuritis, "a form of ascending paralysis which usually requires hospitalization, and in approximately 5% of cases is fatal" (Patterson, ed., *Drugs in Litigation: Damage Awards Involving Prescription and Nonprescription Drugs* (Virginia, The Michie Company, 1992) p. 436).

[6] 42 U.S.C. s.247b(j)–(l), (as amended in 1978).

(B) CHILDHOOD VACCINES

A second American scheme is that established by the National Childhood Vaccine Injury Act of 1986.[7] This provides a no-fault compensation system for injuries caused by certain vaccines,[8] and is paid for by a tax on those vaccines. The Act requires vaccine injury claims to be adjudicated through the Federal Compensation Program before a civil suit may be filed against a manufacturer in the courts. A maximum of $250,000 can be recovered for pain and suffering. A party who decides to take the offer of state compensation is barred from thereafter raising a civil suit.[9] Doctors are required to inform the parents of children who are to be vaccinated about the benefits and risks. The steps taken by this legislation to alleviate plaintiffs' difficulties in establishing causation are described at page 193, below.

(C) AIDS VACCINES

Some American states have developed schemes of their own to encourage the development of a vaccine against AIDS. California has undertaken to pay up to $550,000 in compensation to cover the medical costs and loss of earnings of anyone who sustains injury from an FDA approved AIDS vaccine.[10] An injured party is not precluded from raising a civil action, but the state scheme will recoup any payment it has made to a claimant if a person later succeeds in obtaining damages against a manufacturer.

(D) THE BRITISH VACCINE SCHEME

The Pearson Commission noted that the British government recommended childhood vaccination against certain common infectious illnesses, and that this vaccination policy was designed to improve the

---

[7] N.C.V.I.A., 42 U.S.C.A. ss.300aa–10 to 300aa–34 (West. Supp. 1990).
[8] These are diphtheria and tetanus toxoids (DT); diphtheria, tetanus and pertussis (DTP); measles, mumps and rubella (MMR); and poliomyelitis.
[9] 42 U.S.C. s.300aa–21(a) (1988).
[10] California Health and Safety Code, ss.199.45–199.51 (West. 1990).

general health of the community.[11] The Commission therefore proposed that financial assistance should be made available for children injured by vaccination, where that immunisation had been recommended by public health authorities.

This led to the Vaccine Damage Payments Act 1979, which established a state compensation scheme and provided for a lump sum payment to be made where a child is injured as a result of immunisation by a prescribed vaccine. The prescribed vaccines include those for Diphtheria, Tetanus, Whooping Cough, Poliomyelitis, Measles, Rubella, Tuberculosis, Small-pox and Hib meningitis. The Government has paid out about £6 million under the scheme in cases where it has been satisfied that brain damage has resulted from immunisation. The initial consideration of a claimant's case is made by the Secretary of State, with an appeal lying from this decision to a Vaccine Damage Tribunal. It seems that the failure rate is high, with only 13 per cent of cases resulting in compensation at first instance, and over 70 per cent of all appeals being rejected.[12] Claimants require to show that they have suffered "severe" disability as a result of immunisation. This is defined as 80 per cent disablement.

3. Schemes for all Pharmaceutical Products

(A) THE SWEDISH PHARMACEUTICAL SYSTEM

In 1978 the Swedish pharmaceutical industry set up a voluntary scheme to compensate persons injured as a result of using its products.[13] The scheme is funded by contributions from pharmaceutical companies operating or marketing their products in Sweden. A producer or importer will not be granted a licence unless it is a member of the scheme. Claimants

---

[11] *op. cit.* See, in particular, Chap. 25 of that Report.
[12] See Parliamentary Debates H.C. Session 1981–82, Written Answer, March 2, 1982, Col. 123, cited in Lee, "Vaccine Damages: Adjudicating Scientific Disputes" Chap. 5 in Howells, ed., *Product Liability, Insurance and the Pharmaceutical Industry: an Anglo-American Comparison* (Manchester University Press, 1991) 52 at pp. 53–54.
[13] See Oldertz, "Compensation for Personal Injuries—the Swedish Patient and Pharma Insurance", Chap. 2 of Mann and Havard, eds., *No Fault Compensation in Medicine* (London, Royal Society of Medicine Services, 1989).

require to have been on sick leave for at least 30 days or to have sustained "permanent disability of some significance".

Persons who succeed in being indemnified under this system are required to assign to the insurer any rights they may have to pursue an action in tort. The scheme allows for a maximum compensation of £300,000 per person and sets a maximum annual pay out of £15 million per year. Despite these high sums, the average payment made in 1987 was £5,000.[14] No personal injury suits have been raised against a pharmaceutical company in Sweden since the scheme was established. The pharmaceutical industry's premiums equal about 0.31 to 0.37 per cent of their business. By 1987 there had been 2,026 claims, about half of which had resulted in an award of compensation.

The Swedish scheme defines a "drug related injury" as:

". . . an illness or other bodily injury which with preponderant probability has been caused through the use of a drug. A drug-related injury is *not* considered to include an illness or other bodily injury which

—is due to lack or absence of effect, on the part of the drug, or

—has occurred in the course of an activity which is unsuitable with respect to the intended or predicted effect of the drug in question."[15]

Section 5 provides further restrictions; compensation is not payable if it would have been reasonable for the claimant to accept the injury as a cosequence of taking the drug, due to:

"—the nature and severity of the disease for which the treatment was given,

—the general health status of the injured person,

—the severity of the injury,

—the reason for the medical professional to expect the side-effects of a drug and the possibility for him to foresee the consequences of them."

Section 7 precludes compensation where injury has been caused due to drug misuse. Where the injury has been caused by the failure of a member of the medical profession to follow the manufacturer's instructions for use or heed its warning information then the patient is compensated, not by the

---

[14] Brahams, "The Swedish 'No Fault' Compensation System for Medical Injuries—Part 1" (1988) *N.L.J.*, 138, at 16.

[15] Undertaking to disburse indemnity of drug-related injuries—Indemnity provisions as of January 1, 1988, s.3, emphasis added.

pharmaceutical insurance scheme, but by a separate patient insurance scheme.[16]

(B) The Norwegian and Finnish Schemes

Norway has introduced statutory compensation by way of a Drug Insurance Scheme. The scheme has a number of important exceptions, including injuries caused by the error of a pharmacist or doctor; those due to a pharmaceutical product being used in an unforeseeable manner or contrary to the manufacturer's warnings; and side-effects "which it is reasonable for the injured person to bear the consequences of".[17] It is interesting to note that injured parties may claim against this scheme even if they are unable to identify the manufacturer of the drugs which harmed them.[18]

Since 1984 Finland has operated a similar voluntary scheme, which involves all manufacturers and importers of pharmaceutical products. The scheme covers "illness or bodily injury apparently caused by a drug" where the injury has been caused by a side effect which "was unexpected either at all or in its gravity".[19]

4. "Comprehensive" Schemes

(A) The New Zealand Scheme

A more comprehensive scheme than any of those outlined above was introduced in New Zealand in 1974.[20] It is now regulated by the Accident

---

[16] See Oldertz, "The Swedish Patient Insurance Scheme—8 Years of Experience" (1984) *Medico-Legal Journal*, 52, 43.

[17] See Howells, *Comparative Product Liability* (Aldershot, Dartmouth, 1993) p. 169.

[18] *ibid.* For some American solutions to the problem of identifying a drug's manufacturer see Chap. 9, above.

[19] See Brahams, "No Fault Compensation in Finland with an overview of the Scandinavian approach to compensation of medical and drug injuries" Chap. 5 of Mann and Havard, eds., *op. cit.* p. 86.

[20] See *Compensation for Personal Injury in New Zealand*, Report of the Royal Commission of Inquiry (the Woodhouse Report), 1967. Its recommendations were implemented in the Accident Compensation Act 1972, and the scheme commenced two years after this.

Rehabilitation and Compensation Insurance Act 1992.[21] The scheme has abolished common law actions for personal injuries.[22] It is funded from a number of sources, including a levy from employers, a tax on motor vehicles, and general taxation, and provides up to 80 per cent of the pre-injury earnings of a claimant by means of periodic payments.[23] The scheme is intended to compensate for "personal injury by accident", which includes:

"(i) The physical and mental consequences of any such injury or of the accident.

(ii) Medical, surgical, dental or first aid misadventure.

(iii) Incapacity resulting from an occupational disease or industrial deafness . . .

(iv) Actual bodily harm . . . arising by any act or omission of any other person . . . irrespective of whether or not any person is charged with the offence . . ."

"Medical misadventure" has been defined as occurring where:

"(a) a person suffers bodily or mental injury or damage in the course of, and as part of, the administering to that person of medical aid, care or attention, and

(b) such injury or damage is caused by mischance or accident, unexpected and undesigned, in the nature of a medical error or medical mishap."[24]

---

[21] See also the Accident Compensation Act 1982.

[22] For a criticism of this aspect of the scheme see Mahoney, "Trouble in Paradise: New Zealand's Accident Compensation Scheme" Chap. 3 in McLean, ed., *Law Reform and Medical Injury Litigation* (Aldershot, Dartmouth, 1995).

[23] For more details of this scheme see McLean, "Accident Compensation Liability without Fault—the New Zealand Experience" (1985) *Journal of Social Welfare Law* 31, and Whincup, "Accident Compensation in New Zealand" Chap. 16 of Howells, ed., *Product Liability, Insurance and the Pharmaceutical Industry: an Anglo-American Comparison, op. cit.,* p. 203 on.

[24] Review No. 77/R 1352.

The 1992 Act has restricted claims arising from an adverse consequence of treatment to cases in which the injury was "both rare and severe".[25]

It is clear that the scheme was never intended to compensate people whose medical treatment had simply failed to cure them. In one case it was noted that:

> "all treatment, whether medical or surgical, has a chance of being unsuccessful. There is an expected failure rate in all these matters and such failure may be because no matter how correct the treatment, nature does not always respond the desired way. It would be quite beyond the intention or wording of the Accident Corporation Act that cover should be granted on the basis of personal injury by accident merely because medical treatment was not 100% effective. Certainty cannot be underwritten."[26]

The New Zealand courts have encountered some difficulty in determining the circumstances in which a person may be said to have suffered "personal injury by accident".[27] They have, however, emphasised that an accident is an unlooked-for mishap and an untoward event which is not expected or designed.[28] This must be judged from the point of view of the victim.[29] In the case of *Accident Compensation Corporation v. Mitchell*[30] it was stated that:

> "... a generous, unniggardly interpretation of personal injury by accident is in keeping with the policy underlying the Accident Compensation Act of providing comprehensive cover for all those suffering personal injury by accident in New Zealand *wherever, whenever and however occurring* ..."[31]

However, the Act expressly excludes:

---

[25] s.5. A rare risk is defined as one which occurs in less than 1 per cent of treatments, and a severe injury involves hospitalisation for more than 14 days, is a "significant disability" lasting longer than 28 days, or a 10 per cent disability, according to prescribed injury tables. See Mahoney, *op. cit.* p. 71.

[26] *Accident Compensation Commission v. Auckland Hospital Board* [1980] 2 N.Z.L.R. 748 at 749.

[27] See *Wills v. Attorney-General* [1989] 3 N.Z.L.R. 574; *Dandoroff v. Rogozinoff* [1988] 2 N.Z.L.R. 588; and *Accident Compensation Corporation v. F* [1991] 1 N.Z.L.R. 234.

[28] See *Fenton v. Thorley & Co. Ltd* [1903] A.C. 443, which was applied in *Accident Compensation Corporation v. E* [1992] 2 N.Z.L.R. 426.

[29] *Accident Compensation Corporation v. E, ibid.* at 430.

[30] [1992] 2 N.Z.L.R. 436.

[31] *ibid.* at 438–439, *per* Richardson J., emphasis added.

"(i) Damage to the body or mind caused by a cardio-vascular or cerebro-vascular episode unless the episode is the result of effort, strain, or stress that is abnormal, excessive or unusual for the person suffering it, and the effort, strain, or stress arises out of and in the course of the employment of that person . . .

(ii) Damage to the body or mind caused exclusively by disease, infection, or the ageing process."[32]

The failure of the scheme to provide compensation for injuries caused by illness or disease has been criticised.[33] As Mahoney has pointed out:

"Courts interpreting the Acts governing the scheme are continually forced to deal with the difficulties caused by the disease exclusion, which difficulties stem from not only the basic unfairness of the exclusion but also the impossibility of drawing the bright line of distinction between disease and accident."[34]

The exclusion of disease has important implications for pharmaceutical product injuries since a person who is injured by such a product will almost invariably have been suffering from some pre-existing illness. It seems clear, therefore, that causation remains an issue under the New Zealand scheme, in so far as claimants must satisfy the Compensation Commission that their injuries were caused by "an accident".

(B) A COMPREHENSIVE SCHEME FOR BRITAIN

We have seen that where a mass disaster is occasioned in Britain due to an unforeseen side effect of a drug, the injured parties face considerable obstacles in obtaining compensation through the tort system. The Labour party announced in 1986 that it favoured the introduction of a no-fault scheme for the victims of medical accidents. This was defined to include

---

[32] s.2.
[33] See Ison, *Accident Compensation: A Commentary on the New Zealand Scheme* (London, Croom Helm, 1980) p. 21.
[34] *op. cit.* p. 35. A similar point is made by McLean, "No Fault Liability and Medical Responsibility", in Freeman, ed., *Medicine, Ethics and the Law* (London, Stevens & Sons, 1988) 147 at p. 153.

the unforeseen side effects of drugs. The British Medical Association now favours the introduction of a state funded no-fault compensation scheme for persons injured by "medical mishaps". Again, this scheme would exclude the adverse effects of drugs where they have been used in accordance with the manufacturer's instructions.[35]

The Association of the British Pharmaceutical Industry had urged the Pearson Commission to recommend a government funded system of compensation for persons injured by pharmaceutical products.[36] A patient who sustained serious injury would have to prove that this was due to an accident, and the amount of the loss. The state fund would then provide compensation, and would be able to sue the manufacturer if the latter were at fault. Under this system no account would be taken of any contributory negligence by the injured patient in determining the amount of compensation to be paid—this negligence could only be taken into account if the state exercised its right of subrogation.

5. The Causation Issue

McIntosh has pointed out that, even under a "well thought out no fault scheme ... proof of causation will still be essential and thus cases like pertussis vaccine, Debendox and many of the individual Opren claims would probably not qualify for compensation ...".[37] Commenting on the Vaccine Damage Payments Act 1979, one author has concluded:

"... in view of the unhappy state of medical knowledge in relation to the extent of, and reason for, severe adverse reaction to vaccines, a strict liability system which had at its heart the need to prove causation was never likely to prove satisfactory."[38]

Mention has already been made of the difficulties faced by these victims in

---

[35] For a criticism of this see Mildred, "Reforming the Tort System" (1989) *N.L.J.*, 139, 124.
[36] *Memorandum of Evidence to the Royal Commission on Civil Liability and Compensation for Personal Injury*, (October 1974), paras. 1, 4, and 8.
[37] McIntosh, "A Prescription for Medical Negligence" Chap. 10 of Mann and Havard, *op. cit.* p. 142.
[38] Lee, "Liability for vaccine damage in Great Britain" in *Proceedings VIIth World Congress on Medical Law* (Ghent, 1985) 3, 162–168, quoted in Palmer, "Faults in No Fault Compensation Schemes" Chap. 13 of Mann and Havard, *op. cit.* p. 165.

satisfying the causation test. In the Canadian case of *Rothwell v. Raes*[39] Mr Justice Osler stated:

"Surely it would be worth while for our society to agree to a certain adequate, though not lavish, standard of compensation upon proof of prior good health, the administration of vaccine and catastrophic damage within a limited period of time."

Certain no-fault schemes have attempted to tackle this causation issue. Under the American National Childhood Vaccine scheme a Vaccine Injury Table lists the types of injuries associated with certain vaccinations. These include seizures, convulsions, paralysis, and brain damage. If the injured party can demonstrate that he or she is suffering from a prescribed injury which occurred within the listed time periods, then it is presumed that the vaccine in question caused the injury and the onus of proving that this was *not* the case shifts to the Department of Health.[40]

Similarly, under the Swedish pharmaceutical scheme injured parties must establish that there is a "preponderant probability" that it was a pharmaceutical product which caused their injury. This is less demanding than the usual "on the balance of probability" standard. In practice, liability is frequently accepted where an injury results which is known to be caused by a particular drug, and it cannot be shown that there is another cause which is equally probable. A claim is also likely to be accepted where there is a short time interval between the taking of the drug and the onset of the injury. Thus, as Oldertz has noted:

". . . this more lenient evidentiary requirement has resulted in an acceptance in the individual case of a generally known statistical causal relationship. Causality is accepted if it is not otherwise evident from the investigation that a certain factor or predisposition in the individual case could, in itself, have caused a similar injury. In the same manner, a chronological connection can be given substantial weight. If the injury occurs within a relatively short period of time after the drug has begun to be used, this is taken to be a relatively strong indication of causality."[41]

The adoption of a lower standard of proof in any British scheme would

---

[39] 54 D.L.R. (4th) 193. See p. [130], above.
[40] *ibid.* ss.300aa–12 to 300aa–13.
[41] *op. cit.* (see n. 13, above) at p. 25.

improve an injured party's chances of establishing that his or her injury was caused by the pharmaceutical product, rather than by the pre-existing illness for which the patient was being treated.

As already noted, a precedent for reducing the burden of causation already exists in Britain. Certain industrial injuries are covered by a state-funded compensation scheme which provides compensation for death or long-term disability. A claimant need not show that any party has been at fault, nor need causation be established, since there is often a presumption that the injury was caused by the exposure to the industrial hazard.[42]

This is not the place in which to provide a detailed description of the ideal no-fault compensation system. It is, however, obvious that such a scheme, to be an improvement on existing procedures, would require to tackle the causation issue, and to compensate a person who has been injured as a result of the use or consumption of a drug or device, irrespective of whether that product would generally be regarded as "defective".

6. Deterrence

While both a state funded compensation system or an insurance based scheme paid for by the pharmaceutical industry would increase the number of injured parties who would receive compensation, their impact on deterring harmful conduct is less clear. Oldertz has argued that no-fault compensation systems allow more accurate statistics to be compiled as to the types of treatment which are most prone to cause injury.[43] How best to deter potential tortfeasors from injurious conduct is a problem which is beyond the scope of the present work. It may be noted, however, that the pharmaceutical industry is in an unusual position in this respect. Mention has already been made of the detailed regulations required by the state as to the testing, development and licensing of new drugs.[44] The threat of a personal injury action against a manufacturer of pharmaceutical products may be less of a deterrence than the knowledge that the CSM or licensing

---

[42] See Chap. 9, above.
[43] *op. cit.* (see n. 16, above) at p. 50.
[44] See Chap. 2, above.

authority has the power to impose more restrictive conditions against a company which has been shown to be lax in the past.

The regulatory process could of course be tightened up to make it even more difficult to acquire a licence for all new pharmaceutical products, but this would delay their marketing for a longer period and deprive the population of potentially useful drugs. It would also make drugs more expensive, a burden which we would all share as tax-payers who contribute to the NHS. Furthermore, tougher regulations would mean that the effective patent life of new drugs, that period which is so crucial in allowing companies to recoup the vast sums expended in research and development—would be reduced. Would any of this really ensure that we never again have another Opren or thalidomide tragedy?

7. Justifying Special Treatment

One criticism which advocates of a no-fault system for pharmaceutical products must confront is that it is intrinsically unfair to single out this one group of injured people for special compensation procedures. As Fleming has put it:

> "In what way, one might ask, were the thalidomide children more deserving of public generosity in Britain than the 1,000 other handicapped children born every week or the 100,000 severely handicapped children under sixteen who must be content with the benefits of the general social security program? . . . And on what basis are we to prefer the credentials of cancer victims from drugs to those from leaking x-ray equipment or, for that matter, from microwave ovens?"[45]

There is much force in this observation. It may be argued that our society ought to strive to create a system based on need, which would provide compensation for all persons suffering serious illness or injury, regardless of

---

[45] Fleming, "Drug Injury Compensation Plans" (1982) *The American Journal of Comparative Law*, 30, 297 at 319, n. omitted.

origin.[46] Such a scheme would ideally be wider than the New Zealand one, since it would cover the victims of illness and disease, as well as those injured by "accident".

Pragmatically, however, it must be recognised that a comprehensive system of this nature is unlikely to be implemented in Britain in the foreseeable future.[47] Despite the obvious unfairness in reforming personal injuries law in a piecemeal fashion, one can nevertheless endorse Cane's comment that *any* reform which improves the position of some injured or handicapped people is better than no reform at all. He observed:

> "The waste and inefficiencies of the tort system are continuing realities, and there is only so much that tinkering with the tort system can achieve. Even if all we can realistically hope for is that the funds currently tied up in the tort system as it now operates will be better used, this is enough to justify a limited reform, even at the cost of creating or perpetuating anomalies . . . And in the process the public mind might be sufficiently weaned off the idea of tort rights and onto the notion of no-fault welfare rights, to lead eventually to more comprehensive reform."[48]

Since it is unrealistic to hope for the enactment of a comprehensive compensation system, a case can be made for giving special treatment, at least in the interim, to those who fall victim to the hazards of pharmaceutical products.

In 1961 a working party was commissioned by the government to explore the establishment of a state compensation scheme for persons who were the victims of violent crime. It was unable to find "any constitutional or social principle on which state compensation could be justified" for such persons, other than public sympathy.[49] If public sympathy alone is

---

[46] Of course, a more fundamental question is why it is felt that a person who is injured or ill is more deserving of financial compensation than a person who suffers a bereavement, or who is unable to work due to redundancy. Questions of this nature are beyond the scope of the present work. See, however, Stapleton, "Implications for the Compensation Debate and Beyond" Chap. 7 of *Disease and the Compensation Debate* (Oxford, Clarendon Press, 1986) which provides an excellent critique of the standard approach to compensation.

[47] In September 1988 Edwina Currie, then junior health minister, stated that the British government "considers that the basis for seeking legal compensation for injuries suffered should continue to be through litigation in the courts". See Smith, "No stopping no fault" (1988) *B.M.J.*, 297, p. 935.

[48] *op. cit.* p. 424.

[49] See *Compensation for Victims of Crimes of Violence*, Cmnd. 1406 (1961) paras. 17 and 18. See also Duff, *Criminal Injuries Compensation* (Edinburgh, Butterworths, 1991).

sufficient justification for a state system of compensation in relation to victims of crime, why should similar reasoning not benefit the victims of pharmaceutical drugs?

8. Conclusions

It is not the purpose of the present work to provide a detailed description of the "ideal" no-fault scheme for pharmaceutical injuries. Rather, the intention has been to draw attention to the major deficiencies in current compensation processes, and to engender further debate on these issues. Some thoughts on the principles which might inform such a debate are, however, in order.

Throughout this book, it has been stressed that injury may result from a recognised adverse reaction, as well as from those which are unknown and unforeseeable. In both cases, persons who suffer drug injuries face particular problems. They have sustained the double misfortune of suffering from an illness then being harmed by the treatment designed to cure or alleviate that illness. Mention has been made of the fact that, unlike most product injuries, those caused by pharmaceutical products tend to be of insidious onset. We have also seen that the defects which tend to be associated with pharmaceutical products are commonly of the "design defect" type, rather than manufacturing defects.[50] It follows from this that a defective drug has greater potential to cause injuries on a massive scale than, for example, a defective kettle. While other products are not immune from design defects, it is particularly unlikely that a court will be able to find that a defective pharmaceutical drug could have been better designed. The nature of drugs means that the causation problem is exacerbated, as is the difficulty in identifying and tracing an appropriate defendant.

With respect to unknown risks, it is impossible to spot many of these until a drug has been consumed by a large number of people, hence all patients who are exposed to a new pharmaceutical product in its early marketing stages are to some extent "guinea pigs". There is no fool-proof way of guaranteeing that a new drug is safe; even the very rigorous testing

---

[50] See Chap. 1, above.

procedures which are currently mandated by government regulatory bodies are unable to ensure that a harmful product does not slip through the net. Chapter 1 contained several examples of drugs which fulfilled all the pre-marketing clinical trials, yet nonetheless inflicted serious injuries on a number of their consumers. Such people ought to be compensated from a no-fault scheme. Any scheme would require to have generous causation provisions, similar to those which operate in the Swedish scheme, or the American vaccine scheme.

Where the use of certain drugs is encouraged, as being for the good of society, then it may be suggested that this compensation scheme should also include those who suffer from the side effects of such drugs, *even when* that adverse reaction is a recognised one. The provision of a no-fault scheme for the victims of immunisation programmes can be justified on this basis; society as a whole benefits if everyone is inoculated and should therefore bear the costs of compensation for the inevitable unfortunate minority who are injured as a result. It might be possible to construct a similar argument in favour of the victims of other pharmaceutical products, such as contraceptives. If a society encourages population control then it might be argued that all of its members benefit from the use of contraceptives. Where some of these, such as oral contraceptions and IUDs, are shown to have injured a small proportion of users, then we should accept a responsibility to compensate for this. The problem with this argument is that it is difficult to draw a line; if we are going to compensate the woman who is injured by the contraceptive Pill, why not one who is injured by some other drug?

We have seen that the majority of existing no-fault schemes exclude injuries caused by pharmaceutical products where these were due to adverse reactions which were "not unexpected".[51] Recognised adverse reactions are generally *not* included since the costs of compensating all patients who suffer side effects could be enormous, and it is arguable that patients can be taken to have accepted the possibility of the side effect as one of the risks inherent in taking the product.

Although one would not wish to compensate every patient who suffered a rash or slight discomfort as a side effect of a drug, an exclusion of all known risks seems harsh where the patient suffers serious injury. Ideally, all serious injuries would be compensated, on the basis of need rather than cause. Pragmatically, however, there must be limits to the provision of

---

[51] This applies to the New Zealand, Swedish, Norwegian and Finnish schemes.

compensation, and it may be argued that a person who suffers from a known side effect of a drug, even where this causes serious injury, is in a similar position to a person who is injured by other known hazards of life. If this approach is to be followed, then it is important that patients be fully advised of the risks which are known to be associated with their medications, so that their choice to accept these risks is a genuinely informed one. Recent changes to the legal requirements of drug labels and the provision of detailed leaflets should ensure that patients are aware of any serious side effects which have been recognised at the time of marketing.[52]

---

[52] See Chap. 2, above.

Chapter 13

Conclusions

The difficulties in obtaining compensation faced by the victims of "creeping" disasters or "man-made diseases" generally, have been described in detail elsewhere.[1] The present work has focused on disasters involving pharmaceutical products and has attempted to demonstrate that many of the problems confronting plaintiffs in personal injury actions can be particularly acute for those injured by such products. One aim of this work was to try to ascertain the extent to which legal reforms since the thalidomide disaster have facilitated the provision of compensation for the victims of subsequent pharmaceutical product injuries. This study has illustrated that, while some of the difficulties which confronted the thalidomide victims have been removed, important hurdles remain.

As already mentioned, one of the most serious problems to confront the thalidomide children was the uncertainty as to whether the manufacturer of a pharmaceutical product owed a duty of care to an unborn plaintiff. It is now clear that this duty is recognised by the laws of both England and Scotland. This, then, is one issue which the infant plaintiffs of drugs such as DES and Accutane will not require to confront.

The second burden faced by thalidomide victims was in establishing that the defendant had breached its duty to take reasonable care. Chapter 3 described a number of ways in which the manufacturer of a pharmaceutical drug or device could be negligent—by failing to test its products prior to marketing, by not keeping itself advised of any adverse reactions which subsequently come to light, or by omitting to provide adequate warning

---

[1] See Stapleton, *Disease and the Compensation Debate* (Oxford, Clarendon Press, 1986).

information. As chapter 2 has demonstrated, government licensing authorities have devised very specific and rigorous regulations for the testing of new pharmaceutical products. Since such bodies require to be satisfied of the safety, efficacy and quality of a product before they will be prepared to license it, a plaintiff will find it very difficult to demonstrate that a manufacturer which has complied with government regulations has, nevertheless, been negligent. Indeed, it seems clear that a harmful drug may be marketed *without* there having been any want of care. Furthermore, the discussion of the potential liability of the CSM or licensing authority in chapter 6 has indicated that it is far from certain that such agencies can themselves be subject to suit.

Chapters 4 and 5 have described a number of ways in which members of the medical and pharmacy professions may cause harm in their use or supply of pharmaceutical products. The lack of any contract between doctor and patient or pharmacist and customer in the majority of cases means that plaintiffs must generally rely on the tort of negligence. This emphasis on establishing that a defendant has been negligent may be thought to be misplaced, following the advent of strict liability for products, established by the Consumer Protection Act. However, chapter 7 has drawn attention to some of the weaknesses of this new regime. Central to liability under the 1987 Act is the need for a plaintiff to establish that the product in question was "defective". This requires a court to compare the risks and benefits offered by a product, and it is clear from chapter 8 that establishing defectiveness may be an onerous task for an injured plaintiff, particularly in respect of pharmaceutical products. The vast majority of drugs pose risks, and in many cases the risks to the few are outweighed by the benefits to the majority of users.

It might be suggested that the Dalkon Shield intrauterine device is an example of a product which was clearly defective, in that it failed to offer the safety which "persons generally" were entitled to expect. The behaviour of the Robins company meant that the Shield was an extreme example of a harmful product. It would have been relatively easy for plaintiffs to show that Robins had in fact been *negligent* in marketing this device; the company knew from the outset that there was a problem with the Shield's tail string but gambled that, even if it did have to pay out compensation for injuries, this would be less expensive that the cost of modifying the IUD's design.

The existence of the development risk defence makes it even less likely that a plaintiff will succeed in such a suit. Given that the thalidomide disaster was a major impetus for reform in this area it is of some concern to note that the Lord Chancellor has conceded that this defence could deprive the victims of another thalidomide-type tragedy of a legal remedy.

The impediments which statutes of limitation may pose must not be overlooked. This has not been improved by the Consumer Protection Act, and persons injured by drugs such as DES may find that their actions are time-barred before they are even aware of the fact that they have sustained injury.

A further, important hurdle confronts the injured plaintiff, that of establishing causation. Plaintiffs will have been unwell prior to taking a pharmaceutical product, and drugs operate by changing the physiological functions of the body. As the descriptions of the injuries caused by Opren, the DES litigation and Benzodiazepine addictions have illustrated, adverse reactions tend to be of insidious onset; their harmful effects commonly do not become apparent until a considerable period after a patient has first taken the drug in question.[2] Side effects occasioned by drugs are often similar to naturally occurring illnesses, and chapter 9 has suggested that it may be particularly difficult for injured plaintiffs to establish causation in drug cases.

Worldwide, thalidomide was produced under 51 different names by several pharmaceutical companies. Fortunately for the British plaintiffs, the Distillers Company was the sole manufacturer in this country. Almost 40 per cent of prescriptions in Britain are now written generically, that is, without reference to a drug's brand name.[3] While being cost-effective for the NHS, this increase in generic prescribing means that persons who have been injured by a pharmaceutical product are likely to encounter even greater problems in establishing which company was responsible for manufacturing a particular product.

Such difficulties have faced the victims of defective IUDs; a doctor may have recorded the fact that a device had been inserted in a particular patient, and that it had subsequently been removed, but the make of IUD which the patient had been using may not have been noted. As we have seen, similar problems confronted the victims of DES, and this issue of

---

[2] See Chap. 1, above.
[3] Byran, "Bid to Allay Suspicion of Generics" *GP*, April 7, 1989, p. 67.

identifying the appropriate defendant has been examined in some detail.[4] The Consumer Protection Act should at least improve the position of persons in such a situation in the future, since the supplier of a pharmaceutical drug or device (the patient's doctor or pharmacist) may now be called upon by an injured party to identify that product's manufacturer.

The possibility of group litigation for pharmaceutical product suits was explored in chapter 10. The Opren debacle has illustrated vividly the need for better procedures to be adopted by English law for multi-party actions, and there is little doubt that the Scottish courts and Legal Aid Board are equally incapable of coping. Some possible solutions to these problems have been considered, and adoption of a more rigorous system of strict liability, such as that commonly found in the United States of America, has been rejected, in light of the adverse effect which recent legal developments in that country appear to have had on the availability of new pharmaceutical products.[5] The discussion has illustrated the difficulties involved in legal reform in this area, while trying to provide adequate provision for persons injured by pharmaceutical products, the law must also beware lest it inhibit the introduction of beneficial drugs and devices.

The question of how best to provide compensation for incapacity has traditionally been regarded as within the domain of private law, the province of the laws of contract or tort. Even the strict liability regime established by the Consumer Protection Act requires injured parties to assert their private law rights through the courts. An alternative approach might be to focus on the public law dimension to the compensation question.

The introduction in Britain of a "no-fault" scheme for pharmaceutical product disasters could benefit drug manufacturers, as well as injured plaintiffs. In the early 1980s Fleming suggested that recent litigation in the United States might discourage pharmaceutical manufacturers from developing new products, a fear which seems to have been well founded in light of our discussion in chapter 11. He concluded that reform of the compensation process could provide protection for the pharmaceutical

---

[4] See Chap. 9, above. Some novel solutions to these problems have also been examined—see from p. [137], above.
[5] See Chap. 11, above.

industry.[6] It might be argued that the *British* pharmaceutical industry is not in need of such protection and would have little to gain from a no-fault scheme, particularly if it were to be funded by the industry itself. After all, its members have never been successfully sued in this country. Defending products liability suits can, however, be expensive, even if the company is exonerated at the end of the day. The American Bendectin and Cu-7 IUD cases have shown that suits may be successfully defended, yet a manufacturer may find that it requires to withdraw a pharmaceutical product from the market, on economic grounds.[7] In relation to the recent Myodil litigation against Glaxo, for example, it has been noted that since most of the plaintiffs were in receipt of legal aid, "Glaxo could not have recovered its own costs even if it had succeeded on all or some of the claims . . . "[8]

The brief description in chapter 12 of a number of no-fault schemes which currently operate in other countries serves to illustrate that there may be better ways of compensating injured persons, which are not dependent on an exercise of their private law rights. Given the immense difficulties they face in obtaining redress under the current system, it is concluded that persons injured by pharmaceutical products, in particular, would benefit from alternative methods of providing compensation.

Litigation involving pharmaceutical drugs and devices has had a considerable impact on British laws and court procedures. It was the thalidomide tragedy which led to the establishment of the Pearson Commission and calls for strict liability from product injury. This in turn led to the European Directive on Product Liability, and ultimately to the Consumer Protection Act. Ironically, the pharmaceutical industry was amongst the most ardent lobbyists for the development risk defence to be included in this legislation. The Opren debacle led to the adoption of novel court procedures for actions involving a multiplicity of plaintiffs, and the publication of a Guide to Group Actions by the English courts. It also led to the foundation of CITCOM, the Citizen Compensation Campaigning

---

[6] See Fleming, "Drug Injury Compensation Plans" (1982) *The American Journal of Comparative Law*, 30, 297 at pp. 311–312.

[7] See pp. [175] and [176], above.

[8] Brahams: "U.K. Myodil Arachnoiditis Claims Settle Out of Court", 1995 *Medico-Legal Journal*, 63:3, at 130. See also the more general comments of Dodds-Smith in Chap. 12 of Howells, editor: *Product Liability, Insurance and the Pharmaceutical Industry: an Anglo-American Comparison* (Manchester University Press, 1991) p. 157.

group, and to calls for the reform of the Legal Aid system and the availability of conditional fee actions.

While claims involving pharmaceutical drugs and devices may have had an important role in these changes, it remains the case that none of the suits involving these products has been successfully litigated before a British court. This book began with a quotation from the Pearson Report, which stated that "drugs represent the class of product in respect of which there has been greatest public pressure for surer compensation in cases of injury". It is apparent that, 18 years later, we are little closer to providing surer compensation for such people.

Index